THE
Stilwell
Papers

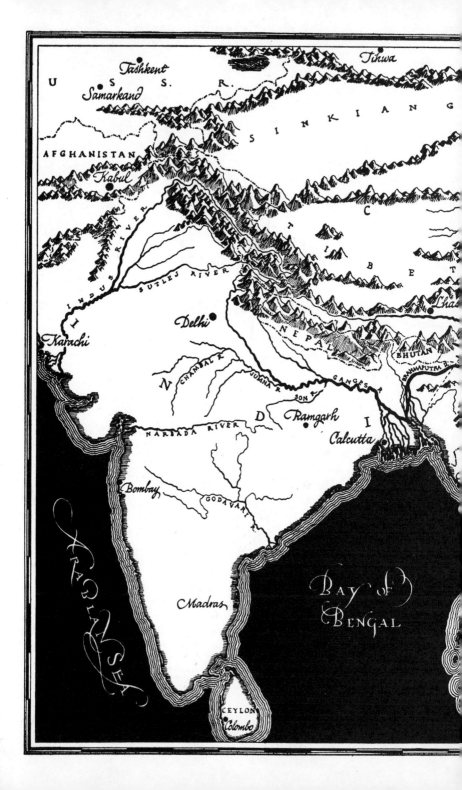

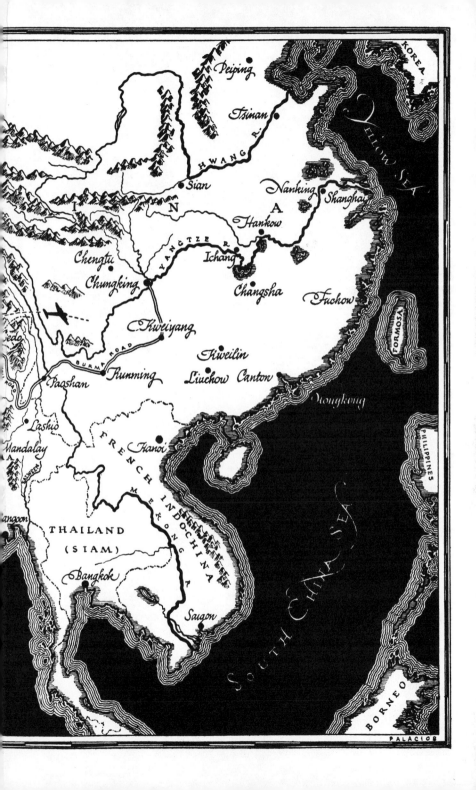

THE
Stilwell
Papers

By JOSEPH W. STILWELL

Arranged and Edited by
THEODORE H. WHITE

New Preface by
ERIC LARRABEE

A DA CAPO PAPERBACK

Library of Congress Cataloging in Publication Data

Stilwell, Joseph Warren, 1883-1946.
  The Stilwell papers / by Joseph W. Stilwell; arranged and edited
by Theodore H. White; new preface by Eric Larrabee.
      p.   cm. — (A Da Capo paperback)
  Reprint. Originally published: New York: Sloane Associates, 1948.
  Includes bibliographical references and index.
  ISBN 0-306-80428-X
    1. Stilwell, Joseph Warren, 1883-1946. 2. World War, 1939-1945 — Campaigns —
Burma. 3. World War, 1939-1945 — China. 4. World War, 1939-1945 — Personal
narratives, American. 5. Generals — United States — Biography. 6. United States.
Army — Biography. 7. Generals — United States — Biography. I. White, Theodore
Harold, 1915-   . II. Title.
D767.6.S74   1991   90-26263
940.54′25 — dc20   CIP

This Da Capo Press paperback edition of *The Stilwell Papers* is an unabridged
republication of the edition published in New York in 1948, here sup-
plemented with a new preface by Eric Larrabee. It is reprinted by arrangement
with William Morrow & Company.

Published by Da Capo Press, Inc.
A Subsidiary of Plenum Publishing Corporation
233 Spring Street, New York, N.Y. 10013

TO MADAME SUN YAT-SEN

Contents

PREFACE

JOSEPH STILWELL went out to China in 1942 with few illusions. He spoke the language fluently and had traveled the interior countryside, observing at close hand the impact of the Kuomintang regime. He did not much care for the Chinese governing class but had developed a profound affection for the ordinary people, among whom he classed the Chinese soldier. He believed that decently led, trained, and equipped, a Chinese military force could fight aggressively and effectively, a conviction he shared at the time with virtually no one else in Asia.

He knew well the inertia, the obsession with appearances ("face"), the corruption, the deeply rooted xenophobia. He knew not to expect too much, not to take anything for granted until it was realized in fact. Hence the incredulous tone with which he greets the news that Chiang Kai-shek has put him in "command" of Chinese armies in Burma. Much of the first part of the book is given over to working out the flimsiness of that "command."

This is General Stillwell's account in every sense, written for his own purposes: to keep a record that would reinforce his memory, to develop logical arguments, to clean his mind of the annoyances and frustrations that accumulate daily in dealing with intractable problems. The mood turns increasingly sour as the war moves on and the problems grow worse. Stilwell's reputation for irascibility and ill-temper finds support in these pages, in the acid of his self-expression and the temptation it poses for other writers to quote him. The Joe Stilwell found here readily passed into common currency — the Vinegar Joe of legend, a sharp-edged and not particularly attractive character.

The reader should be prepared to keep in mind that there were other Stilwells — the professional soldier, the tactician and field commander (one of our best), the diplomat (yes, diplomat!), the gentle and introspective man who worried continually about whether he was doing the right thing. After all, his problems were real; he neither invented them nor could have made them less real by being tactful. One might also note the degree to which he succeeded in playing off the conflicting interests of three major powers in a part of the world to which none of them intended to give priority.

In retrospect it must seem astonishing that so many Americans (George Marshall and Henry Morgan were honorable exceptions) should have been taken in by Chiang's maneuver. His goal was to win the civil war with the Chinese communists that would follow Japan's defeat. For this he needed to squirrel away American equipment that would not be forthcoming if its purpose were known. He must maintain the pretext of a life-and-death struggle with Japan that was in truth by mutual consent a stalemate. Periodically he would threaten to "leave" a war he was not fighting in the first place and could not have "left" if he had wanted to.

Britain and the United States were another matter, Britain because it had more than one policy, the United States because it had none at all. The interests of the Empire as seen from London and those from New Delhi were not the same, New Delhi's if anything the more conservative: it perceived Stilwell like any other threat to India's permanence and immobility. Churchill's view of China might be described as "active indifference." Franklin Roosevelt did not know what to do about China and, having no answers, tended to evade the question. Requests from Stilwell for guidance tended to produce eiher platitudes or stories about the Delano family in the China trade.

Perhaps it might have been better if the army histories of the Stilwell mission had been published first, portraying as they do a Stilwell who is dull by comparison, enveloped at a rarefied height in the endless tedium of his job. All he was supposed to do was create a Chinese army of a competence never before seen and, together with a reluctant ally, fight a ground campaign our own air-minded fellow-countrymen were sure would fail. To acquire a land route to China was central to American military thinking, forced on us by geography and the limited capacity of aircraft. Either you supplied the Chinese through north Burma or else the amounts you could fly in "over the Hump" (the Himalayas) were limited to a trickle.

A fighting Chinese force made a land campaign possible; what had not been anticipated (except by

Stilwell) was that it would win so spectacularly. New Delhi had not expected this; Churchill had not expected it. Had the war lasted longer (and Stilwell been retained) matters would have taken on a very different complexion. He knew what he had done: he had proved countless skeptics wrong. He had made possible, as he put it in a letter to his wife, "the first sustained offensive against a first-class army." Let that be remembered in Chinese history when the cynicism and the pungent language have been forgotten.

Eric Larrabee
New York City
September, 1990

FOREWORD

IT IS with deep feeling and pride that I present these words of my husband, General Joseph W. Stilwell. Because of the many controversies concerning his services in the China-Burma-India theater and his recall in November, 1944, and because he was never allowed to present for himself the true facts of the case, I am giving him this opportunity to speak.

General Stilwell was descended from Nicholas Stillwell (sic) who came to New Amsterdam in 1638. Records and family documents carry the name back to 1456. Among those Stilwells who followed Nicholas, there were many who served this country as soldiers, so it was perhaps natural that my husband chose a military career.

General Stilwell's army life began in 1900, when he entered the United States Military Academy at the age of seventeen. After his graduation in 1904, he saw service in the Philippine Islands with the 12th Infantry. Many interesting years followed and during World War I, he became G-2 of the 4th Corps, under General Briant H. Wells. Between the two World Wars, he was stationed in China three times, for a total of ten years.

In 1921, during his first tour of duty in China as an army language student in Peking, he served in Shansi province as construction engineer on a road being built by the American Red Cross for famine relief. In Shansi, he spent months working and living with Chinese laborers and peasants. In 1927, while stationed in Tientsin, he spent several months as an observer with the Chinese armies, then engaged in Civil War. Because of his intense desire for factual information, he moved continuously on foot within the battle areas. During a later assignment as Military Attaché to the American Embassy in Peking, he learned to know Chinese officials and military leaders of the highest rank. During those years of contact with both the common citizens of China and leaders of wealth and position, General Stilwell developed an intimate understanding of the basic and underlying psychology of China.

Few people realize that General Stilwell, throughout the greatest years of his career, was almost blind. The explosion of an ammunition dump, during World War I at Belrupt, caused a severe injury to the left eye. There was a deformity of the pupil and the growth of a cataract of the lens. The vision of this eye was so impaired that he could not distinguish the fingers on a hand at three feet. The vision of the right eye required heavy correction and constant use of glasses. During the trying days in Chungking, as well as during the jungle campaigns in Burma, where lighting facilities were inadequate, it was often necessary to work by candlelight. His indomitable urge to do his job and do it well forced him to strain the remaining eye. His great hope was that it would last long enough to see him through his mission.

General Stilwell's war journals were written so that he might have a true and factual account of those years. They were put down for his own use. But to me his gallant spirit lives on, encouraging me to bring his journals to publication.

The major problems that confronted General Stilwell during the war are those that essentially confront the representatives of our country in China today. Since a free and great democracy can function successfully only upon the basis of true information, it is my hope that these journals will bring a clearer understanding of the problems America faces in China. We shall then stand much closer to a careful and proper solution.

Winifred A. Stilwell

INTRODUCTION

T HE COMMANDER of a war theater of the United States Army is the most important and most lonesome of all men in whatever area he serves. He can have no intimates or friends to share his fears and worries. The pressures and strains that bear upon him are unrelenting; he must resolve them all in the clarity of decisions upon which the lives of men and the security of the Republic depends.

The quality of introversion that such terrible responsibility brings found its only release in General Stilwell in a series of papers, letters, and journal jottings which were found after his death among his effects. THE STILWELL PAPERS is a collection of these papers covering three years in the history of the last war—from the attack on Pearl Harbor in December, 1941, to the final relief of General Stilwell from command in China in October, 1944.

These papers were written for himself alone—they are presented in this book raw and unformed, torn from the privacy of his emotions. They were written in the sharp, hard language of command and bitterness; they present only one facet of his many-sided character. There is little reflection in them of the generosity, the kindliness, the warmth of love that won him so enduring a loyalty among those who knew him best. It would have been alien to his nature to record those many tendernesses that so naturally complemented his vigor and directness in action.

In this book, his thoughts and reflections are presented as he phrased them in his own words, at whatever penalty the book may suffer by peacetime canons of taste and convention. No change has been made in his text except for certain minor liberties clearly detailed below. Such editorial matter as is added for purposes of background and explanation is clearly marked as such and distinguished from the text proper by this type face.

The papers brought together here come from three sources, each reflecting a lifelong personal habit of General Stilwell.

The first source is his personal command journal, which was kept faithfully throughout the war. The journal entries are usually short, clipped telegraphic entries, serving more as personal symbols of memory than a narrative of events. Frequently they are technical military notes. Only as much of the journals is used in this book as is needed to stitch the sequence of the story together where other sources fail.

The second source consists of longer essays and analyses usually written during periods of reflection when Stilwell, for his own satisfaction, attempted to summarize a situation, sharpen his perception of character, or think through a particularly vexing problem.

The editor has taken the liberty of weaving both diaries and reflective papers together into a single pattern, setting down both diary entry and reflective paper as a single section when they fall under the same date. When the reflective paper is undated, the editor has inserted it where, by the logic of text and events, he believes it properly falls. The third source of material for this book is General Stilwell's letters to Mrs. Stilwell. These are clearly marked with the name of their recipient.

Wherever the name of a Chinese friend of General Stilwell has appeared, and whenever, in the opinion of the editor or Mrs. Stilwell, such a name exposes that friend to danger of reprisal at the hands of the Chinese government, the name has been deleted. Wherever Stilwell, as commanding general, records the shortcomings of United States officers, Mrs. Stilwell has requested that the names of such officers be deleted unless the history of the war makes it essential that the name be retained. The editor has taken it upon himself to fill out the abbreviations of names, or translations of code that Stilwell frequently used. The parentheses in the text are those of Stilwell; but whenever a bracket has been used, the bracketed material is an explanation or translation supplied by the editor. Footnotes also are worded by the editor. Occasionally, writing for his own eyes alone, Stilwell used the harsh descriptive expletives of the soldier. Knowing General Stilwell's reluctance to use such language publicly, the editor has at times cut or softened various easily recognized phrases. Less than half of General Stilwell's wartime writings are embodied in this book; but what has been published is Stilwell's alone, and the liberties mentioned above are the only brief alterations of his original script.

But I remember, when the fight was done,
When I was dry with rage and extreme toil,
Breathless and faint, leaning upon my sword,
Came there a certain lord, neat, trimly dressed,
Fresh as a bridegroom . . .

. . . he smiled and talked;
And as the soldiers bore dead bodies by,
He called them untaught knaves, unmannerly,
To bring a slovenly unhandsome corse,
Betwixt the wind and his nobility.
With many holiday and lady terms
He questioned me; among the rest demanded
My prisoners in your majesty's behalf.
I then, all smarting with my wounds being cold,
To be so pestered with a popinjay,
Out of my grief and my impatience,
Answered neglectingly I know not what;
He should, or he should not;—for he made me mad
To see him shine so brisk, and smell so sweet,
And talk so like a waiting-gentlewoman
Of guns, and drums, and wounds,—God save the mark!—
                    Hotspur to Henry IV
            Henry IV (Part I), Act I, Scene 3

[General Stilwell often declared that this was his
        favorite passage in Shakespeare.]

xviii

THE
Stilwell
Papers

Chapter 1

ON THE DAY the Japanese struck at Pearl Harbor, the United States Army was scattered thin along the Pacific Coast of our country. Four Army and one Marine Corps divisions—in all, some 100,000 men—were spread from Puget Sound, south almost two thousand miles to San Diego, responsible for defending the homeland from an enemy whose first assault was expected anywhere, any time, in any force. These units, in various states of organization and confusion, some half trained, all ill equipped, ungirt and scattered on a peaceful Sunday morning, were under the over-all command of Lieutenant General John L. De-Witt, commander of the Fourth Army.

Major General Joseph Warren Stilwell as senior tactical commander in California was directly responsible to De-Witt. Stilwell's command was the Third Corps with headquarters at Monterey—and his responsibility was the defense of the sea frontier of America from San Luis Obispo through Los Angeles to San Diego. This was an area of some five million people, containing more than 75 per cent of the heavy bomber plants of the United States, some of its most significant oil production, a major naval base, and cut off from the rest of the country by desert and mountain.

On the morning of Pearl Harbor Sunday, General and Mrs. Stilwell were entertaining the officers of the Third Corps staff at their Carmel home. It was the last "at home," the General promised his wife, that she would have to give for his staff. A telephone rang, and Mrs. Stilwell answered it. It was a friend calling—"Turn on your radio," the friend said, "the Japs are attacking Pearl Harbor." Mrs. Stilwell blurted the news to her husband; the party converged on the nearest radio. There was a pause as they listened to the next flash; and then the party dissolved.

Sometime that afternoon or evening, General Stilwell found time to scribble the first entry in his wartime diaries. For the next three weeks his total preoccupation was to be the organization of the defense of the South Pacific Coast. Traveling by plane and road, he inspected the outposts of his command, sorting his units, posting them for action.

DECEMBER 7, 1941   Japs attack Hawaii. [Plan] Rainbow 5 in effect. Three p.m. Goode phoned. Jap fleet 20 miles south, 10 miles out [of Monterey]. Sent Dorn [1] to [Ft.] Ord to call off show and alert garrison. Phoned Hearn [2] to start reconnaissance. Phoned Hearn to have Dorn call enlisted men back to camp.

3:30 phoned White at Ord. White to send reconnaissance troop down Highway No. 1. 3:35 Guam being attacked.

DECEMBER 8 Office in a.m. No further news. Rumors begin. Went to San Francisco and saw DeWitt. Disaster at Honolulu.

Phone from Washington about ammunition. Almost a hatful. Sunday night "air raid" at San Francisco. Two blackouts in San Francisco. Second on account of Navy patrol. Fourth Army kind of jittery. Back at six. Much depressed. Blackout on. Calmed 'em down.

DECEMBER 9 At office in a.m. Arranged to shove off [on inspection trip]. Fleet of thirty-four [Japanese] ships between San Francisco and Los Angeles.

Later—not authentic. (Sinking feeling is growing.) More threats of raids and landings. DeWitt getting four regiments from East. Dorn and I off at 3:45.

DECEMBER 10 Rain all way down. Went by Camp Cooke at 4:00 p.m. Hicks at [Ft.] MacArthur jittery. [Captain] Kaufman, United States Navy, also jittery. News of two British battleships sunk. My God—worse and worse.

On to San Bernardino in heavy rain. All arrangements made. Good job. Had chow at 12:15 a.m. In at one.

DECEMBER 11 Up at 6:30. Saw Moon. No bombers here. Out in desert. But eighty to a hundred B-17s on coast. Navy—no ships, no planes, or very few.

I had just gotten to Mittelstadt's command post in Balboa Park, San Diego, when the phone rang and Dorn was told there was an urgent call for me. He took it down and

---

1 Major Frank "Pinky" Dorn, at the time Stilwell's personal aide. Dorn was to follow Stilwell to China, later to become Brigadier General Dorn, and remained throughout the war closer personally to Stilwell than any other individual in the Army.

2 Colonel Thomas Hearn, chief of staff of III Corps. Hearn accompanied Stilwell to China, and later became Major General Hearn, chief of staff of the CBI theater.

handed it to me. "The main Japanese battle fleet is 164 miles off San Francisco. General alert of all units." I believed it, like a damn fool, and walked around the room trying to figure what to do. I imagined a wild rush up to Frisco with all available troops, and the first thing to do seemed to be to inform the Marines at Camp Elliott. So we dashed out and barged in, and saw General Vogel, a calm, solid citizen who, although under forty-eight hours' notice, agreed at once to play ball and do anything I told him. Then we phoned Army to check on the language and the position, which by latitude was 460 miles out, instead of 160. Then Colonel Howard, Vogel's chief of staff, came in with Navy's estimate of Jap force in Hawaiian waters. (Four heavy ships, two to four aircraft carriers, eight destroyers, some subs.) They guessed it might be this force, in for a raid, and they calmed me down some, enough to get to Dawley's command post without going nuts. The first reaction to that news was like a kick in the stomach—the unthinkable realization that our defenses were down, the enemy at hand, and that we not only had nothing to defend ourselves with, but that Time was against us. We could not ship the ammunition in time, nor could we evacuate the three million people in this area. Had the Japs only known, they could have landed anywhere on the coast, and after our handful of ammunition was gone, they could have shot us like pigs in a pen. (We had about ten million caliber 30 [rifle bullets], a few hundred 75s, and 266 155s. No trench mortars at all. The Coast Artillery Command at Rosecrans and [Ft.] MacArthur had about 180 rds. per [155 mm. gun] and sufficient stuff for their other guns.)

Of course [the 4th] Army passed the buck on this report. They had it from a "usually absolutely reliable source," but they should never have put it out without check. They added that the Fourth Air Force had gone after the Japs, but they did not report results, which of course were negative. Then, when a Navy patrol scoured the area and found nothing, they had to admit the report was not dependable. (I stopped at Encinitas to phone Hearn, and he said then that the Navy had already reported negatively.)

DECEMBER 13   Not content with the above blah, [the 4th] Army pulled another at ten-thirty today. "Reliable information that attack on Los Angeles is imminent. A general alarm being considered." The old sinking feeling again. Ammunition a little better, the 125th [Regiment] due in twenty-four hours, and a division coming in ten days. Got what hope I could from that, and then decided to disbelieve the report. Of course, the attack never materialized, but a "general alarm" would have been just as serious. The plain truth is that it is not possible to evacuate three million people east, over waterless desert, and there would have been frightful casualties if a general exodus had started. What jackass would sound a "general alarm" under the circumstances? The [Fourth] Army G-2 is just another amateur, like all the rest of the staff. RULE: the higher the headquarters, the more important is calm. Nothing should go out unconfirmed. Nothing is ever as bad as it seems at first.

But twelve million 30 caliber [bullets] in hands of troops and three million in reserve. The 125th [Regiment] due tonight. We have two battalions along the coast. Two battalions radioed for Coast Artillery Command defense and two battalions in reserve. For 175 miles of coast. (The old sinking feeling.) Six tanks coming from Ord. (The others won't run.)

Lingayen landing repulsed.

DECEMBER 14   One week gone. What have we done? Reputations blasted and the U.S. united and set for a long hard pull.

Philippine Islands doing fine. Wake and Midway holding. [Secretary of Navy] Knox back in Washington. Still silence from Navy. What a black eye they got. A Coast Artillery Command rookie shot and killed a woman yesterday. DeWitt now in full command on coast.

The Philippine divisions shot 'em up at Lingayen. Caught the Japs coming ashore in launches. Sank 150 boats and contents. Good job. In fact, most of the *despised people* (Chinese, Russians, Greeks, and Filipinos) are doing the best work for civilization.

DECEMBER 15   Dubby day—no scares. Various dopes in to talk. Royse wants to resign—just can't bear it. Told him to wait till tomorrow. The 125th Infantry in. Third Cavalry Battalion arrived at Phoenix and Tucson.

[Secretary of the Navy] Knox back from Hawaii. Statement looks queer. He says *Arizona* and three destroyers and one mine sweeper sunk. *Oklahoma* capsized. *Utah* lost. Others damaged. Whatever that means. Maintains that the Pacific Fleet has gone after the Japs.

The Italians have worked it out. They say the Japs may be considered to be "yellow Aryans."

DECEMBER 16   Admiral Yamamoto, several years back, wrote in a letter that when the Jap war with the U.S. occurred, he did not want to merely take Guam and Wake, and occupy Hawaii and San Francisco. His real ambition was to dictate peace in Washington, D.C.

DECEMBER 17   Off to Santa Monica. Saw Branshaw,[3] all jitters. (One-half our aircraft production localized here in eight plants.) Practically all [the] heavy bombers. My God.

DECEMBER 18 ——[4] came in, and started his worries about Terminal Island.[5] He wanted to evacuate the Jap colony—at least, he wanted me to do it. How and to where, he didn't know. Also, he was afraid the oil stocks at Torrance would be sabotaged and ignited and that a river of flame would pour down through Wilmington, consuming everything in its path, in one gigantic holocaust. To prevent this he wanted to declare a war zone east and west along Imperial Boulevard and north and south along Atlantic [Boulevard] (three hundred square miles), combing the area for aliens, removing them and then preventing them from returning. How this was to be done he did not know. I told him to put some men at Torrance and prevent interference with the oil storage there. We talked till midnight, by which time he was pretty well calmed down.

DECEMBER 19 Flew to Lake Rogers at Muroc to see about request for guard. This is the Air Corps' bombing range on the desert—seventy air miles from San Bernardino. Lieutenant Colonel Smith was much alarmed over the defenseless state of his command; he was sure the Japs could fly in at any moment and shoot his men down. The Engineer Battalion was leaving him, and he didn't see how he could get ditches dug for his men to hide in. The only weapons available were pistols, so he was fearful of a parachute attack that would come in off carriers or from a secret base in Lower California, and murder them all. Or Japs from Los Angeles could sneak

---

[3] Lieutenant Colonel Branshaw of U.S. Air Corps, inspector of airplane manufacture in the Santa Monica area.
[4] A subordinate commander of a southern California sector.
[5] Island in Los Angeles area.

up and sabotage everything. The only remedy seemed to be some infantry to take care of them. The bulk of available heavy bombers in the Army was not reflected in his plan of defense, which left them and the magazine entirely outside his cordon and was confined to the defense of a tent area where the personnel lived. However, Fourth Army has ordered us to send two companies of infantry up to take care of him. (P.S. The colonel has seen some suspicious signaling with flashlights.)

This situation has produced some other strange cases of jitters. Common sense is thrown to the winds and any absurdity is believed.

The wild, farcical and fantastic stuff that G-2 Fourth Army pushes out! The latest is a two-pound bundle of crap. An investigation of a Ph.D. at California Tech., a distinguished research man in weather, who runs a service from California Tech. for orange growers. He voluntarily discontinued his broadcast when the war broke out, but [G-2] had him investigated by FBI.

The frantic struggle of the Army staff to justify General DeWitt's forecast of danger to Alaska has petered out. When they got down to one submarine four hundred miles northeast of Hawaii, that was the end.

DECEMBER 20 Report from a Coast Artillery Command sergeant that his post had been fired on by a passing motorist. (Probable fact—backfire.)

Report from Army that a secret airfield had been reported twenty-odd miles north of Palomar, the planes being concealed under alfalfa, and the probable objective being the Consolidated [Aircraft] plant at San Diego. (An old field where the Ryan Company had some trainers.) [6]

[One] captain and his wife and daughters actually saw three Jap planes at 12:43 a.m. on December 9 outlined against the moon. They were going to bomb Terminal Island but he had had the forethought to order a blackout, and he saw the planes become "confused," then turn back. (N.B. This is apparently the basis of the "confused" report that the Interceptor Command got excited about.)

[The] captain wanted Dawley to put a 75 on a tug and go out after a sub that he knew about. The captain had positive proof that subs were lurking all about him from the frequent "signatures" on his loops in the bay.

General Ryan not only knew that flights of Jap planes were over San Francisco, but explained why they turned back and where they went. It seems they were "homing" on the radio broadcasts, and when these were turned off, they didn't know what to do, and so went away. (If turning off the radio broadcasts will win the war, there will be no objection from me.)

The [XYZ] Fiasco: Rumors of "secret" Jap airfields in Lower California caused Army to organize this expedition of six saps who allegedly spoke Spanish. Two battalions of Mexican infantry were to be brought to Tia Juana over U.S. railways and escort [Lieutenant Colonel XYZ] south on his search (roughly fifty miles by eight hundred!). A liaison post was to be set up, incidentally. [XYZ] to have scout cars and our assistance. Motor transport for the Mexicans, to be furnished by us, in case of need. [XYZ] to *energize* the Mexicans. Christ. The question quickly became who was to energize [XYZ]? His first request was to be made a full colonel, so he could have more face. Well, the Mexi-

* Parenthetical note probably added at some later date by General Stilwell.

cans arrived with seven—count 'em—seven generals, and then the fireworks began. Three changes in command in three days. Objections to [XYZ] going armed, going in uniform, going at all. Messages back and forth to Mexico City, to us, to Mittelstadt, to Army.

[XYZ] backing and filling, asking for planes, then more planes, then amphibians. I had Jeffers fly down about a hundred miles. The Navy flew a PBY well down. All reports negative, of course. Orders and counterorders for [XYZ]. Buy civilian clothes. Leave weapons behind. Paint out designation on cars. Planes fly but not bomb. Can shoot machine guns though. Etc., etc., ad infinitum and ad nauseam. We are now (December 20) so fed up with [XYZ] and his farce and so tired of being a message center that we could scream.

Requests for Army Guards: Terminal Island, shipbuilding plants, commercial radio stations, railroad bridges and tunnels, railroad crossovers, dams, water supply, power plants, oil wells, tanks, and refineries. Aircraft manufacturing plants, hospitals, aqueducts, harbor defenses, airfields, offices of Interceptor Command, etc., etc. Everybody makes a case for his own installation, and nobody gives a damn if the Army bogs down and quits training. Right now (December 20) we have seven regiments of infantry in the area, four of which are on guard duty.

Now we've started giving trucks to General Rico, [XYZ's] friend of Lower California. The rat race continues.

DECEMBER 21 [XYZ] affair getting worse and worse. A stupidity. Now he has planes and is "operating" in two columns. Really was a sub attack yesterday. Or rather two. Attacks on freighters near Santa Cruz and off Eureka yesterday, confirmed today by Western Defense Command and by press tonight. Where is our Navy?

Five Mexican destroyers coming up from Panama to patrol Baja California. (The day has come when we lean on the Mexican Navy!) Our naval "force" based on San Diego is pitiful—twelve PBYs, six fighters, ten bombers. About four destroyers for escort duty. That's all.

DECEMBER 22   How things do fall on you out of a clear sky. Hearn knocked on my door at 6:30 and said Bradley was on the phone. He was. Bryden had called from Washington and I am to shove off at once for work on a war plan, for some expeditionary force which Bradley implied I was to command. He emphasized the fact that *I would be away for some time*. (You can bet on *that*.)

Packed up and shoved off at 1:35. Home at five. Talked and talked. All composed mentally, thank God. *Grand visit*.

DECEMBER 25   The family made it Christmas for me but the clock went too fast. Packed next day and off at 9:30—the family all at the front door to see me off. Not a tear in the crowd—just smiles and waves for good luck. Reached Washington in bright sunshine, 4:00 p.m. Xmas Eve. Reported to Adjutant General. He knew nothing.

Saw ——. He knew nothing, but that was to be expected. I never got anything out of him but silly giggles. His principal worry at the moment was finding out whether or not to wear a black tie to dinner that night. So I went to War Plans Division and found Gerow out but Eisenhower in. Latter gave me the jolt about [Plan] Black. It didn't make me feel any different from before, somehow. From there went down to the War College and saw Malony.[7] That was the 24th and they handed me the first directive, for Dakar.

[7] Colonel Harry Malony, of U.S. War College.

Pretty gloomy. Chow at Pennsylvania Avenue with Smith and Dorn. Had chow at dog-wagon.

LETTER TO MRS. STILWELL   What a brave picture for a guy off to who knows where or what. It meant a lot to me to see you all there at the front door, everybody cheerful and facing the music. Good omen for a good ending to all this crazy business, and you sounded the note of optimism I needed. We may have some dark times ahead, but I'm sure we are coming out of it. This country is a slow starter, but it is full of guts, and *we are going to win.*

LETTER TO MRS. STILWELL   Merry Christmas! Dorn and I went to the War College and read a lot of stuff. Then we had Christmas dinner—and a good one—at a restaurant—and dissipated further by seeing *Dumbo.* I nearly fell off my chair when the elephant pyramid toppled over. We sat through the film twice.

The job I have is very hush-hush and rightly so. Just go along being yourselves. That's as much as anybody can do, and more than most. I'll try and keep you informed as much as possible. You can depend on it that everybody here is most helpful and cordial, in spite of the loads they are carrying and the tremendous job ahead. Everything is going to be O.K. and you are a big factor in making me believe it. I hope you all had a gorgeous Christmas.

Chapter 2

IN WASHINGTON, General Stilwell found that he had been chosen to command the first blow against the enemy.

America's first offensive plans of the war were being put on paper, and Stilwell was charged with organizing the great attack that, a year later, finally resulted in the American campaign in North Africa.

In December, 1941, the outline of the plan was still unclear. No one knew how quickly the pitifully meager resources of the United States could be molded into an effective fighting force. The hour was desperate, but no one knew how much time history would allow for preparation. Nor could anyone clearly tell which point in the enemy front might most easily crumple under an American attack.

The name for the great plan was Gymnast—North Africa. But what North Africa meant no one could say precisely: was it Casablanca, Dakar, Algiers or Tangier? The great plan was composed of variant, alternate, and subordinate plans each one named by color—Plan Black, Plan Gray, Plan Purple. There were combinations and permutations of all these *plans, and every shade and phase of each plan was challenged at every level by the conflicting interests, needs, and resources of the differing service arms and the differing Allied national aims. No one knew what date could be set for action—whether April, May, late summer, or early winter. No one could foretell the reaction of the French, of the Spaniards, or most important, of the enemy.*

Washington was suffused in the first turbulence of war's vast confusion. It was General Stilwell's duty to bring together men, plans, and resources in a draft of action.

DECEMBER 26   (Air has left the Philippine Islands.)
Nobody knows where I'm going. Up to see Gerow at 1:00. Waited till 4:00. No Gerow. Back to War College. "Everybody is in conference," or going to, or coming from. This a.m. it was Dakar, this p.m. it is Casablanca.

DECEMBER 27   Saw Gerow. New directive. Now it's Casablanca or Dakar. The Big Boy [1] thinks it isn't yet the "ripe time" for Casablanca. Good news to me, with 1,100 German planes in Sardinia and Sicily, and 185,000 [troops] in Morocco and 80,000 French in North Africa. 28 divisions [German] in France and 400 planes in Spain, etc. etc. The plain truth is we can do one thing and not several and we'll have to pick it out.

Looked over the operation room with Malony. Apparently we still have 6 wagons and 3 carriers at Pearl Harbor. (The Asiatic crowd is at Soerabaja with 3 cruisers and 21 ships. Why not action? I wonder.)

LETTER TO MRS. STILWELL We have been fumbling with papers, rushing around seeing people and missing people and waiting for people. Getting nothing done. In the evening we had dinner with John Davies [2] and did more talking. Today we continued to rush around and fumble with papers and at 6:00 we quit and had a hot sea-food plate. Then we walked it off.

My impression of Washington is a rush of clerks in and out of doors, swing doors always swinging, people with papers rushing after other people with papers, groups in corners whispering in huddles, everybody jumping up just as you start to talk, buzzers ringing, telephones ringing, rooms crowded, with clerks all banging away at typewriters. "Give me 10 copies of this AT ONCE." "Get that secret file out of the safe." "Where the hell is the Yellow Plan (Blue Plan, Green Plan, Orange Plan, etc.)?" Everybody furiously smoking cigarettes, everybody passing you on to someone else— etc., etc. Someone with a loud voice and a mean look and a big stick ought to appear and yell "HALT. You crazy bastards. SILENCE. You imitation ants. Now half of you get the hell out of town before dark and the other half sit down and don't move for one hour." Then they could burn up all the papers and start fresh.

Well, to hell with 'em. Nothing to report yet. Everything is uncertain and in the "planning stage." But I'll be here for some time yet.

DECEMBER 29 The moving agent of all this is of course the President. The Navy is the apple of his eye and the Army is the stepchild. The Pearl Harbor affair has been a terrific blow to prestige and pride, to such a point that we have orders not to say anything nasty about the Navy. Besides be-

[1] Roosevelt.
[2] Later to be Stilwell's political adviser in China.

ing a rank amateur in all military matters, F.D.R. is apt to act on sudden impulses. On top of that he has been completely hypnotized by the British, who have sold him a bill of goods. It took the disaster in Hawaii to stop the flow of *all* our stuff to the Limeys. What they have gotten must be simply enormous, because just a couple of weeks' production makes us begin to feel rich. Speaking of impulses, last spring the Gray Plan [the South Atlantic islands?] suddenly got hot. War Plans Division was asked how long it would take. They said three months and were told to get it ready in *one*. They nearly went crazy and right in the middle of it word came to lay off, because F.D.R. had another idea. That one was Iceland, so Iceland it was, and the Gray Plan was pigeonholed. The same thing is happening now. We'll do this, we'll do that, we'll do the other. Blow hot, blow cold. And the Limeys have his ear, while we have the hind tit. Events are crowding us into ill-advised and ill-considered projects.

I find there is no basic strategic study in existence. For instance, shall we now go to work and prepare seriously for war, and not undertake any offensive till we can do it properly, or shall we attempt to take the offensive? We should prepare till we can pour it on irresistibly, but that does not appear to be the answer. There is tremendous pressure to *do* something. The Limeys want us in with both feet. So the answer is, we must do something *now*, with our hastily made plans and our half-trained and half-equipped troops.

The next question would naturally be, if we must take the offensive, where shall it be? Because we are not strong enough to do anything serious in *both* the Atlantic and the Pacific, it must be one or the other. The question has not been fairly answered, but the indications are that it will be in the Atlantic (and what will the U.S.A. think of a government that abandons the Philippine Islands and the Netherlands East Indies to their fate?). The British and the Russians argue that Germany is the real menace, and that once we pull her down, everything else is simple. But meanwhile Japan makes it most difficult to visualize how we are going to knock her out unless we keep her out of the East Indies. (A fleet action between the American and Jap navies is the necessary answer in the Pacific. Once we crush the Jap fleet we can relieve the situation, but—is our Navy ever going to get at it?)

It wouldn't be so bad if they would go at it methodically on that side. First, [Plan] Purple, which, it must be admitted, seems to be under way, thus anchoring one flank. Then, [Plan] Gray, so as to anchor the other. Then, and only then, [Plan] Black,[3] with its necessary corollary in the islands. But, here again, the urge to get going before the Germans do is forcing our hand. We can't do all these things alone, so the Limeys must do it jointly. And to hell with these "joint things." I don't like 'em. They are messing around now (Dec. 29) with the idea the Limeys will do Gray and the birds [4] and the wine.[5]

DECEMBER 30 To War Plans Division for talks. Daley with 32nd, 34th, 37th, and 1st Armored [Divisions] going to Ireland.

Secretary of War [Stimson] came in to look us over. Keen mind.

I outlined the [North African] attack in the afternoon and we dug away at [the] dope. I figure we must change the plan to make it snappy in the Cape Verde and get enough space for planes. Left the Hay-Adams [Hotel] and went to the Blackstone. Blackout tonight. We went to newsreel movie.

[3] Probably Dakar.
[4] Probably the Canary Islands.
[5] Probably the Madeira Islands.

DECEMBER 31   Saw George Marshall this a.m. 9:00 to 9:30. Talked over the directive and got some idea of his troubles. The Head Man [Roosevelt] is hard to handle. The Secretary of War being the buffer, who stands up courageously on the big questions. But decisions from the top may very possibly be actually made by the Navy gang.

G-1 is setting up a staff of 139 officers for our show. The air contingent is going to amount to about 30,000 men.

What's the matter with our gang? Out of 35 B-17s in the Philippine Islands, the Japs got 17 on *the ground* the second day of the war.

What is the Navy going to do? 21 ships at Soerabaja, doing exactly nothing. Maybe they took John Paul Jones's slogan seriously—"I have not yet begun to fight!"

NEW YEAR'S EVE, LETTER TO MRS. STILWELL   Happy New Year to all of you, and many of them. I trust we can get this damn war shut down in time for you all to have a few years of peace and quiet. I'd like very much to join you for some of that and I'm sort of an optimist about it. I can't believe this country isn't going to rise up and smite these various brands of bastards, although just now it looks like a long war. But we are beginning to turn stuff out in quantities and when we get to throwing it around, it's going to hit quite a few people. They'll be sorry they started. . . .

JANUARY 1, 1942   Talked with Chief of Staff [Marshall] for an hour on this and that. Trouble with unified command in Far East. Not as between British and ourselves, but among the British! The "Senior Service" [the British Navy] sits disdainfully aloof. Nobody can command *them*—it isn't done. The arrogant Royal Air Force will have none of it.

Only the ground forces co-operate.

George [Marshall] finally got them together by going to

Churchill, whom he caught in bed. Churchill read them the riot act. . . .

Chiang K'ai-shek acting up. Ho Ying-ch'in [6] and he think the U.S. air force should come right over and protect them. Also that they should get everything they ask for. [China] peeved over British grab of *Tulsa* [7] cargo (30 and 50 caliber machine guns) for protection of Rangoon. Chiang K'ai-shek ready to send 100,000 men into Burma, but Wavell refused the help. ("For logical reasons," says Brett—reason not stated.)

George looking for a high-ranking man to go [to China]. Drum? Pompous, stubborn, new to them, high rank. Me? No, thank you. They remember me as a small-fry colonel that they kicked around.[8] They saw me on foot in the mud, consorting with coolies, riding soldier trains. Drum will be ponderous and take time through interpreters; he will decide slowly and insist on his dignity. Drum by all means. To help him? Betts and Boatner. Good solution.

My argument [that] Gymnast [North African expedition] would be threatened by subs was brushed aside by George. "Not a big convoy, guarded. Subs can't get in. Why, there were Jap troopships all around the Philippine Islands and our submarines couldn't get at them, the air and surface defense was so good!" Shades of John Paul Jones. Arnold was in, arguing, not very strongly, against Gymnast.

K—— says the War Department is just like the alimentary canal. You feed it at one end, and nothing comes out at the other but crap.

[6] Chief of staff, Chinese Armies.
[7] The *Tulsa* was a merchant vessel loaded with Lend-Lease arms for the Chinese. The British seized its cargo in Rangoon.
[8] As U.S. military attaché in China, Stilwell had been a colonel in 1937-1938.

JANUARY 2   Manila taken.

Another big powwow on Gymnast. Gerow, Somervell, Arnold, Clark, Chief of Staff, and I. All against it. Limeys claim Spain would "bitterly oppose" Germans. What rot. The Boches *own* the country, Franco must pay the bill for his war. Portal says we can get air superiority at Casablanca with "a couple of squadrons." Also that the Boches wouldn't bother us at all. Their stuff is too transparent for words, but Our Big Boy has swallowed it. (I told 'em we might better go in at Lisbon if Spain is going to fight Schicklgruber.) I also asked George [Marshall] what the basic U.S. objective was in going over there. He said, in effect, to protect the Mediterranean sea lane, which, if it could be used for convoys, would "quadruple the available British shipping." I don't see it. Probably they expect French West Africa to · join the parade as a direct result of Gymnast.

Drum arrived this morning. Quick work.

There are rumors of two new armies. GHQ wants to set up new divisions. Three a month till July, then four a month. Running into equipment difficulties, even for the first ones.

Long talk with Shapiro, Committee of Information boy, on recent trip to Black and Gymnast. He is sure Hitler owns Spain. Black [Dakar?] is bitterly anti-British. The commanding general down there is not so hot, not as aggressive or as alert, civilians all disappointed in him. Good news for us.

JANUARY 3   8: 30 to 12: 00 today on Gymnast with Chief of Staff [Marshall], Gerow, Lee, Somervell, Arnold, and Spaatz. All against and then in and gave the Secretary of War the works. He gets the point all right, but as he says, "It's very hard to always say 'no.' If there were only some alternative . . ."

All agree that any move we make *must* go. All agree that

the means are meager, the transport uncertain, the complications numerous, the main facts unknown, the consequences serious. A few lucky hits will jeopardize the whole affair. We did not take the initiative for our disasters in the Pacific: there is some excuse for us there. But here we are free agents. And we deliberately take serious chances to get ourselves into a rathole that is under the guns, sure of punishment, and hard to supply, and on the outcome of which will depend our prestige—or lack of it—in Europe. I am against this for two main reasons.

1. We know nothing about how the Spanish will react.
2. The affair is highly complicated.

Saw Drum today, and went over his list of personnel [for China] with him. Also gave him a few hints on what to do. He has Pritchard with him.

LETTER TO MRS. STILWELL   Powell brought the envelope with a letter from you and today another one came. The New Year is starting off with luck. Just a note tonight. Wish I could be more definite. This is a planning job I'm on and there's a mess of detail and study connected with it. Pinky, Dick, and I have a two-room suite here. Ben [9] and his shirt with no buttons. What a howl! Don't you know that a happy man has no shirt? Ben is a scientist, not a dude, so don't dress him up too much.

What a relief that Joe [10] is out of danger. I know it has been a big worry for you, and I know you are exhausted. But you'll both stage a quick comeback and everything will be lively again. If it's all the same to you, I'm willing to knock off

[9] The Stilwells' youngest son, then fourteen years old.
[10] Joseph W. Stilwell, Jr., the general's oldest son, later to be a colonel in the Burma campaign, who was, at the time, recovering from a critical operation.

on operations and live without them. I think we've had our full share.

JANUARY 5   The longer I work at this the worse it seems. Here we are, with the Japs giving us hell in the Philippine Islands, and we go on actually sending corps abroad. One of Daley's divisions is on its way. That looks as though we'll go too.

I blocked out the attack and gave it to McCabe to work on. No decision as to whether it's Black or Gymnast or neither.

Full-page ads from various papers about manufacturing concerns, labor unions, etc. "Let's go stuff." When this country once decides to go, we put it on.

JANUARY 6   Some amateur strategist has worked up a grand scheme. We just take Tangier, to which no one could possibly object, and thus begin a triumphal march in North Africa. It's all easy after that. The Americans have already shown up there twice—in 1802 and in Mr. T. Roosevelt's time, and all the natives therefore know that we are bad medicine and will come right over to us. All we have to do is show them how strong we are. The whole paper was a hash of politico-economic military bunk, and of course had War Plans Division and G-2 disapproval.

I saw an amazing document this morning. The notes on the last conference F.D.R., Churchill, Secretary of War, Chief of Staff, and Dill. As well as lesser luminaries. It demonstrated the tremendous hold the Limeys have on Our Boy. They shot off their faces as if they were our delegates and not theirs. So and so simply must be done. The Magnet [11] Plan will relieve several British divisions, which can now go home to jolly old England, thank you. No hint that they might help elsewhere. And we must keep up the Lend-

Lease torrent to our British cousins, even though our people go without.

And the objections to Gymnast are not received very cordially, either. Why, rubbish, we can do that. Our Boy thinks it very queer that ships cannot be unloaded more promptly. "Two weeks seems a long time to a man in a hurry," says he.

That's the trouble with the whole damn thing. The Limeys want us in, committed. They don't care what becomes of us afterward, because they will have shifted the load from their shoulders to ours. So they insist that speed is essential, and [Roosevelt] has acquired this same itch for us to do something, and is continually pressing for action, against the considered opinion of all his advisers. And by God the Limeys now say it is impossible for Great Britain to produce even the munitions she needs for herself, and we must keep up our stream of offerings or else. I don't know what "or else" means, but I would like to ask them. And then tell them what they could do.

JANUARY 9 Saw McNair and talked over Gymnast. He thinks effect would be "electrical" if we could do it. Doesn't worry about Azores and Canaries, will back us for fighter planes (5 groups) and agrees that we *must* have strong anti-aircraft. Is trying to persuade himself that it isn't a wild gamble. Everybody is shrieking for more men, more guns, more planes, more everything. Our small available supply melts as soon as it accumulates. GHQ and the War Department fed up with the howls and a letter has been sent by the Chief of Staff to Drum, DeWitt, and Emmons telling them politely to shut up. McNair says DeWitt has gone crazy and requires ten refusals before he realizes it is "No."

11 Plan for disposition of Americans in North Ireland (?).

JANUARY 10 Called to GHQ at 8:00 p.m. Conference till 11:00. We had to get some dope on dates down on paper. What is necessary, what is available, and when. Our staff just sat and listened. Hayes got the paper ready and proved himself regular. His estimate is six to eight months. The only possible way it could be four [months] would be for everything to function 100 per cent day and night for the entire period, without a hitch or a loss. This meeting, which turned out to be blah, had us a bit apprehensive.

At it till 11:00 p.m. getting data on dates and tonnage, etc.

JANUARY 11 Boy! I got into rarefied atmosphere today. Conference in Stark's office (Marshall, Stark, King, Turner, Holcomb, etc., etc., etc.). Most of the admirals in captivity. My impression was that they were all very conscious of their gold lace, and felt their exalted position greatly. Keenly. All agreed on being disgusted with the British hogging all the material: quite willing to divide ours with us, but never any mention of putting theirs in the pot. Navy aghast at 153,000 men for Magnet. Agreement on token force of 6,000-9,000. That was the only business done.

George [Marshall] tried to pin them on immediate needs, but didn't get anywhere. In answer to question, "Can you hold Hawaii?" King reacted with "Can the Army do it?" The rejoinder was "If the Army says it can hold it, will the Navy say so?" King said "Yes" not too emphatically. Imagine. Doubt about Hawaii. They have the wind up about Australia, yet they are fussing around about the Fiji Islands and Caledonia and what have you. The gist of it is the Navy can't or won't do anything, their only part being the use of available transports and cargo ships. The Army must do anything that is going to be done, and that means principally air, and perhaps some antiaircraft. Three planes a day will arrive in Java from now on . . . via the ferry route.

JANUARY 13   Conference with Chief of Staff, McNair, Malony, Hayes. Questioned about Gymnast. British cooling, in view of Libyan possibility of setback.

The great "presentation" of our [North African] plan began. About six short talks on a lot of economics, ethnological, political, psychological, etc., factors. Also terrain and military considerations.

After our "presentation," Mac and Malony and I were talking, and Mac said we ought to put down on a piece of paper—"not more than one page, or the President won't read it"—65 reasons why we should not do Gymnast—and then propose on another one-page gem, an alternative what we can do, within a reasonable time, or at least start on. So I was detailed to do it, at 5:00 p.m. To be ready tomorrow a.m. Just toss off a campaign, that's all.

Turned in my Dakar and Northern plan of campaign and found it was identical with a plan that GHQ ground out last night.[12]

JANUARY 14   Ordered out to a meeting at Stimson's house at 9:00 p.m. When I got there, found I was the only guest. Henry and I talked for an hour and a half on China. Apparently, he doesn't care for the selection of Drum. Has been looking all over for the right man to go out and run the show. Thinks the Chinese will accept an American commander. Told him I doubted it, but he had that distinct impression. Asked me how I felt, and I told him I'd go where I was sent. He said, "More and more, the finger of destiny is pointing at

12 This paragraph probably added next day.

you." Gave him the lowdown on Gymnast and Black including the Cape Verde Islands. He agrees.

Walked back.

JANUARY 16   Chief of Staff sent for me at 2:30. Up there till 5:00 talking over China and Gymnast and Black.

Stimson didn't want to consider me, "because he had his head down." (Referring to the way I was sitting one day.) George [Marshall] told him the only reason I had my head down was probably because I was getting ready to butt something. So the Secretary [Stimson] said he'd see me, and I went up. Next day Henry [Stimson] said he had been stimulated, and that George should keep his eye on me, because I might be a commander. So George told him, Hell, that's just what he'd been telling Henry. So Henry says Drum won't do, and I believe has told George to sound me out. George said how about it and who else is there. They had considered Joyce and Richardson and Eichelberger and turned them all down.

So I said, "What's the job?" and he gave me the paper. Co-ordinate and smooth out and run the road,[13] and get the various factions together and grab command and in general give 'em the works. Money no object.

Are the chances for getting results good? I said yes if I have command. "What'll we do about that?" Ask Chiang if he'll do it. "O.K. Write out the question." So I went out and wrote it and he's sending it to T. V. Soong.[14] The angle is that I may be appointed chief of staff of Chiang K'ai-shek's joint staff, whatever that is, and in carrying out Chiang K'ai-shek's instructions I exercise command. Well, there it is. Either they refuse and I don't go, or they accept, and maybe I do. Events are moving fast, and so George said, "By the time you get there, you may be in command in Australia."

"Also, we'll make you a lieutenant general." (The Chinese specified a rank above brigadier, on account of the Russian lieutenant generals and full generals.)

JANUARY 18   So they make Mr. Knudsen a lieutenant general. How ducky. Why not Shirley Temple? And for Christ's sake, why not an admiral for once?

JANUARY 19   So they make Pat Hurley a brigadier general. For Christ's sake again.

Rain. Had the Limeys in and squabbled over our convoy list. Dull day.

JANUARY 21   George [Marshall]: "It's hard as hell to find anybody in our high command who's worth a damn. There are plenty of good young ones, but you have to reach too far down."

JANUARY 22   China getting hot again. Chiang K'ai-shek has replied, agreeing to executive control and a United States chief of staff. Brings up point of dual control in Burma. Specifies a lieutenant general and that he must be chief of staff on Chiang K'ai-shek's headquarters staff.

Letter prepared on those lines after a.m. conference with George and p.m. conference with Secretary of War and McCloy. (George had a battle with Henry [Stimson], who was going right to the President and get it fixed up. George told him he'd first have to talk to War Plans Division and to me, and that he couldn't kick administration around like that.)

LETTER TO MRS. STILWELL   Pinky [Dorn], Sandy and I had sea food for dinner and then we went to a movie. *How*

13 The Burma Road, then still in operation and the only communication between China and the West.
14 Chiang K'ai-shek's brother-in-law, then Chinese ambassador in Washington.

Green Was My Valley. It is one of the best films I ever saw, with a lot of background singing by a Welshmen's choir. It doesn't quite touch *The Informer* but it's as good in a different way.

I've spent the day trying to "co-ordinate" with the Navy, and now find they have never even started on what we've been on for weeks.[15] First I got their chief of staff and he said he'd been laid up with a cold and was not familiar with the subject. So he passed me on to Admiral Edwards, their G-3, who did not know what I was talking about. So he asked his assistant G-3 and he didn't know either. Edwards phoned Admiral Turner, of the planning committee, but they couldn't find him. Said they'd call me up when they got the dope. A sample of our "important" work.

You must be sick of the humdrum drool I am reduced to in my letters. My routine is about as interesting as if I were in jail. These lads who are stationed here permanently sure have my sympathy. Six months of this and I'd be screaming in my sleep. Just one month is proving a heavy dose.

LETTER TO MRS. STILWELL   We are still milling around and rushing here and there, waving papers at each other, and not making much progress. However, the general picture is improving and unless the Big Boys kick over the traces, we may in time get down to war. You mention a certain place. Well, it isn't right now but it might be tomorrow, and that may indicate to you just how much we know. When somebody sends for khaki today, it does not mean that he may not send for a fur cap next week. Just take it easy, and after a while the waters will recede and the rocks will stick out. Edwards brought the chocolates and mail. I liked the letter best but am grateful for the peppermints. I hope this does not mean that Garry [16] will be cut down on his rations.

Conferences continue. I had an hour and a half with the Secretary of War, at his home, so you can see your old man has stepped into rarefied atmosphere. Not that that means anything. Everybody "confers" all the time. Outside of these affairs, we scribble plans and then do them over again, or switch to new ones, ad nauseam. I won't be here forever, but that's as much as I can say.

All the while the plans for the future were being shaped on Washington's drafting board, the outline of present events grew worse. The critical point of disaster, for America, seemed to be Asia. There, the Japanese had seized Hong-kong, isolated the Philippines, invaded Malaya, occupied Thailand, and seemed on the point of sweeping away every Allied defense point north of Australia.

Stilwell had had long prewar service in Asia; he was regarded by the Army as its most accomplished student of Oriental affairs. He knew the government of China, had toured its battlefronts in the early years of the war against Japan, spoke and read Chinese. In early January, he had been consulted frequently by the General Staff on its plans for halting the Japanese advance.

The one remaining effective bridge of contact between China and the Allied world was Burma. For American strategy it was vital that China be kept an active fighting power on Japan's farther flank, and it was more vital, then, to keep Burma inviolate than to maintain any other point of danger in the line of defense that stretched from Rangoon in Burma to Port Darwin, Australia, three thousand miles south.

At the end of January, Secretary of War Stimson had invited Stilwell to dinner to discuss the China situation with

[15] That is, the North African campaign.
[16] The Stilwells' giant schnauzer.

him.[17] Their friendship was to grow steadily during the war
years. And to Stimson after their conversation it seemed that
Stilwell could serve the nation more effectively, immediately,
in Burma against the Japanese than in leading the indefinite
and much-debated North African campaign.

A few days after his talk with Stimson, Stilwell was asked
to assume responsibility for the mainland front against the
Japanese. He demanded that he be given full command
powers over the Chinese troops if he were to use them effectively in combat. Chiang K'ai-shek promised these powers.
This was the first of Stilwell's many requests for such authority, the first of Chiang's many promises.

Taken from his planning desk as commander of Operation Gymnast, Stilwell concentrated at once on the Asiatic
front. He threw together a skeleton staff as quickly as he
could and emplaned in mid-February. In Burma, Stilwell
hoped to co-ordinate Chinese and British forces, between
whom a bitter enmity was developing, and with them hold a
front which could be made the jumping-off line for a later
offensive.

JANUARY 23   Here just a month today and the blow fell.
The old gag about "they shall offer up a goat for a burnt sacrifice" is about to apply to my own case. The Chief of Staff
called me in and said that I appeared to be "it," and McCloy
wanted to see me. I went in and he told me he's seen [T. V.]
Soong, who said Chiang K'ai-shek agrees, and no use sending another radio—he himself would O.K. the arrangements.
Also Soong had found out who the United States representative was to be, and had "investigated" my record. He then
said he was perfectly satisfied and knew Chiang K'ai-shek
would be, and thought the best man in the Army for the job
had been chosen. (My God, am I carrying weight.)

So he wrote an answer for Soong to send to Stimson, and I O.K.'d it, and George [Marshall] O.K.'d it and Stimson sent for me and gave me a fatherly talk. He is convinced that this may develop in a big way—he sure wants it to—and gave me the "hand of destiny" stuff. Promised to back me up in every possible way and "God blessed" me out.

So Eisenhower took me down to Drum's office and I moved in. Talked to Ferris and Wyman, and then went down to the War College and told the staff the news. They were sort of stunned and took it in silence. The arrangement is for them to go right ahead, and for Fredendall to come in, transferred from his corps to the III. Probably he'll want to make changes and I can pick up some of the boys. Saw Malony, who giggled and said, "George thought he was going to get rid of Drum in a clever way, and all he's accomplished is to lose his best corps commander—and is he burned up over it." Very flattering, but I'm discounting such remarks.

Went back to the War Department and read the files. Drum sure had big ideas about getting a base in Calcutta and appearing with a big staff and the nucleus of an army and then building up to AEF proportions before he launched his thunderbolts. Some of his yes-men paraphrased his ideas and added similar contributions to the files. None of them seemed to realize that the world is on fire and SOMETHING must be done, NOW. Made a date with Soong for tomorrow.

JANUARY 24   To War Department and War College.

The British have one brigade east of Rangoon and one more on the way. That's what they thought sufficient to hold Burma. And the SUPREME COMMANDER, Wavell, refused Chiang K'ai-shek's offer of two corps. [He] didn't want the dirty Chinese in Burma.

[17] See diary note, Jan. 14, page 25.

Well, this has been a full day. If the Chinese will just play ball maybe we can strike a blow where it will do the most good. Meanwhile, thank God for the Russkies, who got to Kholm today, and who I hope made Mr. Schicklgruber move his command post out of Smolensk.

JANUARY 25   It seems the reason Wavell refused Chinese help for Burma was that the British are afraid of the Burmese civil government. The military have to work through them for use of the railroad. The Burmese hate the Chinese and the British: maybe they are pretty right.

The ABDA [18] setup is defense of the "barrier" (Malaya, Java and North Australia) with its two ends anchored in Burma and Australia. An attempt to push north and fight delaying actions, and also re-establish communications with the Philippine Islands. Wavell in supreme command. Air strength to be built up with the ultimate idea of going after the Japs from China. But the Burma anchor is threatened, and no answer is in yet as to what help Wavell wants from China. What will Chiang K'ai-shek say now, if asked for the two corps [that] Wavell was offered and which he refused? (There is probably one corps of three Jap divisions operating against Burma.)

The AVG [19] is to become the U.S. 23rd Pursuit Group: it will be kept at full strength. Replacements are on the way, by boat. If we can hold on to Rangoon, and develop the bases in China, the bombers can be delivered, and along about summertime the Japs will begin to get it on the nose at home. What a pleasure that would be.

Chiang K'ai-shek commands in China. If Chinese units work in Burma, the United States representative commands them, subject to recall, after Wavell is warned. Indo-China is neutral, although the Japs are there. Siam is a belligerent and can be invaded "legally."

LETTER TO MRS. STILWELL   Three p.m. and I came back to the hotel and left the pot boiling if it will. They have made up their minds about me: First working on one plan then on another, and so on. A new one is now injected and we are setting that up. I think I can take most of the boys along with me. We have to start sooner than I had expected but I will come out to the coast to see you. It is stupid that I can't tell you everything for I know you don't talk. I am going where I believe you would want me to go. A respectable job in a mixed sort of capacity. Now that the load is on me I can feel it and begin to have all sorts of doubts. Can I do anything worth while? Or will I ball it up? What if I don't put it over? etc. Well, that will wear off and, anyway, I can only pitch in and try. It would be bad to let the family down, so I'm expecting everybody to pull hard for the old deck hand. With these few remarks I shall close the book on doubt and worry and just start trying. Everybody here wants to be remembered to you. I am sorry for all of them. They have had to get along all this time without Our Family. I've had the best life of all and we'll see this mess cleared up and still have some time to enjoy our home. I haven't the slightest feeling that I won't and I believe you have transferred the psychic touch to me enough to make it stick.

JANUARY 27, LETTER TO MRS. STILWELL   This has been another of those piddling days. Running around and finding nobody in and phoning vacant offices. It is dull and dis-

[18] American, British, Dutch, Australian joint command for the defense of the South Seas, set up in January of 1942.
[19] General Chennault's famous "Flying Tigers"; AVG abbreviated from American Volunteer Group.

couraging trying to get things done. I gave up and went over
for a few inoculations. Smallpox, typhoid, typhus, and
tetanus. After a few days more—yellow fever, typhus, and
tetanus. Then typhus and tetanus and I'm through. Would
have had cholera also, but they had run out. If they could
inoculate against a pain in the backside, it would be wonderful. Oh, yes, got my blood typed. The doc jammed the wrong
tool into my finger and then found it was broken off anyway,
so we tried again and did better.

The Japs are beginning to get a few slaps, you notice.
There'll be more. It can't be lopsided all the time and they've
had considerable luck already. I hope to find out tomorrow
when I can come and will wire you. The photos of Garry and
Nance's group are grand. Garry sure is a laugh and that's a
cute pup they got for Johnny. Thanks to Doot,[20] as I suspect
she took the snaps.

JANUARY 28 Gradually getting straightened out. The very
uncertain nature of the job, the unknown conditions and
situation, all go to make it a heavy mental load. Will the Chinese play ball? Or will they sit back and let us do it? Will the
Limeys co-operate? Will we arrive to find Rangoon gone?

Saw George. He burned up Wavell on British friction with
Chinese. Limeys sending planes to Rangoon. George says
next two weeks will show whether the Japs can be cracked
soon or not. Can British hold Singapore and Rangoon? Reiterated I might end up in Australia. Admitted the mission
was a big gamble.

Dorn got 27 free games on the pinball machine.

Going home Monday. Whoops.

JANUARY 31 Rainy. Made out priority needs. To PX. Got
blouse, shirts, pen, insignia.

FEBRUARY 2   Saw Chief of Staff about policy, etc. Got some dope. Packed. Office at 1:50. Cold. Haircut. Left at 6:30. Fine dinner.

FEBRUARY 3   Home [Carmel] at 11. Grand day.

FEBRUARY 4   Home.

FEBRUARY 5   Home.

FEBRUARY 7.   Left Monterey at 10:15. Family lined up and waving. Some send-off. Los Angeles, left at 3:30. El Paso, Dallas, Nashville.

LETTER TO MRS. STILWELL   What a send-off! What a family! Perfect. That visit was the all-time high, without any doubt, and you can all write your own tickets. I should have had someone get a picture of you, all lined up, but as usual the best ones get away. I won't need a photo to remember it, however.

FEBRUARY 8   Washington at 9:15.
   Archie [General Wavell] now claims he never refused help. Said he'd take two [Chinese divisions], and for the time being leave the other division where it was. Somebody is a liar. Archie missed Peanut [21] at Lashio and now they are both sore, each thinking the other ducked out on him.
   Henry [Stimson] had me in, to get a "judgment," as Henry put it, on the Jap situation on the coast. What to do about it? Aliens? Citizens? Told them of my experience in Los Angeles. Henry let it drop that the Fourth Army was always exaggerating things, and asked about the "enemy planes." So I told him.
   George [Marshall] cut me down to 200 machine guns,

[20] Nance and Doot: two of the three Stilwell daughters.
[21] From this date on, Chiang K'ai-shek is normally referred to in General Stilwell's papers as Peanut.

20,000 Lee-Enfields, and 5,000 rounds [of ammunition]. No cuts on the artillery, though.

FEBRUARY 9 We go Thursday. We go Wednesday. No, Thursday. No, Wednesday. To New York on Tuesday. 5 go . . . No, 7 go . . . No, 5 . . . No, no, no . . . 14 go. What the hell, let's all go.

Call at White House. 12:00 to 12:20. F.D.R. very pleasant, and very unimpressive. As if I were a constituent in to see him. Rambled on about his idea of the war . . . "a 28,000 mile front is my conception," etc., etc. "The real strategy is to fight them *all*," etc., etc. Just a lot of wind. After I had enough, I broke in and asked him if he had a message for Chiang K'ai-shek. He very obviously had not and talked for five minutes hunting around for something world-shaking to say. Finally he had it—"Tell him we are in this thing for keeps, and we intend to keep at it until China gets back *all* her lost territory." Then he went on to say he thought it best for Madame Chiang not to come here, as invited by some organization or other. It would be too much like a lecture tour of women's clubs. He's right on that. He was cordial and pleasant . . . and frothy.

FEBRUARY 9 Back to White House to see Harry Hopkins, a strange, gnomelike creature. (Stomach ulcers.) Thought it wonderful that at my age, I could shove off on the "great adventure." (*Sic!*) What an opportunity! "You are going to command troops, I believe. In fact, I shouldn't be surprised if Chiang K'ai-shek offered you the command of the Chinese Army." Again, "Is there anything you want the President to do?" and "Do you intend to provide for any American units?" So I shot my wad there. He said that F.D.R. was vitally interested and ready to pull 100 passenger planes off the airlines if we needed them. Wished me luck and promised to help.

Had thought up the idea of using the *Normandie* on the run to India to supply us and Persia. Unfortunately, she was burning at that very moment. (Maybe we can get the other big one—*Queen Liz* or *Queen Mary*.) On the way out, he told me his room had been Lincoln's study, where Lincoln first met Grant. I was slow; I could have said "I'm not Grant, but I can see the resemblance to Lincoln." He had on an old red sweater and crossroads-store shoes, and no garters, and his hair hadn't been cut for eight weeks. I'll forgive him for that if he'll help us out.

McCloy sent for me at 8:30. Worried about the Chennault-Bissell fuss.[22] I told him to let me worry now, and tell Henry so. Henry is quite concerned.

It seems that George Marshall promised Chiang K'ai-shek that Chennault could be the ranking air commander. Soong made an unauthorized statement to me, and then reneged on telling Chiang K'ai-shek he had done so. Then Currie[23] stuck in his wire, urging Chennault to play ball. When Chennault unexpectedly refused to play Bissell bossed him. So we were put in the position of Chinese telling the War Department who could and could not be on my staff.

Currie made a date with Arnold to talk it over and sprang this announcement from Chennault, urging that a man other than Bissell go. Arnold hit the ceiling. I spoke for Bissell, and insisted that he rank Chennault. Arnold so ordered. Currie pulled in his horns. I told him my opinion of

---

[22] Brigadier General Clayton Bissell was General Arnold's choice for command of the Tenth Air Force that was to comprise all U.S. air units in the CBI theater. It was his plan that General Chennault's independent AVG be brought back into United States uniform under the U.S. flag, with Chennault as commander directly subordinate to Bissell.

[23] Dr. Lauchlin Currie, personal assistant to President Roosevelt.

Chennault had dropped a lot since hearing that. It was arranged for Currie to send Chennault another wire telling him to get in the game and play ball or else. They are acting like a couple of kids, and they'll both have to behave.

Our heavy bombers are piling up in India, unable to go farther. If we only had the ground crews, we could use them from where they are. Production is still the trouble, or rather distribution. For instance, for March, April, May, the U.S. gets 60-odd, 70-odd, and 48 fighters. And the Limeys get 400-odd, 325, and 300-odd. (Not accurate, but approximate.) Kee-riste! However, by May we may get a couple of groups with ground crews. The fighters in Australia are being sent to Java boxed, around the south side. The object is to put 2,000 planes in Australia.

Events are forcing all concerned to see the vital importance of Burma. We must get the airline going at once, and also build both the back-country roads.

The smooth efficiency of the Air Transport Command that belted the entire globe at war's end has almost erased the memory of the first weaving of the transport strands. But in February, 1942, when Stilwell left for China, there was no ATC, only a struggling Ferry Command. Pan American Airways' half dozen flying boats—then so new, and now so obsolete—were the single span across the Atlantic to Africa and the Orient. Stilwell's flight from New York to Miami to Brazil to Africa was made at a time when passengers were ordered to stand duty watching the sea for disabled ships or enemy submarines, when a VIP had to be a Very Important Person indeed to fly, when only combat command or emergency air service personnel could crash through the swollen list of waiting priorities. Those were the days when the Vichy

French loosed their antiaircraft on American planes flying over French territory.

From Africa to India the party flew via Kano, Maiduguri, El Fasher, Khartum, Cairo, Bagdad and on across the gulf to Karachi. There were no line messes, no hostels, no accommodations. Even while Stilwell flew, the elements of his strategy were dissolving. Singapore and its 60,000 imperial troops surrendered the day that Stilwell left Miami; he arrived in India to find that the entire Malayan-Indies defense cordon was gone.

FEBRUARY 11   Got to Miami at 6:00 p.m. feeling poisoned. Cool here. Wool is O.K. Columbus Hotel. Had some pompano. Clare Boothe [Luce] gets to ride the plane. Singapore nearly gone.

FEBRUARY 12   To airport at 6:15. Off at 7:30. Turned back after an hour. Engine trouble. 9:00 Miami again. Walked. Movie. Ate. Airport at 6:00. Utter apathy of people about soldiers and the war.

FEBRUARY 13, LETTER TO MRS. STILWELL   This is just like my start for the old war. We left N.Y. on the clipper Wednesday a.m. and sat down in Miami that evening. At sea all the way and saw nothing but water. Stayed overnight at the Columbus and left the next morning, Thursday, from the airport. After an hour and a half, the captain turned back. He didn't like the way the engines were working. So about 11:00 we made our second entrance into Miami. Shoved off again at 7:30 p.m. and at 9:30, damned if we didn't turn around and come back *again*. They had to dump eight tons of gas each time before landing. Today, Friday, they are changing the carburetors and now we expect to leave for the *third* time about 7:00 this evening. Nothing wrong except that spare parts aren't plentiful and they won't send this clipper out unless it's *right*. We should be in Trinidad tomorrow morning and Brazil next day.

FEBRUARY 14   To airport at 6:00 a.m. Off this time at 7:30. On to Port-of-Spain, Trinidad, British West Indies. In after dark.

FEBRUARY 15   Up at 5:00. To airport at 6:00. Got a doctor down for tetanus inoculation. Overland in Guiana. A dreary jungle waste. Across equator at noon. Initiation of pollywogs. The Amazon delta, an immense flat, muddy waste. Over the Pará and in to Belém at about 3:39.

FEBRUARY 16   Off at 4:30. Dozed all a.m. In to Natal at 1:00 p.m. To hotel for lunch. Papaya again. Fairly cool here. Off at 3:30. On out to sea.

FEBRUARY 17   Hit Fisherman's Lake in Liberia right on the nose at 7:30. Big lake landing, shoved off at 12:30. Down the coast over Monrovia. Regular coast line—sandy beaches —flat wooded plain—streams. Out over the water from Ivory Coast (French) on. Dozed. In at Lagos at 11:00 p.m. Got to bed at 2:00.

FEBRUARY 18   Singapore has surrendered—60,000 men. Christ. What the hell is the matter? Hurry-up call at ten. Seven can go—*at once*. Sent five and sure enough word came that only five could go. They got off, *without* baggage. This is all of a piece, everything screwed up. We taxied to office and field. O.K. Baggage *did* go. Reason for cut to five passengers. All set for tomorrow. Kano at noon. 2½ days to Cairo. "Ferry Command" conspicuous by its absence. Hot.

FEBRUARY 19   Maiduguri (300 miles) about 4:30. Outside beds, all in a row. Excellent chow, electric stove and four Frigidaires, cook from N.Y. Cool and dry, delightful air.

Usual Limey stories everywhere, apathetic and snooty. Pan American gang at swords' points with them.

FEBRUARY 20   Khartum at 4:00 p.m. The night was made hideous by howling drunks. I fear the Pan American gang. But hope it was Royal Air Force.

FEBRUARY 21   Up at 6:00—cool and dusty—off at 8:00. The Nubian Desert is a hot sand waste, with black rocks sticking up here and there.

FEBRUARY 22, CAIRO   To [American] mission at 9:00. Beautiful fall weather. Session with Fellers till 12:30. All about how the Germans have put it on the British. 17,000 Boches plus about 26,000 Italians—vs. 80,000 English, Australians, American Air Force, New Zealanders and Indians. British have lost at least 1,000 tanks. Have about 200 now. Germans have about 400 tanks. Germans have 200 planes, constant level. Italians have 400 planes. British about 700. German methods and equipment better. Rommel equals another 50,000 men. British command not unified, Royal Air Force, Navy, Army all independent. Cairo is wide open if Rommel gets reinforcements. British don't think he will; they say he needs Benghazi first, and they interfere with its use. All told, today not more than 100,000 British fighting outside England. Fleet completely bottled. *Queen Elizabeth* and *Valiant* wrecked at Alexandria. (*Hood, Barham, Royal Oak, Repulse, Prince of Wales, Royal Ark, Illustrious, Malaya*, all out of action.) Ninety per cent of Germans getting across to Tripoli from Italy. Malta completely blanketed. German tank recovery service excellent. British poor. What a chance for the Germans unless the Russians can hold them to it. Jumbo Wilson came in. He's defensive too. No apprehension. "Will take six to eight weeks for Rommel to build up and no indication yet. How can Germans use air force in Libya and Russia as well?" etc., etc.

Back for lunch at 2:00 p.m.; to [Minister Alexander] Kirk's house for tea. Pyramids right there, outlined against the sunset. Back to hotel; then to Fellers' house for dinner. Back to hotel at midnight.

FEBRUARY 23   Up at 6:30 and off at 9:30. Over Suez Canal at Ismailia, then the desert. Soon green patches appeared along the coast to Gaza and Jaffa. Turned in at Jaffa, went over Jerusalem, and Jordan River. Dead Sea to south. Arrived Bagdad at 2:30.

FEBRUARY 24, BASRA AIRPORT, IRAQ: LETTER TO MRS. STIL-WELL   Just shoving off again. Yesterday was our most interesting day. Suez Canal, Gaza, Jaffa, Jerusalem, River Jordan, and Bagdad. Had a good look at them all. Cairo rated more than the one day we had there, but compared with Peking—phooey. From here on it won't be as interesting as it has been up to date. This is a surprisingly modern hotel, run by the Iraq government. Queerly enough the best chow we have had was at Maiduguri in Nigeria, where the Pan American had put a cook who used to be in the New Yorker Hotel. There were hyenas all around camp, but the cook had an electric stove and four Frigidaires. Karachi in India tonight. Cheerio and love to you all by kind permission of the censor.

FEBRUARY 24   Up at 5:00. Off at 6:05. Across Persian Gulf to Sharja in Arabia. Arab guard of honor. Silver knives and eye blackeners. They sang for us. The agent, Barrington, a live wire. Showed us everything. Natives live on fish and dates. Off for Karachi at noon. Along coast all way. Arrived 5:20. Adler says only nine B-17s in India. Karachi resembles North China or North Mexico. Much as imagined. Good port. Big military installations. Can handle anything.

Chapter 3

STILWELL'S PLANE touched ground in India ten days before Rangoon was lost to the Japanese. The Philippines were lost, Java was being invaded, Burma was crumbling. Commanderless soldiers, civilian officials, armyless commanders, hordes of refugees, individual planes and plane crews, all falling back in confusion before the Japanese advance, were choking India's highways, railways, airlanes, her streets, hotels, and communications.

The nominal British commander of the Imperial defenses of India and Malaya was General Sir Archibald Percival Wavell, the desert warrior. The commander of the China theater was Generalissimo Chiang K'ai-shek. Between these two theaters lay the Burma front, the only land bridge between China and the Western Allies.

The British were responsible for the defense of Burma—but Burma's importance was far greater to the Chinese than to the British. Already the Chinese had sent two armies—seven divisions in all—to the Burma border; one of these divisions was already in line of battle, 400 miles to the south. The British, under the command of Lieutenant General

T. J. Hutton, had two divisions and a brigade of tanks disposed against the Japanese drive. The British and Chinese cordially disliked and sometimes actively hated each other. The Burmese hated both British and Chinese.

America's contributions to the defense of Burma were the hundred old P-40s and the hundred-odd pilots of the American Volunteer Group, commanded by General Chennault. The AVG made a spectacular fight against odds, writing the finest record of any Allied unit in the campaign. But outnumbered, without secure bases, undermanned, they were forced back in the general retreat so that the Japanese dominated the air over the battlefront and in the rear. There was no over-all commander nor any strategic plans for opposition to the Japanese.

Stilwell made his stay in India as brief as possible. A pause in Delhi, a pause in Calcutta, and then he was off across Burma, flying to Chungking to consult with Chiang.

In Chungking, Stilwell found the Chinese courteous, friendly, and planless. Stilwell wanted to learn immediately precisely what his authority was in the Chinese Army and what strategic plans were being formulated. Several conferences with Chiang K'ai-shek seemingly gave him command of the Chinese Fifth and Sixth Armies, and a cloudy directive to inch these armies down through central Burma toward the enemy. Stilwell left for the front to survey his command in person.

Some names that appear again and again in the course of the diaries are here prominently mentioned for the first time. Among them were:

Ho Ying-ch'in, Chief of Staff of the Chinese Army and Minister of War. Ho, a round-faced bespectacled soldier of 53, had been Chiang K'ai-shek's chief of staff for five years and an intimate of the Generalissimo's for eighteen. His career had been graced by no distinction of combat command, but a skill at paper work and military administration had made him the Number 1 man of the Chinese Army administration.

Shang Chen, Director of the Foreign Affairs Bureau of the Chinese general staff, was a northern soldier who had been withdrawn from the front to the staff the preceding spring. Shang was a rather jovial, straightforward man, with a penchant for polo playing and some command of English. He was charged with all liaison between the Chinese Army and foreign forces. He was one of the Chinese with whom Stilwell worked most closely for the next ten months.

Ambassador Clarence Gauss. After diplomatic service of thirty years in the Far East, Gauss had been nominated United States ambassador to China in the spring of 1941.

FEBRUARY 25   In at Delhi at 12:30. Hearn and I to commander in chief's house.

At 3:00 to the conference. Room full of [British] lieutenant generals and major generals and brigadiers, etc. After I made my speech I started asking questions and nobody but the quartermaster knew anything at all. They will play ball, but cannot help. I made it plain where our stuff had gone.

Painfully small remnants in Burma; they will pivot on flank (left) and retire north.

This GHQ is an enormous affair, big enough to run our War Department. And [only] 3 brigades at the front.

Seventy fighters on way, and 77 coming in two months.
Dinner with the Hartleys [1] and Lady Wavell and daughter.
Quiet and unconstrained. No pomp or ceremony. Wavell
has been hit all right.[2] Lady Hartley let it out. Letter
had come saying his back was improving. Lady Wavell evidently under a strain. Turned in at ten.

FEBRUARY 26, COMMANDER IN CHIEF'S HOUSE, NEW DELHI:
LETTER TO MRS. STILWELL   Getting farther along now.
Stopped here to confer with the commander in chief of the
Indian Army, General Hartley, and iron out a few points
that have come up. Will go to Calcutta tomorrow. We hit
India at Karachi yesterday and had an interesting trip up to
Delhi this morning. General and Lady Hartley have been
very kind: we must have met Lady Hartley in Peking in the
spring of 1936, at our embassy.

Delhi, being the capital, is of course a magnificent layout,
done beautifully with spacious grounds and fine approaches
to all the government buildings. It was started in 1920, so
everything is new and modern. Surprisingly enough, it is
cool and we are wearing wool uniforms.

Tomorrow we will fly past the Taj Mahal and get a look at
it from the air. That will be something I have waited for for a
long time, and I am wondering if it will compare with the
Temple of Heaven.[3] I am inclined to doubt it.

After Calcutta, our plans are rather indefinite, due to
events farther east and doubts as to transportation, but we
have hopes that our own planes will catch up with us soon.

Everybody is well and having a grand time seeing the
world and this is the way to see it. My love to everybody, including the censor, who can hardly take exception to that.

FEBRUARY 26   Yesterday when I looked down my nose at
his one brigade General Hartley said, "Well, it *might* just

turn the scale. Miracles do happen in wah, don't they?" And at lunch, "One *does* enjoy a cawktail, doesn't one? It's so seldom one gets a chawnce. In my own case, I hardly have time for a glahss of bee-ah!"

To airport. Over Calcutta at 5:45. Our plane is to take Wavell to Delhi. Same old story about British. No casualties. No fight. To Great Eastern Rookery.[4]

FEBRUARY 27, LETTER TO MRS. STILWELL   Calcutta at last, one day's flight to go. Arrived yesterday and had to give up our plane, so we're stuck here till Monday. By good luck, I have caught some people here who can help setting up our layout for the future. Have made necessary arrangements with the British command and if it works out equally well where we are going, then I'll feel better. Until today we were rather gloomy, but now the clouds are lifting a bit. Calcutta is a hole, and India in general holds little attraction for anyone who has been spoiled by Peking.

This is a lieutenant general [5] writing you. Just a Mex one, and rather under false pretenses but the grandchildren won't know that.

They are very jumpy here. The population won't stand bombing the way the Chinese have, and the means to prevent it being rather meager, there may be trouble ahead. However, we can expect trouble for a few months before we get to sock back.

I have been so busy picking up the strings everywhere and getting acquainted with all the various agencies we shall

[1] General Sir Alan Hartley was commander in chief of the Indian Army.
[2] Wavell was wounded in Java early in the war.
[3] The famous Chinese antiquity at Peking.
[4] Stilwell is referring to the crowded and expensive Great Eastern Hotel in Calcutta.
[5] Official confirmation of his promotion to the rank of lieutenant general reached Stilwell in Calcutta.

have to deal with that I hardly know what day it is. Our crowd is very keen about the trip and the job and anxious to get down to business. We should arrive with fourteen in our party.

Tell Garry that I expect him to take good care of you all. The more I see of the world, the less I care for any part of it except Carmel. If we can just get this dirty job done and have a little pleasure loafing there, it will be heavenly.

FEBRUARY 27 Shopped for sun hat, sleeping bag, and chow. Big lunch. Nap.

FEBRUARY 28 Woke up with the skitters, dizzy and weak. 1:00 p.m. coming out of it. Wavell and Brereton [6] coming this p.m. Got up at 2:00—to airport. Wavell's plane late. Finally, at 5:30 it came in and they got off. Brereton slapping his fanny with his riding crop and darting around importantly. Finally we went up and introduced ourselves. Arranged a talk at 6:30 at Government House. Wavell gave us the story [of the East Indies campaign].

A shock to Brereton to learn he had anyone over him. Expected to be the Big Boy [U.S. commander in chief] here. I arranged to accompany Wavell tomorrow, but was told by Brereton later that the plane would hold only five and as Wavell wanted Brereton to go, I could stay put.

MARCH 1, CALCUTTA: LETTER TO MRS. STILWELL Just a chance to maybe get a line back to you by "safe hand." We may be where we are going day after tomorrow night. The Big Boy left a greeting here for me and directed that anything I told them, be done.

Yesterday, met General Wavell, who flew down from Delhi on his way to Burma. Had a talk with him at "Government House." He's a tired, depressed man, pretty well beaten down. We have had a ray of hope in the promise of backing from some of our people.

When I think of how these bowlegged cockroaches have ruined our calm lives it makes me want to wrap Jap guts around every lamppost in Asia.

MARCH 3 Usual fuss of departure. Saw Wavell at airfield. More hopeful. Had to buck them up. They were shy of information, to say the least. Off in the hotbox [7] at 2:20 [for China]. Delta region, short water hop, then Assam hills. Burmese villages on hilltops. Lashio at 7:00. Chiang K'ai-shek there. Impressions of Lashio: strained attention of Fifth and Sixth Army commanders while Chiang K'ai-shek was talking to them; sharp, clipped staccato voice of Chiang K'ai-shek on upper porch of Porter House; hushed quiet below; small fry whispering and keeping me from pushing in. Cordial welcome by Chiang K'ai-shek and Shang Chen. "Riot" reported at Porter's house was crowd cheering Chinese troops on way to railroad. Shoved off at 8:10. Kunming at 10:30. To AVG place at Agricultural College. Had Chennault's room. Cool.

MARCH 4 To airfield to wait for Chennault. Had a talk. He'll be O.K. Met a group of the pilots, they look damn good. Off at noon. Rough. Chinese passengers all puking. Quick trip of two hours, fifteen minutes. Hell of a bumpy landing [at Chungking]. Met by Mayer,[8] McHugh,[9] and

[6] Brereton, later Lieutenant General Lewis Brereton, commander of the First Airborne Army in Europe, was at the beginning of the war commander of the Tenth Air Force of the CBI theater, subordinate to Stilwell. Brereton and Wavell were both arriving from the Netherlands Indies, whence the Allied collapse had forced them to flee.
[7] The Indian sun usually baked the aluminum transport planes on the ground till they were almost perilously hot. Entering a grounded plane before flight was like entering an oven chamber.
[8] Colonel William Mayer, U.S. military attaché.
[9] Colonel James McHugh, U.S. naval attaché.

Magruder's stooges. Same old tough climb up the hill, to Lattimore's house.

MARCH 5   On plane, as I was admiring the view of the river and hills and fields, Magruder [10] said, "Isn't that a hell of a looking country?" Gloomy Gus.

To office at 9:00. Called on [Ambassador] Gauss. Lunch there. Gauss is fed up. Back at 3:00.

Back and called on Ho Ying-ch'in. Did it in Chinese. Ho very pleasant. Belden [11] and Fisher [12] in till 11:00 p.m.

MARCH 6   Conference with Chiang K'ai-shek. Dorn had talked to Shang Chen, but we did not *know* anything about Chiang K'ai-shek's intentions as to command, etc. It has been a hell of a mental load wondering how to put it over. Apparently, he [Chiang] told the Fifth and Sixth [Chinese] Armies [in Burma] to take orders only from me as soon as I arrived. He seems willing to fight and is fed up with the British retreat and lethargy. Also extremely suspicious of their motives and intentions. Anxious to know if our Service of Supply in India would be for their use and if they were to have the supplies. Reassured him. Anxious to know if Naiden [13] or Brereton was to be under British command. Reassured him. Told him I commanded them and he commanded me. He said, "Isn't General Stilwell my chief?"

I asked about the general plan for operations in Burma and he said there was none. Wavell had not made any agreement with him, so the Chinese troops are just waiting for direction. Went over the President's message and my orders and explained the setup and help now on the way.

Tong [14] had trouble translating, so Madame [Chiang K'ai-shek] took over and Tong made notes. Tong was nervous and sweating. Madame made some caustic remarks about the British, and their broken promises. She kept me after the conference to talk about Chennault. Worried for fear he would be pushed aside. No objections when I said the AVG was to be inducted [into U.S. Army]. G-mo said we'd set up the joint staff next day. It was a relief to find that the G-mo contemplates command in Burma for me. Now I don't have to wake up in a blue funk every morning and wonder what the hell I can do to justify my existence. That has been a load.

Chungking isn't half bad when the sun shines. The city lies on a rock promontory and we live on the Kia-ling [river] side. Views up and down the stream which is busy with boat traffic. Clear water. Prices are fantastic: $80 for a pair of garters; $200 for a charcoal iron. Coolies go around with $50 bills. Clothes are not to be had.

Lovat-Fraser [15] in to beg for planes. Brushed him off O.K. and gave him an answer to send back. He looked as if he had been in the ash can—old khaki pants, gray sweater with a hole in it. Lost all his stuff on the Burma Road. I remember him in his Indian Army uniform and swanky helmet.

MARCH 7 Waiting.

MARCH 8 A.m. at office. Conferring and studying map. P.m. ride around city.

[10] Brigadier General John Magruder was chief of the U.S. Military Mission in China in the fall and winter of 1941-1942.
[11] Jack Belden, author of *Retreat with Stilwell, Still Time to Die*, who was to accompany the general all through the Burma campaign.
[12] F. McCracken Fisher, Far Eastern correspondent of the United Press, later to be chief of the China division of the OWI.
[13] Brigadier General Earl L. Naiden was chief of staff to Brereton in the Tenth Air Force.
[14] Dr. Hollington Tong—vice-minister in charge of propaganda during the war; he was a personal friend of the Generalissimo, and frequently served as interpreter at conferences with foreigners.
[15] Lieutenant Colonel William Alexander Lovat-Fraser, British military attaché.

MARCH 9   The outlook is obscure, but if the Japs push, we can't do anything. Rangoon is the vital point. Without it, supply stops. If the Japs go to Mandalay, we'll have to build up in India. Chinese munitions are running short (3 months' activity or 6 months if we piddle) . Although I imagine there is a lot of stuff squirreled away. [Chinese] divisional and army commanders are prone to hang on to weapons and ammunition, and not acknowledge how much they have. If we could get everything together, it might be a respectable total. Our important questions are to get a man with authority to handle *all* the engineering and construction [for the Burma Road] and to formulate plans that the British will accept for pushing the Japs back. The Japs have been strangely quiet. They may be building up for an offensive, or they may be too weak to make one. Nobody knows. The British haven't taken a single prisoner as yet, and estimates of Jap strength are mere guesses. I have a hunch the Japs are weak: if they have the men, why not go into Rangoon at once, and establish water communication? Chiang K'ai-shek thinks they won't move farther west.

The Chinese had a grand time in India.[16] The Limeys thought they were impressing their guests, but the Chinese were laughing most of the time. Actually Chiang K'ai-shek was much more impressed with Gandhi and Nehru than with the whole damn British Raj.

Poor old General Hartley thought he'd made a tremendous hit with Chiang K'ai-shek because he shook hands twice on leaving. Tong said, to Hartley, "You have captured the Generalissimo's heart." (Incidentally, while we were at breakfast, recently, Hollington Tong suddenly barged right into the room and announced that he had come to get his breakfast. He has some delusions that have got to be knocked out of him.)

[LATER]   Saturday and Sunday were blank, waiting for word from Chiang; today also. Got word from Shang Chen he would be in with the staff setup. At 7:00 he came, with the expected abortion, making everyone equal and with me the chief of staff for Allied forces alone. Well, hell. I was to suggest any changes I thought suitable. . . . We went on to dinner at Chiang K'ai-shek's. I was the guest of honor —on Chiang's right, and Gauss on Madame's. Simple chow but very good. Li Tsung-jen next to me. He and Pai [Chunghsi] seem like good eggs: it was strange to see them there, after '36,[17] at Chiang's table. Pai and Li are very quiet, thinking their own thoughts.

They told me to stay after dinner "for a few moments." It ran into two hours and turned out to be a session of amateur tactics by Chiang K'ai-shek, backed up by a stooge staff general. Chiang K'ai-shek gave me a long lecture on the situation and picked on Mandalay as the danger point. "If the British run away, the Japs will get to Mandalay and crucify us." I showed him the solution, but [the] stooge jumped in and made a long harangue about how right Chiang K'ai-shek was. I let them rant. Madame said, "How do you like it?" and I had sense enough to say I preferred the G-mo's first plan . . . ATTACK. "But you must remember, one *chün* [Chinese army] is only as strong as one Jap division." "We haven't the *ping li*" [troop strength]. "We don't know the strength." (Chiang K'ai-shek had told me he thought they [the Japs] were weak.)

I said, "Let's go before they build up." No [said Chiang], we must wait, and if they don't reinforce, then we can at-

[16] Stilwell is here referring to Chiang K'ai-shek and Madame Chiang's flying visit of state to India in February, 1942.
[17] In 1936 Pai Chung-hsi and Li Tsung-jen had led a military uprising against Chiang K'ai-shek's government, accusing it of appeasing Japan.

tack. "But if they do," I said, "then they'll be too strong so we must defend." The way to defend, it seems, is by the good old *chung shen p'ei pei* [defense in depth]. A column of divisions about 50 miles apart. After we make sure of our base and get all set, if the Japs don't move, we can move. But not until; and Chiang K'ai-shek doesn't like this flanking counterattack: it's too risky over ground we don't know and over such great distances.

So anyway, the British are s.o.b.'s and he won't take their orders. God damn 'em, they left Rangoon and didn't tell the liaison officer. (I told them we made that the duty of the liaison officer.) Well, anyway, [said Chiang] they won't fight. I ventured the suggestion that they might, and if they did, we might as well take advantage of it. Also that they had tanks and we could use them. That was O.K. Get their tanks to support us. Also the bastards had promised gas for our tanks and trucks and hadn't delivered. Also they were putting Burmese in Mandalay and that was no good. If they did that, we wouldn't play. They would have to hold Mandalay strongly, or else let the Chinese do it. And God damn it, we [Chinese] weren't asking them to let a Chinese command them, but a third power man, and anyway, the Chinese had the most men. (All he wanted was everything.) Anyway, by Jesus, Chiang K'ai-shek was going to send a radio to Roosevelt and tell him to tell Churchill that I would have to command or else Chiang K'ai-shek would take the Chinese troops out of Burma. I said we wanted Rangoon above all, and we must remember our interest there: all the British need is a wall in front of India, but we want the port for our supplies. Yes, but he was going to send the telegram anyway.

O.K. then. Exactly what am I to do? Take a plane and go down there and find out:

1. Will they hold Mandalay or shall we?

2. Will they give us gas or not?

3. Will they give us their tanks (support) or not?

4. Look out for fifth column.

5. Study terrain, weather, nature of the people and what have you.

6. Use the old old *chung shen p'ei pei* and inch down along a string of bases.

What a directive. What a mess. How they hate the Limeys. And what a sucker I am. Well, at least, Chiang K'ai-shek is sticking to one part of the agreement. Never before has a foreigner been allowed any control over Chinese troops. Hedged around as it is, it's much more than I expected this afternoon. I thought I was destined to be a tailor's dummy and go to Tuesday meetings. Maybe the Japs will go after us and solve it for us.

MARCH 10, LETTER TO MRS. STILWELL   Back to the old stand, and find not much change, except the fantastic money situation. We are comfortably located in a government house with a view up and down the river. No bombing yet—wrong season. The town has been plastered, but they are working at it. Chinese spirit strong, but they are tired. Of course, my job is just endless grief, and it's too early to say if I can do anything, but I've put over one or two things and we may get somewhere. I go from one conference to another, sandwich in some courtesy calls and try to keep on an even keel. Leaving tomorrow to see the British [in Burma] and try and arrange some general plans which are lacking. Everybody well, and working hard to get hep to the situation. It's the hardest job I ever had handed to me.

MARCH 10   Talk with Chiang K'ai-shek. Lecture about Chinese temperament and limitations. Why they can't attack. What they *will* do. Won't retreat until ordered out, etc.,

etc. But defeat in Burma would be disastrous shock to morale. Fifth and Sixth [are] "cream of Army." Must be careful, etc., etc. I put up a stout plea to use the British as far as possible, and not expose Chiang K'ai-shek to criticism by reneging on his commitments. He had a lot of good sense in his talk. Importance of making good—first foreigner to handle Chinese troops. Impression made on these troops will make or break me. Must look to future. I repeated instructions and went over all the points he had made. Look at it coldly, and the Chinese are doing a big thing from their point of view in handing over this force to a *lao mao-tzu* [old hat] they don't know very well. It must be a wrench for them, and they should be given due credit, in spite of all the restrictions they have put on me.

22nd and 96th Divisions (of Fifth Army) edge in when chow is provided. Sixth Army stays put. Hold Toungoo-Prome line till British leave Prome. Then back to Thazi line. Hold at Thazi and concentrate for counterattack.

When Stilwell arrived in Burma to assume combat duties in March he found a country whose civil population, both rear and front, festered with discontent and treachery.

The strategy of the entire Burma campaign spun itself about the north-south railway line that ran three hundred miles from Rangoon to Mandalay, and then in meter gauge, two hundred fifty miles more to Myitkyina. Somewhere in central Burma the Allies hoped to establish a front cutting from east to west across the railway, where the Japanese might be held. Meanwhile the actual line of combat was some hundred miles north of Rangoon, running east and west for roughly one hundred miles. This front was being pushed north by the Japanese, but the Allies were trying to shield the railway as they withdrew to

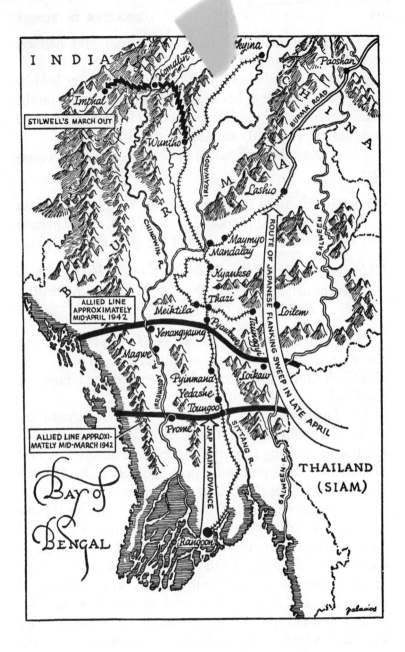

INDIA

STILWELL'S MARCH OUT

Imphal

Myitkyina

Paoshan

Homalin

Wuntho

BURMA ROAD

IRRAWADDY R.

CHINDWIN R.

B U R M A

Lashio

C H I N A

SALWEEN R.

Maymyo
Mandalay

Kyaukse

ALLIED LINE
APPROXIMATELY
MID-APRIL 1942

Meiktila

Thazi

Pyawbwe

Loilem

Yenangyaung

Taunggyi

Magwe

IRRAWADDY R.

Pyinmana

Loikaw

ROUTE OF JAPANESE FLANKING SWEEP IN LATE APRIL

Yedashe
Toungoo

ALLIED LINE APPROXI-
MATELY MID-MARCH 1942

Prome

JAP MAIN ADVANCE

SITTANG R.

SALWEEN R.

THAILAND
(SIAM)

Bay of
Bengal

Rangoon

galacios

keep retreat from degenerating into a rout over pathless mountains and jungles.

The western end of the front (nearest India) was held by the British at Prome. The center, at Toungoo directly on the railway, was held by the Chinese 200th Division, the eastern end (nearest Thailand) was held by the British again.

The forces at Stilwell's command consisted of the following:

Chinese Fifth Army (Commander: Tu Yü-ming) which in turn commanded the 200th Division (Tai), 22nd Division (Liao), 96th Division (Yu), and the 38th Division (Sun)

Chinese Sixth Army (Commander: Kan Li-ch'u) which in turn commanded the 55th Division (Chen), 28th Division (?), and the 49th Division (?)

The 200th Division was in the line. The rest of the Fifth Army was in north Burma several hundred miles to the rear. The Sixth Army was disposed along the border of China and Thailand.

The Japanese in their swift drive north had almost encircled the 200th division (Chinese) at Toungoo in the center. But in so doing they had also exposed themselves, and Stilwell saw an opportunity for a counterattack. As commander in chief of the Burma Expeditionary Forces of the Chinese Armies he wanted to concentrate his forces at Pyinmana on the railway 60 miles north of the front. He wanted particularly to bring down the 22nd and 96th Divisions of General Tu Yü-ming's Fifth Army from the north, where they were useless, to the Pyinmana area, where they could rescue the 200th Division. Scattered across Burma, the Chinese divisions would be destroyed one by one—concentrated and used in battle, they might check the Japanese advance.

It might even be possible to recapture Rangoon and reopen the port.

The plan depended on two things: the ability of the British to hold the western flank at Prome and the swiftness and diligence of the Chinese in moving to execute orders for a counterattack.

To the Chinese, however, concentration of divisions in the battle zone for a counterattack meant not a multiplication of opportunity, but a multiplication of risk of loss. Reluctance to attack seemed to drench the spirit of the Chinese command beyond any measure of encouragement Stilwell could give. In the course of the next two weeks Stilwell found that his authority to command was an authority of courtesy, not an authority of action. He decided then to fly back to Chungking and discuss the matter with Chiang K'ai-shek.

MARCH 11   We hopped off at noon [from Chungking] and got to Lashio at 7:00.

Yü Fei-p'eng gave me a shock. Is this fat man Magruder's idea of a traffic director? I believe he's just a damn glutton.

Mr. Porter's [18] welcome for the night was very cool indeed, but Dorn and I had to sleep somewhere, so we stayed. Dennys [19] gave us a tirade on the "bastardly Chinese" till 12:30 a.m. The British *always* keep their promises, according to Dennys. It didn't sound very generous.

MARCH 12   At Maymyo, Merrill's [20] story of the Burma campaign: no plan, no reconnaissance, no security, no intelli-

---

[18] A Lashio missionary whose home was the scene of frequent military conferences.

[19] Major General Dennys, British military attaché in China; killed a few days later.

[20] Major, later Major General, Frank Merrill, who was to command Merrill's Marauders in the Second Burma campaign.

gence, no prisoners. Left flank wide open at the Salween. Vigorous Jap reconnaissance and patrols; none by the British. Rough estimate 14,000 British against 26,000 Japs. Merrill believes he has been deliberately misinformed.

Talked with Sir Reginald Dorman-Smith, the [civil] governor, and gave him the works. Told him we'd start in shooting the Burmese if they got tough with us. He said O.K. Agreed to help in any way he could and told me to call on him direct. Astounded at my commanding the Chinese troops.

Dennys came in, breathing fire and destruction. The goddam Chinese won't rush in and save the British Empire. He's going up to tell Chiang K'ai-shek what to do, and Chiang K'ai-shek can jolly well better do it. (Dennys might better have let Chiang K'ai-shek alone—he was killed at Kunming in the plane crash on his way up.) [21]

MARCH 13   Friday the 13th. Alexander [22] arrived. Very cautious. Long sharp nose. Rather brusque and *yang ch'i* [standoffish]. Let me stand around while waiting for Shang Chen to come. Uninterested when Shang did come. Astonished to find ME—mere me, a goddam American—in command of Chinese troops. "Extrawdinery!" Looked me over as if I had just crawled out from under a rock.

2:00 p.m. Brigadier Clark and Colonel Jones about maintenance. They agreed to do it. Also will repair ordnance and operating instruments. Damn nice of them. In fact, all the British are now co-operating. If Chiang K'ai-shek will only say "Go" we're off. The press is after me now. Dorn is keeping them off.

About midnight, Major Miller, from the governor's office, barged into my *bedroom*, woke me up and said General Morris was in from India, and that he and General Alexander wanted to see me at 10:00 in the morning at "Flagstaff House." Can you beat it? I wonder what those babies would have said if I had sent Dorn on a similar errand to them? It's just the superior race complex, for which they will pay dearly.

The situation down front looked bad, so I radioed Chiang K'ai-shek over Hou's secret set, to release the 22nd and 96th Divisions to go to Pyinmana and back up the 200th.

MARCH 14   Conference with Morris and Alexander. Latter was half hour late. When he fully understood the command business, he was shocked. "That makes my position impossible from the start." So I gave him a dirty look and said I wasn't exactly on a bed of roses, myself. He just stared blankly at me, as much as to say, "I wonder what the bounder means?"

70,000 [men] on the [British] rations [list] in Burma and [only] 12,000 at the front! The difference is scattered around over the country in Frontier Guard detachments and the Burma Auxiliary Forces. Every "home guard" puts on shorts and a Sam Browne belt and climbs on the ration wagon. But nobody goes up front. There it's just a couple of brigades of Indian troops, one brigade of tanks, and about five battalions of British troops. G-2 [intelligence] had no idea how many Jap divisions are in Burma. Neither did assistant G-2. They finally found a guy who did.

One Limey division is coming to India. Released, I suppose, by our force in Ireland. Morris laughed about that, at me. "Why," said he, "your President arranged that." The Limeys sure have economy of force down to a fine point. (It never came, of course.) [23]

[21] This sentence added later.
[22] Field Marshal Sir Harold Alexander—later commander of all Allied forces in the Mediterranean.
[23] Sentence added later.

This job is a bitch. The Limeys are providing [for the Chinese] rice and gas and transport and maintenance. We have a few radios; no other means of communication. The usual lack of medical facilities, no medicine. Malaria, scabies, blackwater fever already appearing. Wired Merrill in Calcutta to buy a lot of stuff. We are requisitioning this mission and buying all the food on sale near Mandalay. No police yet set up. We are grabbing cars. Everybody else has stolen a jeep. Civil officials with each division. Ammunition will have to last.

Tu [Yü-ming] (5th Army) is O.K. Solid on tactics. Ready to fight. Kan [Li-ch'u] (6th Army) seems O.K. too. Lin and Hsiao, after a long talk, agreed that we ought to fight at Toungoo. Shang Chen also agreed. The only trouble is up top. I am amazed the way the Chinese accept me. At 11:30 decided to act. Got Shang Chen and went to Hou's office. Called Lashio. No word there. Told Lin Wei [24] to start troops [moving south]. Got Tu out of bed. He agreed at once to move right down to Mandalay. Better than my plan of Lashio only. To bed at 1:00. Die is cast.

MARCH 15 (9 A.M.)   Morris, Hutton, Alexander, at Flagstaff House. Told them the news. They were much relieved. Alexander now pleasanter. (Morris has talked to him.) They had the instructions out studying them. Alexander tried to joke about my stealing his Chinese troops. [He] wanted to wear some Chinese insignia. Sent word to Wavell and Brereton. . . . Asked for air support.

Alex says he has just 4,000 fighting men. Alex says he now perfectly understands and we will co-operate alongside each other.

Move of 22nd and 96th Divisions under way. Leading elements here tomorrow. Tu came over at 5:00. He had to shoot a man of the 55th Division at Lashio for hell-raising. I told him to keep it up. DC-3 crash at Kunming. General Dennys killed, on way to tell Chiang K'ai-shek to send more troops.

Got Tu over, went over plan, wrote order for Tu.

MARCH 16 Talk with Brink.[25] He says Japs are good. Fine communications, great aggressiveness, high mobility. Tree fighters. Rush through jungle. Be set on flanks. There is no pause for development [of] counterattack. Use their own tactics on them. Off at 10:30. Dusty ride. At Lashio at 4:00. Long talk with Hsiao and Lin Wei and Shang Chen, [about] tactics and command and move. I'll have to go to Chungking.

Long talk with Yü Fei-p'eng. Usual mess on evacuation. Usual faultfinding about British setup. Seagrave [26] here.

MARCH 17 Chinese breakfast, peanuts and congee. To field at 6:00. At Chungking at 2:30.

MARCH 18 Up at 7:00. In the dumps over the outlook. 10:30 Shang Chen came and we saw Chiang K'ai-shek at 11:00 until 1:00. We had a battle and every point he set up I knocked down. Just kept at it and at it. He'll consider the command suggestion. Exhausted.

Shang to confer with *Chün ling pu* [Bureau of Operations]. He did and at 6:30 came in and told me to my astonishment that Ho, Pai, Hsü, and Liu Fei *all* agreed with my arguments. They will see Chiang K'ai-shek tomorrow and propose consent.

[24] Chief of the Chinese staff mission sent to Burma to assist Stilwell in command functions.
[25] Colonel Francis Brink, U.S. Army, who had participated in Java campaign and was a member of Wavell's staff in early South Seas fighting.
[26] Dr. Gordon Seagrave, author of *A Burma Surgeon*.

Astounding. My first reassuring moment in months. I felt as if I had had a reprieve.

Got to bed early. First time in weeks.

MARCH 19   Had a night's sleep—first time since Calcutta. Woke up without feeling all was lost. At 11:00 saw Chiang K'ai-shek again. Stubborn bugger. But he gave in a bit. 22nd Division can go to Taungdwingyi and can support 200th, or help British out of a mess if they lose Prome. [See map, page 57.] Under my command only, and only in emergency. It's to be morale mainly.

96th Division must stay in Mandalay, but one division of Sixth Army will be sent to Maymyo. Later two more will go to border. In a month, *if nothing happens*, maybe we can take the offensive. (He wants to be sure it will be easy.) Again told me Fifth and Sixth must not be defeated, so I told him to send someone who could guarantee that, because I couldn't. In war, we'd have to do our best and take what came. He laughed. Said he had bowed in some part to my recommendations, but insisted he knew what he was talking about. Told him when fighting started, I would have to be free to act, and he agreed. Of course under the general restrictions of defensive attitude, one division in Mandalay, no British command, and help for British only in an emergency. It's pretty bad, but maybe it will get better. All I can do is try.

59 today. Very nice message from Marshall.

Q. Am I getting anywhere? A. Compared to two weeks ago, decidedly. Appointment as *Chief of Staff, (Creation of) Joint Staff, and Commanding General of Fifth and Sixth Armies.* Of course there are many restrictions, but not so many as at first. Continued butting is wearing down resistance. Repeated arguments are shaking Madame somewhat. (In fact she told me to keep it up.) And Ho Ying-ch'in, Pai Chung-hsi, Liu Fei, and Hsü Yung-ch'ang unanimously approved my argument. That might be considered a major victory. Even Chiang K'ai-shek has yielded on some points—he is sending more troops, he has released a division to Taungdwingyi, and I can even use it to help the British at Prome. He will consider an offensive if there is quiet, or a successful defense—after another month. The supply is arranged, the medical people are stirred up, and the British understand how they must work. The Chinese accept my status, which is close to a miracle, since it is the first time in modern history that a foreigner has commanded regular Chinese troops.

MARCH 20   Tong and George Yeh in. Tong is nosy. Tried to get a paper from me after conference yesterday.

Press conference at 4:00. Not bad; got off easy.

At dinner—called to Chiang K'ai-shek's—more stuff about operations and command, etc. He can't make up his mind. Changeable. If I had said, "British command," he'd have accepted, but when I told him Alexander would move the 96th, he got his back up. Now he's going to pull out entirely if the British give up Prome. And I'm to tell them so.

[This undated paper, found in General Stilwell's files, was probably written shortly after the close of the first Burma campaign.]

When Chiang K'ai-shek told me I was to take command of the Chinese Army in Burma I found that he expected to give me the benefit of his advice and experiences. At the time, the 200th Division was at Toungoo, and the 22nd going into Mandalay and the 96th near Lashio.

He asked me what my plan was and I told him I wanted to concentrate the three divisions near Toungoo. This was not the approved solution: Mandalay, he insisted, was the key to the situation, and he preferred to put both the 22nd and the 96th there, so as to have a strong garrison. We were told to hold Mandalay at all costs. I told him that this would mean that the 200th Division would be beaten[27] and the Japs could then march to Mandalay unopposed. I wanted to fight as far forward as possible, after concentrating all available force there. If we could get three divisions concentrated, we would have some chance of holding the Japs, whereas leaving the 200th Division unsupported would mean losing it and having to oppose the Japs later with only the other two. No, that was not the way it would work. He would give me an instance in his own experience. He had just such a case at Chengchow,[28] which the Japs were approaching from the east. There were three divisions available, but he was too crafty to put them all out there at once. He put one of them in Chengchow, with orders to defend to the last, and drew the other two back to the west about 50 miles. The Japs attacked and destroyed the division in Chengchow. But they went no farther. And do you know why? This, he announced, was a matter of psychology—the Japs were so impressed with the determined defense put up by one division that they simply did not have the heart to go and attack the other two. So really he had stopped the Jap attack with the sacrifice of only one-third of his force.

This dazzling victory left me cold: I told him the 200th Division was in a very exposed advanced position and should be supported; it was a good division and we could not afford to lose it; its morale would suffer if it were left to bear the brunt of the Jap attack. Chiang K'ai-shek said not to worry about that; I could feel free to order the division to stay and fight to the last man, and I should not be squeamish about it; there would be many times I would have to harden my heart and refuse to listen to calls for help. The thing to do was to let the 200th do the best they could, and hold on to Mandalay itself.

Actually, Mandalay had no military significance and offered no advantages as a position for defense. Chiang had never seen it, but apparently thought of it as a walled city and therefore a strong point. He drew a circle around it on the map and pointed to it dramatically saying, "There is the key to the defense of Burma. Never mind what happens south of it: we must put a strong garrison in Mandalay and hold it." Since we had already arranged with the British to attempt to hold the Prome-Toungoo line, I kept at him and asked for three more divisions to be sent down. These could make Mandalay safe, while we were fighting to the south. The other units were promised and I finally got permission to move the 22nd to support the 200th, but beyond this he would not go, and it was plain that he was making a concession against his better judgment.

Even after he, the G-mo, had shown me the key to the situation, I was insisting on a different plan and what did it amount to? In spite of his uneasiness, he was letting me move another division forward: this would reduce the garrison of Mandalay to one division, and when we were defeated at Toungoo, we would have lost two divisions instead of only one. In rebuttal, I ventured to say that if we had all three divisions at Toungoo, maybe we would beat the Japs, but this horrified him because it would

[27] Which it was.
[28] A provincial town in north China, near the Yellow River.

leave Mandalay (200 miles in the rear) temporarily unoc-
cupied. In this connection, there was an important thing
he wanted me to remember, and that was that because of
their deficiencies in armament, equipment and transport,
it took three Chinese divisions to hold off one Jap division,
and an attack on that basis was out of the question. Five
Chinese divisions were necessary before an attack could
have any hope of success. This was the doctrine that the
Chinese Army was saturated with: with the G-mo giving
such a lead, the fearful and the incompetent always had a
good reason for retreat, and this fitted in with the natural
desire of the Chinese commanders to keep their units at
as great a strength as possible. The G-mo gave me further
instructions in psychology and tactics, and told me if I
would observe him and listen for only six months, I could
myself learn something of both arts. I emerged from this
conference with permission to move one division up
behind the 200th in case I felt it desirable on my arrival
at the front. Considering his feeling about the matter,
this was a handsome concession to make. And in all fair-
ness, it must have been a severe strain on him to put a
foreigner in command of regular Chinese troops in action
at all. It had never been done before, and he was trying it
on short acquaintance with a man he knew little about.
Even though, as I found out later, he had ways of effectively circumscribing the authority he apparently delegated
without restrictions, the face of the Chinese high command was severely affected, and it put an extra burden on
me in my efforts to gain their confidence. I left, feeling
that maybe some real executive authority might be ultimately forthcoming, as agreed, in spite of the cockeyed
conception of warfare I had been listening to: it was lucky

I did not know then what a long and bitter struggle was going to be necessary.

MARCH 21   At Kunming saw Chennault and agreed on May 1 for induction [of AVG]. Arranged air support. Off [over Hump] at 3:20. Snowstorm about halfway—Lashio at 6:00. To command post and went over the stuff. Yesterday the 200th Division (Cavalry) surrounded a big patrol and got 'em.

MARCH 22   Last night Hsiao got out the order for the [divisional] moves [to the front] and I signed. Arrived Maymyo at 10:00. Saw Alexander. He's O.K. now. Took everything nicely. Going to see Chiang K'ai-shek.

Off at 5:00—down through Mandalay over the twisting grade—Meiktila at 10:00. Pyawbwe at 11:00. Saw Sibert and Co. Tu [Fifth Army commander] in. Mosquitoes thick. 12:30 to bed.

MARCH 23   Toungoo being attacked. Tu [of Fifth Army] worried. Talked it over. Will send 22nd Division to Pyinmana and Yedashe and prepare to counterattack to support 200th.

  1. 55th Division hurry to Pyawbwe.
  2. 22nd Division hurry to Pyinmana and south.
  3. Radio Chiang K'ai-shek that Tu wants help near-by and I agree.

Rushed back to Maymyo to get things going. Arrived 4:30. No air support left now. Tai's tanks on way [to front], 30 miles south of Mandalay at 2:30. Bed at 12:00.

MARCH 24   Situation: 200th Division hang on [at Toungoo] till 22nd Division gets set at Pyinmana [to support it]. [22nd] can't be sent to Taungdwingyi now, no water there anyway. Push out a regiment south, and then tell 200th Division to break out and join at Pyinmana. Put 55th Division in at Pyawbwe and hang on at Pyinmana. (Use 96th and 38th Divisions similarly and delay back to Mandalay. This is the best we can hope for.) Wrote letters. Haircut. Nap. Japs north of Toungoo.

The suspense till the 22nd [Division] gets going is bad.

MARCH 24, MAYMYO: LETTER TO MRS. STILWELL You may imagine that I keep busy. There are so many things to do that I never know what day it is, but we are getting organized now and the staff is beginning to take a little of it off my back. You will know long before you get this what I'm up against, and it's not a pretty picture. The Jap air raids on Magwe about cleaned out our meager support, and now we'll be taking it on the nose for some time with no answer available. However, the Chinese have had a lot of that, and I believe, can take more without cracking.

We have a dandy command post here, up in the hills, about 3,000 feet elevation. Unfortunately, most of my time will be forward, in the low country, at least for a while, but I can always run up and get a bath and cool off. The rains are due in about a month and for once I wish they'd start tomorrow. It would help us in the air.

I think of you often and picture the scenes in Carmel. What a paradise. My traveling is done now, definitely, and if I can just get back there, you won't be able to throw me out.

MARCH 25 Situation confused. Got it straight with Tu. He is quite cheerful with 22nd [Division] coming down. General Scott, 1st Burmese Division, in. Looking for 4 guns and 200 men. Caught in surprise at Toungoo airfield yesterday.

Nap. Scott back. Got his guns. Tu has report [Chinese] counterattack has reached point just north of [Toungoo] airfield.

9:00 p.m. to see Tu—he had scheme of attack ready for the 27th. Exactly like my solution. Whole of 22nd Division will attack from Kyundon south. (If the Japs will stay put tomorrow.) Chiang K'ai-shek has changed his mind. Three [radio] letters on the 23rd. 3:00 p.m., 5:00 p.m. and 9:00 p.m. Full of all kinds of warnings, admonition, and caution. Then, at last, at 9:00 p.m., he said, "Use your judgment and give 'em hell." Apparently the fight here has pepped him up. [He says] we can use the 22nd. (Which I had already ordered in.) And I told Tu to take the 96th and bring it along also. The 55th is already turned over to Tu. Whoops. WHAT A RELIEF.

Chiang K'ai-shek and his changeable mind had me worried. I was deadly afraid he would call off this attack. But the seed has apparently taken root, and as Tu says, now we can work my plan. Christ. The mental load on a commander who has strings tied to him. Now Chiang K'ai-shek is concerned about pursuit before we even stop the Japs. If I had done what he wanted and put the 22nd in Taungdwingyi, the 200th would have been lost and God knows what might have happened. It may still be bad, but it couldn't be that bad. Three newspaper boys [in for interviews.]

MARCH 26   If the Japs will only subside just for today, we have a chance. Hot day.

I believe the crisis in this business was when Chiang K'ai-shek said he would pull the troops out entirely if the British didn't hold Prome. He'd have done it too, no matter how hard the British fought. It was essential to get the Chinese committed, and that was my worry when he tied me up and

would not release the 22nd and 96th. (The way to handle
him is undoubtedly the slow way, letting the ideas trickle.
Therefore always be slow to *put an unacceptable plan into
action*.)

Japs were active all night.

Pyawbwe road—riot among British soldiers at Yenangyaung. *British destroying the oil fields*. GOOD GOD. What
are we fighting for? Civil government orders. Hell to pay on
the railroad. Crews running away. No trains below Pyinmana. No trucks.

How [shall I] get the 22nd [Division] in? Report of Japs
at Yedashe [see map, page 57] cutting road, and railroad.
Finally got phone call to Liao [29]—groundless. Long belly-
ache back and forth.

Tu had one of his depressed fits and everything was wrong.
The track might spread, the trip was dangerous, how protect the trains, etc., etc. Everything was against attack. "*Mei
yu pan fa*" [It's impossible]. Christ, he's terrible when he's
like that. Arranged for shuttle, Pyinmana to Yedashe. Told
Martin to hold a gun on the crews and get the trains through.
Captain Snow working on it. We are staying here tonight
and will let it simmer. Tomorrow *tsai shuo* [we will discuss
again]. (Tu is a hard guy to handle; he must have everything just so.) Sent Wyman and Haymaker to Pyinmana to
report. Last train of 22nd passed Pyawbwe at 7:00. Looks a
bit better. Snow phoned he could get them through. Wyman back at 10:45. Encouraging.

Went to see Tu. Queer reception. (Lin, Tu, Shao, all in
the dumps.) It came out that they thought the 200th had
been wiped out. 12:30 last message. Was to be every two
hours and they had given up mentally. I felt the 200th was
still there and kept talking attack. Argument after argument.
Tu went into his room and wouldn't come out.

At 1:00 a.m. a message from Tai [the commanding general of the 200th]. O.K. in Toungoo. Well, once again, gloom to joy. "Now we can do it," etc. I insisted that we attack on the 27th, early or late *pu yao chin* [it makes no difference] but ATTACK. Tu said *"Ming T'ien i ting kung chi"* [Tomorrow we certainly attack]. Well, a terrific load rolled off me. I had visions of the 200th gone, and the 22nd compromised and what not. Now it's just a question of getting the 22nd in. A report at 3:00 a.m. from Lin indicated that two trains were still at Pyinmana. (Anybody that wants my job can have it.) At 9:00, Snow reported *all* five trains *had* cleared. Now Tu says he isn't concerned about troops, but rations. Holy Christ.

The basic cause is Chiang K'ai-shek's refusal to me to concentrate at Pyinmana. Everything trails from that and the delay by Chiang K'ai-shek of the 22nd at Mandalay. Some bastard at Pyinmana stopped the move from 1:00 to 4:00 a.m. *Who was it?* (Tu is too far back, too lackadaisical, doesn't supervise execution. To think that a victory can be compromised by a goddam slip on the railroad.)

MARCH 27   To bed at 2:30. Conflicting reports at 9:00 a.m. of [22nd Division] move through Pyinmana. Finally sure that two trains are still there. 2:00 p.m. Everything is optimism once more. 65th and 64th [Regiments] in position, 66th behind them, guns and tanks, ready. Jump-off at 4:00 p.m. Japs burning outskirts. *Leaving?* Too much to expect.

Later. It *was* too good. Now they [the Chinese] are down again. "They have 49 tanks," "They have 105's etc.",—Tu. Wants to wait till situation gets tough, I guess. 200th easier.

[29] Commander of the 22nd Division.

22nd can be ready tomorrow a.m. "Will they attack then?" "Well, don't know. Must *shang liang* [think it over]." Tu again went into his room. I guess it's impossible.

At 6:00 Martin in to say that the British *had started to withdraw from Prome.* Well, this will raise hell. Martin much ashamed about it. *What to do?* Tu is too much for me. I can announce that I can't command troops that won't attack. Showdown on Tu. What can Chiang K'ai-shek do? Long talk with him. Tu and Lin are playing politics, of course. And Chiang K'ai-shek corresponds with both. So they try to kick me around. Lin Wei shoved off without telling me; he was afraid of being pinned. Left at 10:00.

MARCH 28   In [Maymyo] at 3:30 a.m. Saw Alexander. Alex said Chiang K'ai-shek agreed to command by British.

British planes all gone to India. No one at headquarters knew about it. Oh, you independent air force.

Saw Lin Wei, who agreed with me throughout. Kept at him till he agreed to [transmit] the *ming ling* [the order] to Tu. *So he takes orders, finally and under pressure.* O.K. I won't fool with Tu but make Lin do it: 22nd [Division] to attack. 96th to hurry in and back up. 55th to dig at Pyinmana. Will they get it off? I wonder. Letter from Madame [Chiang]. British command accepted by Chiang K'ai-shek. Talked with staff. Notified Alexander and Lin Wei.

Shoved off at 4:00. Reached Pyawbwe at 10:00 (rock on road—just a bit of sabotage). Tu came in and talked about the situation and the attack tomorrow. He accepts the order all right. *Thinks we've lost our chance.* (Whose fault is that?) We will go around the salient and cut in from three directions—at midnight phoned Maymyo to have Gruber call on Alexander for a real attack, not just a piddle. Major Hill took the message.

MARCH 29 (2:00 A.M.) Maymyo called. "Message delivered. They promise to do it." (Hot day.) Left at 9:30. Yedashe at 12:40. As usual, they are dogging it. General Liao, the 22nd Division's commanding general, is a colorless bird. He wants to wait for the 96th [Division] and I suppose the commanding general of the 96th for the 55th, etc. Full of excuses—how strong the Jap positions are, and how reinforcements are coming to them, etc. Two days ago it would have been easy, but now. . . . They'll drag it out and do nothing, unless I can somehow kick them into it. The order read: "Push in outpost either tomorrow or day after, attack in force toward Toungoo."

Tu goes back [to rear]; I must also, or be thought to be interfering [with his troops] behind his back. O.K. I'll try to be patient a bit longer. HOT as hell. We were all dried out and exhausted. I am mentally about shot. Merrill back at 9:00. Limeys will attack in force with all tanks. Good old Slim. Maybe he's all right after all. Order of the day is that "Chinese are attacking under extreme difficulties and it's up to the British to follow the example." Gave this to Tu in plain language and called on him for a real effort. Full of excuses as usual. Now wants to go back to Pyinmana and has held the 2nd Regiment of the 96th Division there, thus making it impossible to concentrate at Yedashe in time. [See map, page 57.] (Wind up on sabotage.) Also the 1st regiment is being held at Yedashe because a Jap flank detachment is out there somewhere. It's all a bunch of crap. By Jesus, I'm about fed up.

MARCH 30 To bed at 1:30 as usual. Alternatives now at hand. Let it ride and do nothing. Resign flatly. Ooze out and demand own force (make a statement "Now that command is unified [under Alexander] I believe it would unnecessarily complicate the situation if I or third country national remain").

Shoved off at 9:30. Liao and Tu have dogged it again. The pusillanimous bastards. No attack at all. Front quiet, no Jap reaction. Just craven. Liao [commander of 22nd Division] moved command post back a mile. Tu ordered him *not* to attack till 96th and 55th get in. Wavell here.

MARCH 31   Saw Wavell and Alexander. Explained the situation. Shoved off at 12:00.

Chungking at 2:00 a.m.

[UNDATED] THE "SYSTEM"

Chiang K'ai-shek says "J. W. Stilwell can command the Fifth and Sixth Armies." Then I get lengthy harangues on the psychology of the Chinese soldier, and how the Fifth and Sixth must not be defeated or the morale of the Army and the nation will crumble, together with a cockeyed strategical conception based on the importance of Mandalay. Then I have a chief of staff assignment from Chiang K'ai-shek's headquarters. So I go to work.

Then the flood of letters begins. To Tu. To Lin Wei. To me. All of them direct. I never see half of them. They direct all sorts of action and preparation with radical changes based on minor changes in the situation. The Chinese commanders are up and down—highly optimistic one minute; in the depths of gloom the next. They feel, of course, the urgent necessity of pleasing the Generalissimo, and if my suggestions or orders run counter to what they *think* he wants they offer endless objections. When I brush off these objections, they proceed to positive measures—for instance, stopping the move of a regiment until it is too late to bring it to bear —or just fail to get the order out, or getting it out with a lot of "ifs" and "ands" in it, or when pushed, simply telling lower commanders to lay off and not carry it out. Or just put on a demonstration and report opposition too strong. I can't shoot them; I can't relieve them; and just talking to them does no good. So the upshot of it is that I am the stooge who does the dirty work and takes the rap. (This is what I hope will be corrected by the conference April 1.)

APRIL 1—APRIL FOOL DAY Am I the April fool? From 3/19 to 4/1 in Burma, struggling with the Chinese, the British, my own people, the supply, the medical service, etc., etc. Incidentally, with the Japs.

Through stupidity, fear, and the defensive attitude we have lost a grand chance to slap the Japs back at Toungoo. The basic reason is Chiang K'ai-shek's meddling. Had he let me concentrate at Pyinmana, we would have been set to attack. Had he not stopped the 22nd Division when I ordered it in, we would have had plenty of force to cut off the Japs when they first went around Toungoo. Had he not gone behind my back to Tu and Lin Wei, they might have obeyed my orders. He can't keep his hands off: 1,600 miles from the front, he writes endless instructions to do this and that, based on fragmentary information and a cockeyed conception of tactics. He thinks he knows psychology; in fact, he thinks he knows everything, and he wobbles this way and that, changing his mind at every change in the action. We hang on, and he says, "Get all set for a push right into Rangoon." He gets a gloomy report and sends word to dig in at Pyinmana. He curses the British for falling back, and does the same thing himself without reference to them. He is *hipped* on holding Mandalay and can't see that the way to hold it is to lick the Japs at Toungoo. He lets the native sabotage decide the strategy of the campaign. He tells me to keep in my own sector and have nothing to do with the British and then says Alexander can command. He lets Yü Fei-p'eng send me 50 trucks when I tell him I need 150.

His constant interference and letter writing have the effect of completely nullifying my little authority. I have no troops, no bodyguard, no authority to shoot anybody. The army and division commanders are vitally interested in doing what they think he wants them to do. Why should they obey me?

Saw ———.[30] He knows. Spilled the beans. Said Chiang K'ai-shek himself was ordering retirement to Pyinmana line.

At 12:00 went down [to Chiang K'ai-shek] and threw the raw meat on the floor. It was quite a shock. Pulled no punches and said I'd have to be relieved. He said, "Why won't they obey?" "I'll investigate and if the divisional commander disobeyed, I'll shoot him." "Did General Tu order a retreat?" "I can tell them they *must* obey and we can straighten it out," etc., etc. I asked him to think it over and proposed a new army of Burma, under my command. Asked him to consider that too. Said probably I would not be accepted now, anyway, and that since Chinese had accepted British command presence of a third country national was no longer necessary. Told him, however, I couldn't put American air units in support of troops in whose commanders I had no confidence.

It was a very frank interview, and the bombs burst rather loudly. In plain words, the army and division commanders had failed to obey, and I had insufficient authority to force them to obey. Shang Chen is shocked and Chiang K'ai-shek and Madame are worried.

How to evade obeying an order? By General Tu, commanding the Fifth Army. "How can we attack? They have 105s and we have only 75s," or "They have 49 tanks," or "The 96th can't get here in time." (Create a condition by failing to act, and then plead it as an excuse for not acting. For instance, fail to move the leading regiment of the 96th by truck.) Or "They have a flank detachment out there." ("Well, put a battalion against it and go ahead." "But it takes a regiment to hold a Jap battalion.") Or "These are new troops; we have to give them a chance to get used to it," or "The Burmese are making trouble in our rear," or "The trains will run off the track," (actually). Or "There is a break on the Taunggyi line which will take three days to repair," etc., etc.

Tu's method of getting rid of my impertinent suggestions for attacks was to go out and telephone. He would scream and yell over the phone endlessly, sometimes not even appearing when I left. My nominal position being his *tsung ssu ling* [commander in chief], this was of course a serious breach of manners. Lin Wei, my alleged chief of staff, simply ran away from Pyawbwe to Maymyo without telling me he was going. This was when he felt the attack by the 22nd was going to be forced. I chased right after him and caught him at midnight in Maymyo. Away from Tu, he agreed absolutely with me, and got the order out. Then, of course, the "system" got going, and Tu nullified the order by telling Liao to simply put on an act.

The fact that Tu felt he could treat me with gross discourtesy indicates that he took his cue from the highest quarters. What a gag. I have to tell Chiang K'ai-shek with a straight face that his subordinates are not carrying out his orders, when in all probability they are doing just what he tells them. In justice to all of them, however, it is expecting a great deal to have them turn over a couple of armies in a vital area to a goddam foreigner that they don't know and in whom they can't have much confidence.

[30] A Chinese officer.

The worst has happened in the press. Before I have a chance to get my feet on the ground, a flood of crap is released, to justify which I would have to be in Rangoon within a week. What a sucker I'll look like if the Japs run me out of Burma. I hope this command business is settled promptly, so I can go back to the front and hide.

MADAMISSIMA [Madame Chiang K'ai-shek]

A clever, brainy woman. Sees the Western viewpoint. (By this I mean she can appreciate the mental reactions of a foreigner to the twisting, indirect, and undercover methods of Chinese politics and warmaking.) Direct, forceful, energetic, loves power, eats up publicity and flattery, pretty weak on her history. No concessions to the Western viewpoint in all China's foreign relations. The Chinese were always right: the foreigners were always wrong. Writes entertainingly but superficially, with plenty of sarcasm for Western failings but without mention of any of China's little faults. Can turn on charm at will. And knows it. Great influence on Chiang K'ai-shek mostly along the right lines, too. A great help on several occasions.

Chiang K'ai-shek has been boss so long and has so many yes-men around him that he has the idea he is infallible on any subject. He is, however, determined and forceful, and wants to get on with the war. He is not mentally stable, and he will say many things to your face that he doesn't mean fully or exactly. My only concern is to tell him the truth and go about my business. If I can't get by that way, the hell with it: it is patently impossible for me to compete with the swarms of parasites and sycophants that surround him.

APRIL 2   I am always wondering what the hell I will have to put down next. And usually expecting the worst. Went over to Huang Shan [Generalissimo's summer residence] to get the answer, which is the appointment of Lo Cho-ying as my executive officer. Lo is a snappy, energetic, forceful character, about 45. Cantonese. Commanded at Changsha. Generalissimo and Madame both lined him up, and he said he would *fu tsung ming ling* [obey orders]. Tu has previously been under him. He is to tell me everything and we are to be together. Lin Wei is to be relieved. It was obvious that Lin could not handle Tu, but I rather think Lo is a tough bird and can do it.

Anyway, this is a major victory for me and I hope it will clear the air. The G-mo will himself go down and make it very plain to the boys that I am the boss.

When you consider their history and experiences with foreigners, this is really a handsome gesture that Chiang K'ai-shek is making. Of course, the flood of letters will continue, but maybe even that will be tempered a bit by this visit. Madame understands what it means and promises to help in any way she can, which is a whole lot.

APRIL 3 Good sleep at last. Woke up without a worry. What a wonderful feeling. To office. Nap. (Puked my breakfast—bad orange juice.)

APRIL 4 To office. Chiu Lung P'o [air] field at 11:30. Waited at field till 2:00 p.m. Flight called off. Back home. Nap. Tomorrow is Easter.

We are making arrangements for the April 8/9 party [the Doolittle raid on Tokyo] but the three essential fields have all been bombed.[31] Leak? Or just precaution by the Japs? Suspect talk in Washington.

---

[31] The Doolittle raiders were to land in Chekiang, one of China's eastern provinces, where usable airfields awaited them.

APRIL 5   Bad weather. Off at 11:00 a.m. Lunch at Kunming at 2:00. Lung Yun [the governor of Yünnan province]
in. Comical little duck.

Lashio at 6:00. Burma rifles and bagpipes for G-mo. To
Porter House for Lin Wei's exposition of the sichyation.
Clare Luce here. No change in Yedashe front.

*On Stilwell's return he found the front had withdrawn to
the north but was still intact. He proceeded swiftly with his
plans, hoping to fall back on Pyinmana where his main
forces were concentrated; draw the Japanese after him into
a trap; bloody their noses; and then, if necessary, retire in
orderly fashion toward Mandalay.*

*His first action, however, was to make a swift inspection
of the eastern flank of the Sixth Army (fronting Thailand) to
ensure its security. Having disposed the Sixth Army on the
Thai border and left behind several American officers to
make sure that his directions for security should be enforced,
he returned to headquarters at Kyaukse to put the finishing
touches on his countermove.*

APRIL 6   Off at 5:30 for Maymyo. Took [Clare] Luce
along. Arrived at 11:00. Situation about the same. We *still*
have a chance.

7:00 p.m. Meeting with Alexander, Chiang K'ai-shek, etc.
Chiang K'ai-shek laid it on thick and Alex told his side of the
story; parted in amity. Chiang K'ai-shek said, "Consult
General Stilwell: he has full powers to handle the Chinese
troops."

APRIL 7   Chiang K'ai-shek at 12:30. Tu [Yü-ming], Lo
[Cho-ying], Madame, Chiang K'ai-shek, and I. (Photos
with the Chiang K'ai-sheks.) Then talk with the boys, who
were told in plain words that I was the boss—that they would

take orders without question—that I would handle the British, that I had full power to promote, relieve, and punish any officer in the Chinese Expeditionary Force. (Jesus.) This is a new note in Chinese history. Chiang K'ai-shek has come around to my contention: i.e., it is necessary to fight where we are, to hold the oil and food; we *must* fight a decisive battle now. Lo Cho-ying and Tu Yü-ming are all for it now.

Madame told them that this is just what I've been telling them from the beginning, and if they'd done as I said, we'd have been better off. 96th to go at once to Gatthwa. British to hold till we get there. When we get set, ATTACK.

Well, a month ago, this would have seemed incredible, and I wouldn't have believed it would ever come out. Now, Tu and Lo say they don't want to go home if we don't beat the Japs. Baloney, maybe, but they have committed themselves. Pumped by Mrs. Luce for *Life* article. (Chiang K'ai-shek wore his teeth for lunch.) Deathly afraid of this damn publicity; what a flop I'll look like if the Japs just run me up in the hills. Why can't they wait till after the event, and give me a chance to escape the fiasco I may be inviting?

APRIL 8   Yü Fei-p'eng in, trying to pin me down on details of transport. Chiang K'ai-shek sent for me at 10:30. Went over his plan of operations. The usual crap but not so bad, beyond tying up the 38th [Division] in Mandalay. Poor Sun [32] condemned to defend Mandalay.

Kan (commander Sixth Army) in to report; I didn't recognize him. Air raid. We took to the woods and Kan explained the situation under a tree. Twenty-eight planes dumped a full load with a hell of a swoosh. One dud near us—the town took quite a beating; many casualties; one lad going for the

[32] Sun Li-jen, commander of the Chinese 38th Division; two years later he was to rise to be the senior Chinese commander in the reconquest of Burma; Stilwell regarded Sun as the ablest of his officers in Burma.

culvert didn't make it. Several bombs around our headquarters; no hits; a second alarm was a false alarm.

Shoved off at 2:30 for Mandalay. Poor Sun is in a stew.
Reassured Sun and left. Mandalay a shambles. Still burning
and stinking. We finally got out and made Pyawbwe at
11:00. Got some chow. Bed at 12:30. (Jumpy Burma Rifle
guards, along the road, cocking their guns and aiming at us.)
Front fairly quiet. I expected hell to pay.

APRIL 9   Up at 8:00. [Jap] plane over for an hour. Long
talk with Lo and Tu about the situation. The boys are
breathing death and destruction. Concentrate [Fifth Army]
in Pyinmana area and fight. Kan [Sixth Army] to fight south
of Loikaw and watch approaches. The whole point, of
course, is making them stick to the plan. 4:00 p.m. Chow
with Tu.

5:30 shoved off for "front." 200th Division formed up
north of Pyinmana. Fine-looking lot of soldiers. We all
made speeches. Mine was very *chien tan* [simple]. Lo
screamed for 30 minutes. Then Tu for 15. On to 96th [Divi-
sion]. Officers lined up in dark at Pyinmana. Yü is commanding general, schoolteacher type. Indecisive, looks weak.
On to 22nd Division. Liao talked and talked. A lot of crap at
high speed. He impresses me as being empty. The usual
bunk about losses: 14 days in line, and 1,300 casualties.
They got a live Jap today. All the villages burning. Stink of
corpses and burnt wood. Back at 4:34 a.m.

APRIL 10   Air alarm. Lo and Tu in to talk. Letter from
Chiang K'ai-shek welshing on agreement with British about
96th [Division]. Now says one battalion is enough. And
wants British to send their tanks over. Fat chance.

APRIL 11   Filthy breakfast. Off [for eastern flank] at 8:15.
Loikaw at 11:30. Kan [commander, 6th Army] feels O.K.

about dispositions. [Sixth Army] command post is 42 miles from the phone at the forward command post! Ten miles more to regimental command posts. They sure play safe. Left Loikaw at 4:00. Loilem at 9:00 (132 miles). Very pretty country. Hilly and wooded. Cool. Kan put on a good dinner—serving crème de menthe as wine. Good sleeping.

APRIL 12   Pyawbwe at 6:30.

APRIL 13   Dubbed around all day playing rummy. Hot night. Ants got all over me.

APRIL 14   Hot. Air alarms at 8:00. Tu in at 9:00 with deep gloom. Saw British yesterday at Magwe—complete demoralization. British destroying the oil fields. The 17th Division [British] pulling out of Taungdwingyi. Expects prompt breakdown on British front. Pyawbwe bombed and burned today. Message from Lo Cho-ying—Alex wants me at once to Maymyo. Shoved off at 10:30.

APRIL 15   Arrived Maymyo at 4:30 a.m. Slept till 7:30. Air alarm. With Lo and party saw Alexander at 9:30 to 11:00. Did Aleck have the wind up! Disaster and gloom. No fight left in British. "Afraid of the Japs" who dress as natives and live openly in the villages. Magwe lost and nothing there to stop the Japs. Fears a division is pouring up the road. (According to the escaped Indian prisoner, one battalion.)

Situation very bad. If Mandalay is lost, one Indian brigade and the tanks [are to] cover our rear at Lashio.[33] The rest of the British go to Kalewa and Myitkyina.

Alex calls me "Joe" now. Letter from G-mo, full of crap and nonsense—"Give each squad a watermelon." Lo agreed readily to several suggestions: he may be O.K. Nap. Air

[33] The Chinese were to withdraw eastward up the Burma Road to China. Lashio, the entry to the road, was the key spot in the withdrawal.

alarm. Wrote radio to War Department with many inter-
ruptions.

APRIL 16   Pyawbwe at 7:45. Governor's suggestion that
we transport to India, *by air*, 60,000 to 100,000 Indian
refugees.

LETTER TO MRS. STILWELL   Have been up here on business
and am going back to the front this afternoon. We are about
to take a beating, I think, but maybe somebody else will
get hurt too. Already quite a few Japs have decided to stay
in Burma permanently. The Chinese troops have been doing pretty damn well, but you can't expect too much fancy
work without at least a few fancy tools. (If you get the idea.)
Just imagine us as doing our best and if we get run up into
the hills it won't be for lack of trying.

We are getting plenty to eat and I manage to keep busy
as you may imagine. Also, I'm keeping well and not losing
as much weight as I am sleep. I have been well received by
the people I am working for, and if I can do anything for
them, the loss of sleep is a small item. The rains are due in a
few weeks now and that may mean an enforced rest, anyway.

Carmel! I don't dare think too much about that, or even
about the family. But I am happy in knowing you are all together there. Enjoy it and someday I'll be back and look you
up. With a long white beard and a bent back!! Give Garry
some coffee with my best wishes.

APRIL 17   Merrill told me the Governor [Dorman-Smith]
has one of our scout cars. Can you beat it? Radioed to grab
it. Merrill to British front. Tu is now breathing fire through
both nostrils and mouth. (It may be coming out of his backside soon.) ("Total victory" is one of his code words for air
support.) Lo Cho-ying in for a talk. Went over the situation.

Lo is sound. Has reprimanded Kan. I recommended general court-martial for Ch'en.[34]

Alexander in. Got promise of half his tanks. Still doesn't know much about his front. General outlook much more promising. Actually, victory or defeat depends on the character of a few men: Tu, Yü, Liao, Tai, Kan, Ch'en, and Lo. Lo is beginning to pass back to me stuff I planted in him a week or ten days ago.

Alexander impressed me as sucking a lot of moral support out of being around us. His own surroundings are constant deep gloom.

4:00 p.m. shoved off for [Fifth] Army command post at Yezin. Tu out to [visit] 96th [Division] and saw Yü, who had shot a captain and a lieutenant for retiring without orders. Good job. Went all around Pyinmana, looking for defense works. Yü got bawled out. Has not done much of a job. 96th not so hot today. Lost its outposts at Ela and Lewe: at Lewe without much of a fight. Back to Chün pu (Army headquarters) and talked till 10:30.

Tu has the wind up already: they have artillery, they have a reserve, they may do this or that. He's howling for the 28th [Division] now. He's a crybaby, not a commander. Lo didn't take much of his crap, but just the same, he ought to be shot. Chow. Bed at 11:30.

Before any of the slow maturing plans for the Pyinmana trap could come to fruit, the Japanese, by now heavily reinforced, struck at the British flank in the west at Yenangyaung, the oil center. There in the searing heat of the Burmese spring they trapped and all but destroyed the polyglot 1st Burmese Division. Stilwell sped the Chinese reserve to the rescue of the British. No sooner had they been saved,

[34] Commander of the 55th division which the Japanese destroyed in the following week.

however, than the critical blow of the campaign fell: the Japanese pressing through the dirt roads and jungle of the Thailand border fell on the eastern flank in Burma and ripped the Chinese line wide open at Loilem. Destroying the Chinese 55th Division so completely that it never thereafter was listed again on Chinese military records, they raced north through the Sixth Army front toward Lashio and the unprotected Burma Road.

The objective of the campaign thereafter became elemental survival. The line had been turned beyond any hope of reconstruction, and the Allied command problem became simply the withdrawal of its troops up the railway to Mandalay and Myitkyina before the flanking Japanese should cut them off. It was hoped that from Mandalay the Chinese might fall back to China up the road, the British back to India across the mountains.

Stilwell raced the 200th Division by foot, train and truck eastward toward the open flank hoping to slow the enemy column speeding north. The 200th Division arrived late. Stilwell demanded from Chinese civilian agencies in the rear use of their trucks to rush troops to shore up the gaps in his crumbling front. These he was denied, for Chinese trucks were too busy evacuating goods that would be commercially priceless in China to spare transport for military purposes.

The Japanese controlled the air, civil administration had collapsed, and refugees clogged the roads. Military discipline began to dissolve; Chinese generals refused to obey the orders of their own senior commanders as they struggled in panic to flee as fast as they could.

As Stilwell struggled back with his Chinese troops through Mandalay and Shwebo to the north, he learned that the Japanese had seized Lashio, thus effectively cutting *the Burma Road and the escape route by which he had planned to withdraw his men to China.*

APRIL 18   Dorn woke me at 3:00. Merrill back. British in hell of a jam [at Yenangyaung]. Got up; got Lo up and got going. [I ordered] 200th Division to Meiktila by truck and train. One battalion of 38th to Myingyan. 22nd and 96th Divisions delay back to Pyawbwe. [See map page 57.] There is a hole from Ywanua to Kyaukpadaung and beyond.

Lo & Co. took this blow well. All our plans knocked to pieces. And in three days the picture might have been so different. To bed at 5:30.

Up at 7:30. Three AVGs for breakfast. (N.B. The way the boys look at me in the jams, dead-pan, to see how I take it. "Now what are you going to do?" and "Will it break you down I wonder?" I feel like an animal in the zoo.) 200th moving. (Three trains tonight, I *hope*. It's a hell of a strain to just sit helpless, and wonder if that 60-mile hole can be filled up in time.)

Report of Tokyo bombing on radio.

Merrill in at 10:30. Much better news. Burmese in Yenangyaung, Japs—1,500—south of it. British closing in on Magwe. Christ—what a relief! Still critical, but by the 19th the 200th will be in position to smack 3,000 [Japs] reported moving on Kyaukpadaung (maybe).

APRIL 19   Hot as hell. Jap over, strafing.

Lo and Tu in at 10:30. Now the boys are all smiles. We have another wonderful chance for a killing [at Yenangyaung]. Alexander and Slim and Lo and Tu, Winterton,[35] etc., in. "My men are simply afraid of the Japs." Long belly-ache. Well, they delayed lunch till 3:15. Not so good today

[35] Major General Thomas J. W. Winterton, British Army, chief of staff to Alexander.

at Yenangyaung. Chinese attack went too wide. Slim worried the Burmese division will fold.

10:30 p.m. that bastard Tu came in. Same old crap. Can't take the responsibility. Jap will rush up behind us. It will take two weeks to fight them. The Japs will bomb the roads etc., etc. The bastard did not use the trains last night. Discipline was terrible. I told him to go ahead and fight. Christ, he's a headache. It kept up till *midnight*.

APRIL 20   Spear in at 8:00. 200th Division hasn't moved! Order was issued at 4 p.m. yesterday, but Tu has told troops not to move!

38th [Sun Li-jen's Division] retook Yenangyaung, got 400 Japs. Burmese out to Gwegyo. So that's cleared up. Spear in with tales of disobedience and absence.

[LATER] Disaster at Loikaw [on Eastern flank]. 55th [Division] completely smashed, Japs above Loikaw [see map, page 57]. Only two battalions left. Kan (commander of 6th Army) terrified. I ordered Yang to have Kan get a regiment of the 49th Division to Loilem at once, and to order a regiment of the 200th to go to Kalaw. Wild tales of the Jap tank division at Loikaw. Aiming at Lashio? Jesus. This may screw us completely.

Later. 96th [at the center of the front] is in trouble. Japs around them on flanks. This looks like a collapse here, too. Jesus again. Sent Sibert down to find out. Burmese fired Pyawbwe today. Getting out their knives now. Phone wires all cut. Are the British going to run out on us? Yes. The outcome is becoming apparent. Sibert back at 1:00 a.m. 96th about as we figured.

APRIL 21   Battle with planes over our house. No hits. Two

bombs. Lo came in at breakfast. Decided to send Tu to Kalaw with 200th. First priority, plug the Loikaw break. Went on to Maymyo—passed many trucks of gas and rice. Q. The Chinese commanders getting rich? That's why we can't get trucks at the front. Bath. Haircut.

Conference with Winterton and Alexander the Great, 9:30-11:30. Winterton had to write a "directive" which Alexander considered necessary, but was unable to find words to express his "ideas." The directive is that the troops are to occupy positions *where they already are.*

APRIL 22 Up at 6:00. Reached Kyaukse at 8:30. Nap. Alexander came down. Got Lo and "conferred." Alexander will do anything I tell him to. Had him radio Wavell for two reconnaissance planes. Told Lo we'd go to Kalaw [on eastern flank] and check [action of] 200th Division. He couldn't refuse, but he wasn't going himself.

Shoved off at 7:15. On road, stopped and found 114th Regiment in a jam. So stayed behind to straighten them out. (What if I hadn't stopped?)

At Meiktila found Tu by the lake. Tai [commander of the 200th Division] has started, he says, and one infantry regiment has reached Taunggyi. [See map, page 57.] No new developments. Tu sour at being chased to the front. Lo made a speech (spoke of my "determination" in these operations). Bustle during the night, getting 2nd Regiment started. Tu wanted to wait till tomorrow.

APRIL 23 Slept on porch by Meiktila Lake. Cool. Up at 5:20. Hard to get the boys going. Kalaw at 9:00. Tea. On to pass 18 miles west of Taunggyi. Tai there sitting on his ass. Japs in Taunggyi. Hesitating tactics. (Tai's advance guard stopped after two casualties.)

Contact with Japs about 10 miles west of Taunggyi. Surround Taunggyi tonight. Attack at daylight. Went up front
in scout car. Brisk exchange of fire. Too thick to see much.
The boys were still at mile 7, which was kind of slow going.
A good deal of ducking and starting back going on. Fairly
steady, on the whole. Brought back two [casualties]—leg
wounds. 200th *must* take Taunggyi or be caught fore and
aft.[36]

Drove all night. Kyaukse at 6:00.

APRIL 24   No news from Tu or Kan. No news till late at
night.

APRIL 25 (2:00 A.M.)   Message the Japs are 40 miles
north of Loilem. 5:30 a.m. message from Lo, says he has very
important news. Must confer. 96th [at center] chewed up.
So Meiktila is wide open. Must get a garrison somewhere.
Called Alexander to come down. O.K. 200th got to 4 miles
west of Taunggyi.

Alexander and Winterton in. Will send a brigade of
17th Division [British] to Meiktila at once. Winterton
had to write out a Leavenworth order, the jackass. Liao in
from 22nd [Division], heavily attacked at Pyawbwe. Will
hang on till tomorrow night. That may let the Fifth Army
special troops and trucks, and the 66th Infantry (Regiment)
slip back through the hole east of Thazi. It will be a close
call. Then we all fade for Mandalay and its one bridge. I
hope it's still there. The 200th did not get Taunggyi and
will go on for Hopong. A glimmer of hope there.

But all we can get to Mandalay will be the 38th, 22nd,
scraps of 96th. This has been a horrible mental day, and at
lunch if six Jap planes didn't dump a load almost on us. How
the boys did jump for cover. (65,000 gallons of gas and 850
trucks at Lashio about April 18. 105 [trucks] came down

to haul rice and gas. 55 of Yü Fei-p'eng and 50 he borrowed from the Central Bank, food administrator.) [37]

APRIL 27   Left at 4:00 a.m. Came on across Ava bridge at daylight. Car going bad. In Shwebo at 8:00. Bawled the hell out of Lo, who shoved off to get Tu going. 6:00 p.m. Alexander, Winterton, and Lo in. Chewed over the situation. Q. Reconnaissance? No got. Limeys as usual knew nothing. Asked Alec about original plan of withdrawal. [38] "Oh, tanks can't operate over there now, it's too wet." Very loath to turn 38th Division loose.

We will use 22nd and 96th with one regiment of 28th to delay on Myiting [River]. Then cross over and go up the railroad to Bhamo. (Letter from Chiang K'ai-shek. His system is to get a wire about what we've done and then issue instructions to do it. Anyway, he says, to stay in Burma, which is more than British will do. They are on their way.) Lo accepts everything I say, now.

APRIL 28   Japs halfway to Hsipaw, both roads blocked. If 200th gets to Loilem, [39] the Japs will be in trouble.

The division commander of the 28th [Division] refused to obey Tu's order and Chang [commanding officer] 66th Regiment refused to obey Lo's order. Lin Wei is issuing orders also. It promises to be a mess.

Went to 96th [Division] command post at mile 9 on Maymyo road. Yü [commander, 96th Division] is a pitiful object. Entirely oblivious of his troops, he was drinking tea

[36] It was this action for which General Stilwell later received the Distinguished Service Cross. Finding the Chinese confused and laggard, he went to the front and, under intense fire, personally directed the infantry counterattack on the Japanese.
[37] This, at a time when Stilwell was desperately demanding trucks to move his divisions to plug up the various Jap advances.
[38] See April 15 entry.
[39] South and in rear of Jap column moving on Hsipaw.

and fanning himself. Cried all over the place. I got disgusted
and left. Dumb Tu gave the 96th [Division] (1,000 fighting men) 20 miles of front [to defend], and the 22nd [Divi-
sion], with two regiments (4,000 men) , about 5 miles. Back
in Shwebo at 3:20.

APRIL 29 Got Lo over and gave him the dope. He had already issued orders for the 96th to go to Myitkyina and the
22nd to fight delaying action so I left it alone. Sending bulk
of our command post upriver tomorrow. Shwebo bombed
by 27 Jap bastards today. Ugly rumor from Limey liaison
officer that Chinese are leaving Lashio. Radioed Chiang
K'ai-shek about General Lu of 28th Division disobedience.
God, if we can only get those 100,000 Chinese to India,
we'll have something.

APRIL 30 They will blow the bridge [40] tonight. Last night
word came that Lashio was taken. (Chiang K'ai-shek sent a
radio that we were to hold Mandalay!! This a.m. he sent
another that we need *not* hold Mandalay.) Alex and Winterton in. Aleck's wind is up. Now it looks as if the Japs
would rush to Bhamo. Radioed for plane to go back to
Lashio front. Lo wanted to go by railroad for some reason or
other. His gang will, but he and I will take the plane. Our
crowd direct to Myitkyina. Asked War Department where
to go—India or China. (Alex has 36,000 men to take out!
Where in the hell have they all been?)

Imminent danger of disintegration and collapse. I hope
the 22nd [Division] stands up. We are sending 40 people
[Americans] to Myitkyina, 12 to Katha, and leaving 20
here. Dorn and I and Tseng and Belden to Loiwing, May
1, a.m.

Lo over, and obviously averse to the plane. Wants to ooze
out of Myitkyina, leaving the baby with Tu. Finally told him

O.K. he could go to Katha if the plane didn't come, and I'd stay over. Loilem taken by 200th, which moved on north.

Since his command authority over the Chinese had evaporated, Stilwell now sought to save the U.S. Army personnel that had been confided to his care. He hoped that he could send them north over the meter-gauge railway from Mandalay to Myitkyina, where one airfield still remained operational. But the single-track rail line was in chaos; the rail route was infested with troops of various armies, and commanders of differing degrees of authority were all seizing rolling stock and using it according to the logic of individual necessity. Stilwell's plans were suddenly cut short when a head-on collision occurred on the railway north of the town of Wuntho. The tracks became useless. Since there was no highway through the jungle to Myitkyina, American headquarters personnel had been trapped. Stilwell's comment in his diaries on the information was a single word: HELL.

It was now a matter of walking out of Burma, or of waiting to be seized by the Japanese.

Stilwell chose to walk.

The long walk out of Burma was an agony that Stilwell shared with all those other hundreds of thousands who were fleeing the Japanese. The Stilwell party was numbered among the few that survived. Their route was a matter of simple geography—simply to walk through the jungle, wade down the rivers, climb over the tropical mountains that formed the almost uncharted border of Burma and India. Chinese troops, some heroically led and nobly organized, others stumbling forward in barbarian undiscipline, followed along behind in the same trail. Civilian refugees suffered their way forward, dying by the road.

[40] The Ava railway bridge south of Mandalay.

There was in Stilwell less of the martinet, perhaps, than in any other American officer of so high a rank. But the march and the survival of his party depended precisely on their strictest obedience and cohesion. There was disease, jungle, enemy, elephants, tigers, snakes—and most of all hunger and exhaustion—to meet or avoid. Stilwell bound the party together with the thongs of his spirit. His was a polyglot crew—26 Americans, 13 British, 16 Chinese, a bevy of Burmese nurses from the Seagrave military hospital, several civilians, some Indian cooks and mechanics. He led the daily treks, counting cadence. He checked baggage and marching order. He inspected food and rationed the individual portions. He cursed, snarled, tongue-lashed his people—and brought every man through alive.

The march took him over the dirt roads and jungle trails from Wuntho to the Uyu River. There the party fashioned rafts and poled downstream for two days to the Chindwin. They crossed the Chindwin and then for eight days climbed up and down the razorback forested mountains of the Indian border. They arrived finally at Imphal, where the British hurried them on to an airfield and contact with the world.

MAY 1 Loiwing is now closed. No radio communications last night.

Neither plane from Chungking nor Calcutta had appeared before 8:00 a.m. So I'm stuck on the western front. Sixth Army [headquarters] at Zigon. So we'll go too. Lo shoved off by train. He never intended to go on the plane at all. At 10:00, 27 bombers went up and worked on Kinu. At 11:00 [American] plane in from Yünnanyi! Sent bulk of headquarters crowd out to Calcutta. Plane to be back tonight. Sent for three planes to come in tonight. We can get some British women out anyway. (The crowd that shoved

off were plenty pleased. We are now down to twelve officers,
plus hangers-on.)

Lo's train collided last night with another. Unfortunately,
he was not killed.

Went to British headquarters about the planes for British
families. Dumb Limeys sitting around. Got a captain finally.
Not interested, don't you know. "Our people are all out, I
believe." Then the goddam car stalled and we went back to
get it fixed, then three hours to Zigon. Got the Burmese
division and all codes.

MAY 2   Tu in at 6:00. Had breakfast with us. Shoved off.
Battled along the ox trails till 10:00. Hot. 3:40 off again.
Bitch of a "road." Got to Pintha at 7:00. Supper at 11:00
p.m. Lo's train in. Talked to him: he was secretly ashamed
of himself.

MAY 3   Off at 6:30. Sibert and I and [Paul] Jones by railroad auto. Nice ride to Karolin. Road blocked by *two* cars.
Limey was just looking at them. Jones rooted them out and
pushed the cars up. Did the Limey push? NO. (No news
from anywhere. Japs may be in Bhamo for all we know.)
Got to Wuntho at 9:30. Lo's train is in.

Letter from Chiang K'ai-shek to go to Myitkyina with
Fifth Army and *not lose time*. Rain. 22nd coming over the
river. It is now apparent that we can no longer be of much
use. Tu is doing just as [he] pleases. Lo has no control over
him. Lin Hsiang is doing nothing. Why keep Americans in
hot water?

Went at 8:00 to see Lo. House dark—everybody gone.
Went to train and talked supply. Lin Hsiang had no plan.
I told him we had several. Should we work or not? Oh, of
course. We are just bothering them now. "Fifth Army will
bring their own food," etc., etc. Lo wants a plane at Myit-

kyina. Lo was leaving without notice. No news. Three garbled wires from Chiang K'ai-shek. Decided to send our
crowd out.

MAY 4   Radios from Marshall. Indefinite. London radio.
"General Alexander, a bold and resourceful commander,
has fought one of the great defensive battles of the war."
And a lot of other crap about what the Limeys have been doing. Martin in. Disintegration at Shwebo. Chinese out of
control. Fifth column busy. Decided to take train if possible
[to Myitkyina]. If not, go west to Tamu.

Jones reported railroad jammed. Hell.

Reconnoitered Katha Road for an hour. Looked good.
We'll go that way. Off at 3:30. Fair road to Lingon, where I
had a hunch and inquired. We were 6 miles past the turnoff,
Colonel Holcombe being the guide. Pooped around the
wrong turn and got stuck and got out. Finally got back, dug
up a forestry guide, and had 12 miles of good road to the
forest bungalow. Arrived at 10:30.

MAY 5   Nap. Breakfast at 1:00 a.m. Off at 1:45. Good road
into Nankan. On to Meza. One bad bridge. Repaired it and
got over in 40 minutes. Bridge at Meza was a fright. Chinese
trucks barging in over a plank makeshift. *Mileage yesterday
was 52.* Elephants trumpeting in the woods. Wonderful big
trees. Fine big bungalow. Guide lost us twice.

Meza to Indaw 18 miles. We got a couple of cars over.
Dorn, Jones and I went to Indaw about a train. A joke of
course. Road jammed both north and south. Everybody piling out the Indaw road. Lo is sunk, he has to be a refugee.
Back to the gang, worried sick about the bridge. Thank God,
they were nearly over. Price: rupees 100 for quick repair.
Set up the column and went back. Waited and waited, imagining all sorts of calamities. Finally at 2:00 McCabe came

in. Broken gas line. Instead of junking the goddam truck, they were tinkering on it. Christ. If I can only get them *around the corner*. Went up 3 miles to wait—Dorn put the car in the soup. Got dragged out. Then waited and waited and waited. Finally got them up and on the way. Battled all p.m. to get them forward, ahead of Chinese rush. We got out after dark and went on till 11:00 p.m. At camp 14 kilometers beyond Banmauk. I think we are ahead of the deluge.

MAY 6   Late start. 3:30 a.m. Lost four trucks yesterday and one sedan, but have the *food* and the *jeeps* and the *party is together*, and still ahead of the deluge. Three serious fords yesterday. Through Thayetkow before dawn. Hit Mansi about 8:00. Got guide. On to Magyigan. Bamboo bridge two miles east stopped us. Checked up on personnel, and found eight Limey stowaways. Abandoned the trucks, harangued the troops, and went to Magyigan while the chow was shifted. Of course, no rafts, coolies all gone downstream already. Ten days to get rafts. Down to next village and saw headman. *Ting*'ed [hired] sixty carriers for tomorrow. Good eggs here (the people). Papayas. We go two days on foot, then on boats to Homalin. We are off the main refugee route. We are ahead of the Chinese horde as yet. If we push hard we can make it.

P.m. getting bearers, arranging food, etc. By chance a herd of pack horses came by, and we took after them and captured them. Oh, boy, what a break. Last messages by radio. Several in.

MAY 7   Out at 6:30. A mess. Start ordered for 5:00. Easy pace down the river. Till 11:00. Holcombe out. Merrill out; heat exhaustion. Lee out. Sliney pooped. Nowakowski same. Christ, but we are a poor lot. Hard going in the river all the way. Cooler. All packs reduced to ten pounds.

MAY 8   Start ordered for 5:00. Off at 5:45. Delay in kitchen. Made Dorn mess officer. No guard on food. No check. Did four marches to Saingkyu. Arrived 10:15. Limeys' feet all shot. Our people tired. Damn poor show of physique. Chattering monkeys in the jungle. Bombers over, reminder that we're not yet out. Hot camp. Insects. Long delay with coolies. March downriver to next village and camped. Pleasant grassy camp. Soaked in the river. Had tea and a good sleep. Merrill and Holcombe better. Nowakowski still shot.

MAY 9   Were to start at 5:00. Got off at 6:30, all over fussing around with the bearers' loads. Dry hike today. Gradually getting some discipline. Sibert pooped out. Rogue elephant flushed the column. We ganged up on him, but he didn't bother us. Smarty Colonel Davidson-Huston couldn't see what we were up to—the elephant had a bell on him didn't he?[41] Left camp at 4:30, on time for once. Arrived Maing Kaing at 5:45. Some rafts ready. No boats. Had a swim. We can start tomorrow.

MAY 10   Overcast. Mules by land with Chinese. They left at 8:30. Sun came out. Nurses put the roofs on the rafts. Long scramble getting rafts ready. Mat sheds by Seagrave's group. Always willing. We have a couple of gentlemen who can't be bothered with work. Four-piece rafts and an advance guard of one piece. Ten polers. First raft off at 10:30. Paul [Jones] says, "Can this be an appointment in Samara?" Christ. Nice ride, but too damn slow. Swim, nap. At dark, supper, then at 10:00 off again. All night poling and pushing.

MAY 11   Showers. That is ominous. Stop for breakfast ten miles from Maing Kaing. Limey officer told me the deputy commissioner at Homalin strongly recommends *against* the direct route. Rafts all split, of course. Seagrave's [party] and the Limeys lagging. Had a hell of a job collecting the gang and getting on our way. Off at 10:00. Made good time to the 6-mile village.

Rumor that preparations for us have been made in Homalin.

Had tea at 4:30. Made a mile or so, and wind stopped us. So we stopped for a big chow. Tea, chicken and rice, green tomatoes, and jungle spinach.

Off again at 10:00, and struggled through the night. Many snags and the rafts are breaking up. I dead beat all night.

MAY 12   Rain at daylight. Mountains now in plain view. 8:00 a.m. about 4 miles from Homalin. In at noon, maybe.

Got there at 2:00. It was 6 miles at least. Contact with mules, kitchen raft, and advance guard. No one in Homalin. Commissioner upriver with a launch. I bet he's beaten it. Telephone office shut. Suspicious. Mules went on and crossed the Chindwin. Sent Jones to direct them upriver. Usual fuss getting started. Off about 7:00 p.m.

Had an arms inspection. Limeys astounded: their guns were in terrible shape. Hiked to village about 3 miles above Homalin. Camped in temple. Slept on concrete floor.

MAY 13   Off at 6:30. Two miles to ferry. Over the Chindwin by dugouts and freight boat. Laiborne not yet up with mules. He's thinking, I suppose. Waited till 1:00 p.m. then Jones came in. Mules coming up west bank. Off at 2:00 p.m. Met mules at top of hill. Took it easy over good trail,

---

[41] A belled elephant is a rogue elephant. The Indians hang a bell about the neck of a domesticated elephant that has become savage to warn strangers that the beast is dangerous to life.

but the sissies are pooped out. They can't take it. Huston
tried to lead his horse through the mess line. "What will I
do with him?" And he's a guerrilla leader. Well, by 5:00
p.m. everybody was tired and snappy, so I stopped at 6:00
and camped. *Cool pool* of water, and a swim. Thunderstorm, but we were just off the edge of it.

MAY 14   Off at 7:15. Sikh fired off his rifle by "accident."
Three slow marches through cool shady jungle at 10:30. Big
bright green sucker about 8 inches long.

Noon halt at 12:15 p.m. Off at 3:30, long climb up to
Kawlum. Heavy rain caught us just as we arrived. Soaked.
Well, we were met at Kawlum by the British from Imphal.
Food, doctor, ponies, and everything. Quite a relief.

Had chow with the British. Canned sausage, while our
people had pig. Jones, Sibert, and I struggled up the mountain and back to be polite. Rained like hell. All of us in a
nipa shack.

MAY 15   Time changed back an hour. Slow start. Off at
7:45, made 7 miles up and down by 12:00. Off at 2:00 for
the climb to 6,500. Not bad. Right over the top of the peak.
Beautiful view over Manipur Hills. In at 5:30, 14 miles.
The cream puffs are doing better. Private shack for the night.

MAY 16   Off at 5:45. Easy pleasant going till about 10:00.
Then a bitch of a hill. Four and a half hours of steady up.
Not yesterday's hummock. Reached Chammu over the top
at 12:45. Greeted by headman in brilliant red blanket, with
bottle of rice beer. Had tea and crackers. Headman of last
village presented me with a goat. I reciprocated with cigarettes.

Off at 2:15 and in camp at Matiang at 4:00. All downhill. Congested camp with horses, mules and 200 bearers.

Soaked feet in brook. Rocky hillside in gorge. Tangkhuls squatting around their rice pots and fires. Lean-to shacks. What a picture, if we only had a movie camera. Thatched covered bridge. Chinese soldiers. Burmese girls. Americans and Limeys, all in the brook washing and shaving and soaking feet. Rough sleeping (14 miles).

MAY 17   Seventeen miles to Pushing on the hilltop. Stiff climb at start, then a long loop down to camp at 14 miles. Beautiful location: gorgeous view out south over a mass of ridges. Noon stop just across the valley. The Nagas come out at each village with a bottle of rice wine, to welcome.

Pushing has a touch of Alaska. The side walls of the houses have upright boards carved like totems. The trees at the top are all cut in notches, with the top branches cut off.

MAY 18   Noisy night with bugs. Off at 5:30, for once on time. Long zigzag climb, which flattened off for a couple of miles at 8:00 a.m. Sharp says this is the best route across hills. Continued receptions, rice wine, seats, and red blankets at all villages. Getting to like the wine. Pretty country; rice terraces, more villages. Made 11 miles by 11 o'clock and had lunch. Cripples getting fewer. 6 miles to Ukhrul. Off at 1:15, climbed for three-quarters of an hour, then leveled off. In Ukhrul at 4:00. More headmen with cider and chickens. Jones got the Assam Rifles' salute! Beautiful place, much like Baguio, 6,400 foot elevation. Myitha [42] meat for supper.

MAY 19   Bad start. Off at 5:50. Ran into rain. Piked on and passed through Limpo without being stopped. So we went on and on and on—15, 16 miles, and then found we'd have

[42] An aboriginal cowlike animal eaten by the Nagas; its flesh is similar in texture to veal.

to go all the way. Had a cracker and a piece of meat. Rolled in at 4:00 p.m., 21 miles. Two-thirds of the Limeys on ponies. None of our people. Sharp started for Imphal to get the trucks out. Paid the bonuses. Eckert and Arnold came in. They *had* been looking for us, after all; at Tamu and here. Cigs and chocolate.

MAY 20   Rained all night. Seven trucks came in but it's going to be "push" most of the way. We put the stuff out and shoved off at 10:00 a.m. Only one bad place, where everybody pulled and pushed and waded in mud up to their knees. We got in at 3:00 and had chow at the old fort. Cordial reception by the Limeys. The provincial administrator, an old fool, named Jimson, failed to send our messages. The colossal jackass. "Oh, were they to be forwarded?" he says. Jesus. Chow at fort and to bed with hell of a cold. Mosquitoes inside the net. (Nice message from War Department and George Marshall. Why?)

MAY 21   Rain. Breakfast at "A" mess. Not such a hot impression. Indefinite about transportation.
    British have no contact with Japs, who appear to be going for China. Chinese troops not heard from. Alexander in New Delhi. Feeling like hell with a cold. Had lunch at "A" mess, a most casual business. (I almost walked out.) In bed all afternoon. Got dinner from Jimson (punk) and took 10 grains of quinine, 10 grains aspirin and luminol tablet and turned in.

MAY 22   Breakfast at 4:00. Party left at 4:30 by truck. Sibert and I with Allen at 5:30. So doped up I dozed all the way to Dinapur. Meeting Wavell tomorrow at Dinjan.
    At 8:00 six of us got a special car and went to bed. Pretty soft.

MAY 23 Train pulled out at 3:00 a.m. Lunch out of cans. Tea gardens all along the railroad. Rice paddy everywhere. Got to Tinsukia about 5:00. No one around. Phoned to field and Brereton, Gruber, Scott came in and got us. They had been about to turn out the entire bomber command to look us up. To Mr. Reynolds' house (tea planter hospitality at 5 rupees each) had bath and chow. Wavell and Alexander came up and talked. Decided to go to Delhi first. Talked to Gruber, Bissell, Naiden, Wheeler, Brereton.

MAY 24 Off at 8:30 in Brereton's plane for Delhi. Rest of party just arrived at Dinjan. (Four sick.) Gruber says everything will be O.K. Good dopey trip to Delhi. In at 4:30. Flock of newsmen at airport taking pictures. Into Imperial Hotel. Press conference at 7:00 p.m. to 8:00. Hell of a lot of mail. Two letters from home, that was good.

MAY 26 (7 A.M.), NEW DELHI: LETTER TO MRS. STILWELL
Ole Pappy calling from India, and reporting in from Burma. Everything O.K. I'm a little underweight—to be quite truthful I look a good deal like the guy in the medical book with his skin off, showing the next layer of what have you. However, I'm eating it on again fast. I was damn glad to get my gang out of the jungle. Most of them now consider me more of a mean old s.o.b. than ever, because I made them all play ball. Rank or no rank. We had quite a trip, which I suppose will now be exaggerated, as usual, till it's unrecognizable.

Tomorrow or next day I'll be going back to report to the G-mo and I sure have an earful for him. He's going to hear stuff he never heard before and it's going to be interesting to see how he takes it.

I have hopes that someday we can step on these bastards (Japs) and end the war, and if I am lucky enough I can go back and have a few days at a place called Carmel, where there are a few people I know who will welcome a vulgar old man, even though he has proven a flop and has been kicked around by the Japs. Meanwhile, the vulgar old man is trying to think up a scheme to kick them around.

On May 26, 1942, American newspapers carried their first direct report from Stilwell on the Burma campaign. The following is an excerpt from the Associated Press dispatch:

"New Delhi, India, May 25—Still full of fight after a 'hell of a beating' in Burma and a weary march of 140 miles through wild Burmese jungles, Lieutenant General Joseph W. Stilwell declared today that Burma could be—and must be—retaken from the Japanese.

". . . He said he regarded Burma as a vitally important area for re-entry into China, now blocked from the Burma Road supply route. . . . Here, in his own salty words, is what happened to the Allies in Burma:

" 'I claim we got a hell of a beating. We got run out of Burma and it is humiliating as hell. I think we ought to find out what caused it, go back and retake it.' "

Chapter 4

FOR EIGHTEEN MONTHS—from late spring 1942 to early winter 1944—General Stilwell was not again to hear the sound of enemy fire. His war, instead, was to be a war of tangled wills, of staff conferences, of desk drudgery, of intrigue, ambition, and politics.

The outlines of the struggle that was to occupy and absorb all Stilwell's energy were established within a few weeks of his escape from the jungle. Its military elements remained unchanged until war's end. Its political elements remain unchanged today, perplexing and confounding all those who have succeeded Stilwell at the helm of American policy in China. The struggle took form about the basic strategy of the war; as Stilwell attempted to translate strategy to action, he found himself meshed ever more intricately in the underlying politics of China and Asia.

The grand strategy was the defeat of Japan. China's role was to be the anvil upon which the hammers of American power in the Pacific might shatter Japan's armies. Stilwell as commander in chief of America's CBI theater was responsible for providing the supply, training and leadership to go with China's huge pool of peasant muscle and courage.

The problem of supply was linked directly to combat. Immediately after the Japanese victory in Burma, America put through an airline over the Himalayan Hump which, under legendary conditions of difficulty and hazard, began to fly supplies to West China. But the Hump airline was an emergency expedient. The ultimate solution, everyone knew, was to cut a way through the Japanese blockade so that a supply-flow great enough to equip entire armies by land or sea could begin. Burma seemed the logical place to begin, and therefore the reconquest of Burma became an obsession, a primitive, single-minded passion at Stilwell's headquarters.

Burma was a great Japanese-occupied wedge thrust north between British India on the west and China on the east. To drive the Japanese from the jungle of North Burma and cut a road across its mountains required the co-operation of both the British and Chinese. Stilwell's assignment was to urge, plead, threaten and beg both Chinese and British— over whom he had no real command power—to organize for the immediate reconquest of North Burma to end the blockade.

The map shaped the strategy of the Burma campaign that Stilwell planned. It would require a Chinese drive into eastern Burma from her own Yünnan frontier; a co-ordinate drive by the British into South Burma from the Indian frontier or from the sea; and a third drive into northwestern Burma from Assam province in northern India. This last drive Stilwell hoped to mount with a joint Chinese-American force. (See map, page 243.)

Theoretically, both British and Chinese agreed on the necessity and urgency of the campaign. But neither the British nor the Chinese were willing to put up the troops necessary for the operation. Stilwell fought a continuing battle to make his allies bring their promises to fulfillment.

While he urged combat to end the blockade, he devoted himself simultaneously to the twin problems of training and leadership within the Chinese Armies. This task brought Stilwell to politics. The long war in China had seen the troops gathered in pulpy groupings and fixed immobile in the provinces they occupied. Their officers twined in political intrigue: almost every province had as its civil governor an Army general. Over the years, Army politicians had won the upper hand over line commanders. As Stilwell tried to regroup and retrain Chinese units he found himself shaking the inner structure of the Chinese command, and inevitably he was drawn closer and closer to an examination of the politics and government that had produced such an army.

Underweight from his ordeal in Burma, exhausted by his march out, his wiry frame worn thin by dysentery and jaundice, Stilwell entered on his work in the summer of 1942 with no pause to recover his health and strength. By the end of May, he was already planning the details of reconquest. Nine thousand Chinese troops had escaped from the Burmese disaster. Stilwell wished to make these the nucleus of a well-trained Chinese-American force to strike back toward the Burma Road from upper Assam. He was to get Chiang's assent to the training of these troops at a military camp in Central India called Ramgarh.

MAY 25, DELHI   All morning on paper work, figuring the angles. Dinner with Bosshardt and journalists. Kind of tiresome. Dorn fell asleep.

MAY 26   A.m. papers. P.m. same.

MAY 27   Now —— wants to go home, on account of his belly. Englehart in, apologetic about going home and lack of accomplishment in China. Sent in script for broadcast on "March of Time" and at 5:00 recorded it. British censor wanted to revamp it; Fisher wouldn't let him.

Date with Wavell at 7:30. "Hello, Joe" stuff. He mumbled around and I didn't get very far. WILL go back for [reconquest of] Burma. From there to Davies' dinner at Naiden's Hotel, a God-awful affair. Dust storm, lights failed, waiters banged into my chair. Christ, I left early.

MAY 28   Personal letter from Gruber. "Please ask for my relief." Christ again. Isn't there one of them that puts the war first and himself second? Shoved off at 11:00 [for Assam][1] in a B-25 (250 miles per hour—1,150 miles from 11:03 to 4:30 p.m.). Not so comfortable but fast as hell. Beat the transport in.

MAY 29   Goddam boy woke us at 5:30 instead of 6:30. *The pest.* We shoved off in B-25 at 9:00,[2] and reached Kunming at 11:30. Rode at 17,000-20,000 feet and got cold. Took the oxygen. At Kunming found that weather at Chungking was impossible. Went to bed with some aspirin.

MAY 30   Fine day. Feeling better. Bad weather in Chungking. Can't land. To bed at 10:00 a.m.—soup and coffee.

MAY 31   Still bad at Chungking. Stayed in bed.

JUNE 1   Zero-zero [3] at Chungking.

JUNE 3   I don't believe we'll get off. We did, about 4:00, pulling ten Limey soldiers off the CNAC [4] plane.

Fine weather at Chungking. Late afternoon light, on spring crops, very pretty sight. Shang Chen and Ho Yao-tsu met plane. Back to No. 3 [the Stilwell residence in Chungking].

General Stilwell's home and headquarters in Chungking clung to the side of one of the city's tumbling hills. From its flat, terraced roof one could sight directly through the great cleft in the mountains out of which swept the Chialing River from the north; in summer the green rounded slopes of valley gap and the lazy muddy waters far below speckled with Chinese junks soothed the spirit with their endless quiet; and in winter, when gray fog closed down over the hills, the river seemed to be winding out of a curtained tunnel that stretched away, one thought, as far as the cliffs of Tibet.

Originally, the concrete, modernistic house had been built to the taste and order of T. V. Soong who planned to make it his home upon his return from his long stay in Washington. But prior to Stilwell's arrival the government

[1] In this province of Northwest India for the rest of the war were operated the western terminals of the great airline over the Hump.
[2] For the trip across the Hump.
[3] Flight conditions impossible.
[4] The China National Aviation Company, a joint Sino-American airline founded in 1931, and the outstanding pioneer of civilian aviation in the Orient for fifteen years.

had taken over the house as residence for a list of distinguished foreigners that included Owen Lattimore and Lauchlin Currie. When General Stilwell arrived it was turned over to him as personal headquarters and staffed by the government with twenty-nine servants—seven gatemen, two gardeners, four houseboys, one cook and two kitchenmen, four water boys to haul water to the rooftop tanks, three general servants, and odds and ends whose function was never defined. Their duties were as much to watch Stilwell as to care for him. The Chinese espionage system kept him under surveillance and on at least one occasion he found agents shuffling through his desk papers. Stilwell reduced this staff as soon as possible and, while he was there, it operated with reasonable efficiency. The cook considered Stilwell a deputy of God and, when he was in Chungking, produced spectacular dishes of Chinese-American cuisine. The service staff was constantly quarreling; on one occasion a houseboy cut off the ear of one of the general service staff with a meat cleaver. A foul-tempered monkey, which had the run of the house, bit everyone except General Stilwell, General Dorn (its owner), and one of the servants.

Stilwell's staff lived in the various rooms in the basement and on the first floor. His own suite consisted of a very large and very gloomy bedroom into which the sun never entered, a bathroom with wretched plumbing, and a small office in which he did most of his work and thinking. The maproom was in the basement and was sometimes used as a movie projection room. Of the two and a half years in the CBI theater, Stilwell probably spent no more than eight months in this house; but it was more home than any other spot in Asia, and to it he always returned from his long trips. It was his first lodging when he arrived; and there, late in 1944, he received the telegram relieving him from command.

JUNE 4, CHUNGKING Got [Dr.] Mendelsohn to look me over. He says jaundice, perhaps due to bad yellow fever serum last February. To bed and a purge in the morning. At 12:30 to see Chiang K'ai-shek and Madame. Both very pleasant. He invited me to Huang Shan for weekend. I gave them the full story, pulling no punches, and naming names. Left the paper with Madame. She took a quick look and said, "Why, that's what the German advisers told him!" Shoved off at 2:30.

JUNE 5 Stayed in bed.

JUNE 6 Reneged on dinner at Chiang K'ai-shek's tonight.

JUNE 7, CHUNGKING: LETTER TO MRS. STILWELL When I got here I was met by letters from you and it sure was good to have them. Your letters are the only bright spot in a drab existence, so send me one occasionally. I am enclosing a few photos taken at Dinjan just after I had gotten out of the jungle, to prove to you that I am not nearly dead yet, although I am a bit skinny. Dorn and I dropped about 20 pounds apiece, but we'll get it all back. I didn't waste much time in India. Took three days to polish off the paper work at Delhi; and then shoved off.

We are oppressed by the magnificence and grandiose style of the Delhi headquarters. Both American [Air] and British. The Limey layout is simply stupendous, you trip over lieutenant generals on every floor, most of them doing captain's work, or none at all. Came to Kunming in a bomber and then got stuck there for five days on account of bad weather here at Chungking. We finally got here on June 3, and next day I made a report to the Big Boy. I told him the whole truth, and it was like kicking an old lady in the stomach. However, as far as I can find out, *no one else* dares to tell him the truth, so it's up to me all the more. He has of course kept an eye on me all the time through certain agencies which I know are always present, but which I cannot identify very well. In fact, I pay no attention to them at all—just go ahead and let nature take its course. There are several things cooking now which will take a lot of talk: I hope some good will come of them, but my recommendations are so radical that it will be a wrench for him to put them into effect. Very cordial welcome from both him and Madame. Whether it means anything or not I of course don't know as yet.

Last February, when they inoculated us against yellow fever, they had some bad serum, which is now causing jaundice. This delayed jaundice apparently caught up with me at Kunming and after I got here the doc took over. I am taking it easy and coming out of it and only speak of it to let you know, in case you hear I've been sick.

JUNE 8   Doc says I'm better. Maybe. Slept, dubbed, and read.

JUNE 10   More of the same. Not such a good day.

JUNE 11   Slept badly. Doubt if medicos know what they're doing.

JUNE 14   Not so good this a.m. Better in p.m. Conference —Chennault, Brereton, Wheeler, Strahm, Gruber, Bissell.

JUNE 15   Talk with Chiang K'ai-shek about this and that. Fifth Army to stay in India. I to retain command, because that will make it easy for the Chinese; they won't have to deal with British. Tu [Yü-ming] to remain. (His face is to be saved, the hell with mine.)

He greeted with derisive laughter [the suggestion] that the Limeys might come back into Burma, grab Siam and

Saigon. "Why," he laughed merrily, "they can't think of such a thing without the help of the Chinese Army." (Jesus Christ.) They have the same old complex—planes, tanks, guns, etc., will win the war. I got a bit hot and told him that the only way to do it was to thoroughly reorganize the ground forces. Madame jumped up and came over and sat by me and said the G-mo had to consider "certain influences," etc. I told her I, of course, understood all that. But with the U.S. on his side and backing him, the stupid little ass fails to grasp the big opportunity of his life.

JUNE 16   Rotten day. Felt worse than any time during the siege. Little better at night.

JUNE 17   Two weeks of this goddam jaundice. All Mendel-sohn can suggest is to go away.

JUNE 19   ——[5] came in. Asked him if Chiang K'ai-shek could be moved [to attack Burma]. He said I might be able to do it—certainly nobody else could. Reiterated that no one dares tell him anything unpleasant. "Ho Ying-ch'in is the leader of the military group but he does not dare tell the G-mo there is anything wrong." Asked him if the G-mo was really worried. He said "in his heart" he thinks he is, but he is putting on a big front of being in full control. The Chinese government is a structure based on fear and favor, in the hands of an ignorant, arbitrary, stubborn man. It is interlaced with family and financial ties and influences, which could easily tear it to pieces if pulled out. Faced with emergency, it has no alternative but to go on, and none of these interlocking interests predominate to the extent that any one of them could take over and clean house, even if the necessary patriotism were present, which it isn't. Only out-

[5] A Chinese general.

side influence can do anything for China—either enemy action will smash her or some regenerative idea must be formed and put into effect at once.

How does Chiang K'ai-shek look at me? I believe he realizes I tell him the truth, which so far he ignores. I am [a] convenient means by which he can sidestep the British. He thinks that by an order to me (Aren't you my chief of staff?) he can make use of any American supplies and units available. He knows I am friendly to China and expects me to present the Chinese side of any question favorably; I am the visible sign of American support.

But he double-crossed me in Burma. He never gave me [the] *kuan fang* [official seal][6] as *tsung ssu ling* [commander in chief]. He worked direct with Tu, Lin Wei, and Hou. He did not act on Yü Fei-p'eng[7] or Yü [96th Division] or Tu.

He has never taken the trouble to answer any memo I have given him. He won't clean up the Chinese Army.

The question now is, What do I do next? Just sit here, or resign?

JUNE 21   Better and better now. Appetite improving. Doc brought some candy. Radioed Brereton: No women to China.

JUNE 22   Surprise radio from T. V. Soong [in Washington]. Through Madame [Chiang]. Emptied a bucket of soft soap all over me. First word I've had from him. It seems they all listen to me in the U.S. and won't I get busy and wire the War Department to keep on sending stuff to China. Maybe he has had word of the serious shipping situation. But something is up and some leverage may come out of it.

JUNE 24   Madame Chiang at 5:00. She made a few cracks and I came back at her. Chiang K'ai-shek came in early.

Conference started badly. [Chinese] troops in India just rest and I look out for them.

Get busy on the Big picture (!) (1) Plan for stabilization as is. (2) Plan for the counteroffensive. (Basis of 500 planes [in China] and 5,000 tons a month [over Hump].) I threw in the artillery training scheme and it caught Chiang K'ai-shek's fancy. He would think about it. Well, yes, it could be done. He'd think some more.

Then the old question of command [for the Chinese Army in India] came up. I said leave Sun [Li-jen]. "Too junior." Well, he'd mull it over. Then he pulled out.

Madame went over the scheme again and I said Tu would have to come home. Would I accept Lo [Cho-ying]? O.K. if I controlled the training.

So she went and talked to Chiang K'ai-shek and that's the agreement. I command; I control training; Lo runs administration and discipline. (It was one of those sudden turn-arounds and Chiang K'ai-shek even went so far as to say we could send in 50,000 [Chinese troops to India] by air.)

LESSON IN PSYCHOLOGY How to handle Chinese command-ers. [Chiang K'ai-shek speaking:] "I have to lie awake nights, thinking what fool things they may do. Then I write and tell them not to do these things. But they are so dumb, they will do a lot of foolishness unless you anticipate them. This is the secret of handling them—you must imagine everything that they can do that would be wrong, and warn them against it. That is why I have to write so many letters."

[6] Command orders were made official in China by the large official *kuan fang*. This was a 2" by 2" seal which, when stamped in vermilion ink on any paper, made it an effective document. It was the most important single tool in the kit the Chinese high command used for war.
[7] Yü Fei-p'eng—the Chinese military traffic director in Burma who had refused Stilwell trucks during the Jap breakthrough in Burma. Yü was an old friend of the Generalissimo.

(Apparently, my dig got under his skin, and he felt called on to explain himself a bit.)

In late June, an incident occurred that was to signal the beginning of the long personal struggle between Chiang and Stilwell. This was the sudden withdrawal of American air units from India to bolster the perilous situation in the Middle East, where Rommel beat on the gates of Alexandria. When this happened, Stilwell found himself suddenly confronted with a Chinese ultimatum—the famous Three Demands: Chiang demanded that three United States divisions be dispatched forthwith to the Burma front; that 500 planes with concomitant replacements be assured him; that the United States guarantee him 5,000 tons a month of airborne supplies over the Hump by August.

This ultimatum was presented to the United States with guarded threats of Chinese defection from the Allied cause. At this time—the sad summer of 1942—all the resources America could spare from her own campaigns were going to the embattled British at Cairo and the Russians at Stalingrad. Three U.S. divisions were nowhere available. Plane production had not yet hit its stride. Transport carriers designed to fly the tremendous heights of the Hump had not yet been designed and wornout C-47's were bringing into China approximately 100 tons a month. The American government was forced to reject Chiang's demands, and Chiang's incandescent wrath was focused on Stilwell.

From then on, though Chiang's suspicion of Stilwell fluctuated in intensity, it was never to rest permanently. His longing for Stilwell's removal was conceived. In Stilwell's mind, at the same time, grew the feeling that he was webbed about with plot and conspiracy. A message of President Roosevelt to Chiang firmly supporting Stilwell was never delivered to Chungking by the Chinese Embassy in Washington. Distinguished emissaries flew from Washington to soothe and placate Chiang, but Washington failed to offer the China theater even a minimum of the supplies necessary for waging war. The CBI theater had a priority listing lower than that of the Caribbean. Stilwell was left to argue the Chinese Army into reorganization and battle by persuasion alone.

JUNE 25 Bang! Brereton to go to Egypt with all the heavy bombers and all the transports he needs. Bang! The A-29s are to be held at Khartum and diverted to the British. Now what can I say to the G-mo? We fail in all our commitments, and blithely tell him to just carry on, old top. The AVG is breaking up, our people are dead slow about replacing it, the radio net operators don't arrive, and our boys are brand new at the game. All we have on the record is the sad Lashio show.[8]

JUNE 26 (11:00 a.m.) Put the hard word on Chiang K'ai-shek. He was primed, I believe. Said the President had assured him the Tenth Air Force was for use in China. Why, then, was part of it diverted without notifying him? He was fed up and couldn't believe the President knew the facts. In any case, I was to radio and ask for Yes or No on the question, "Is the U.S. interested in maintaining the China theater?" (So I did.)

(5:00 p.m.) Madame called. Long radio from T. V. [Soong]. Now I'm the villain. I sabotaged the [Chinese] transport grab by saying we couldn't use more than 100

[8] The first American bombing raid on Lashio by B-25s; nine B-25s set out on this mission from India planning to bomb Lashio, and then land in China. Only two planes landed successfully in China, the radio operator of one of them dead at his panel.

[transport planes]. I sabotaged the 4-engine bomber transport [scheme] by saying we didn't want them. I won't ask
for anything, so of course the War Department won't send
it. In general, I'm an s.o.b. I threw it right back at them,
telling them what I had asked for, and inviting attention to
priorities and tonnage allotted for May to October period.
Explained the gas bottleneck, and the airfield bottleneck.
Madame cooled off rapidly and finally came down to a walk,
but I'm afraid I am now suspect. Also, I'm afraid the War
Department is using me as a whipping boy. "In a jam, blame
it on Stilwell."

JUNE 30 Lo Cho-ying in. Long talk about India. He was
more concerned about the name of the center than about
the training. Worked on back papers. Gradually clearing up.

JULY 1 Conference. Madame Chiang, Chou, Mao,[9]
Chennault, Bissell, and I. All rigged beforehand. "How
many planes do you want, Mao?" "200, with 20 per cent
monthly replacements." "How many do you want, Chennault?" "300, with 20 per cent ditto." "All right, now we'll
tell Washington, and T. V. will put on pressure, and *General Stilwell can get busy and tell them, too.*" (In substance.)
This was an elucidation of the second of the three minimum
demands. What they want now is P-51s or P-47s, or as third
choice, P-38s. That's all. They ignore entirely the limit on
stocks of bombs, ammunition, and gas. As Madame says,
"We won't talk about that. That's your job to get it in."

Madame made a bad break. She got me alone, and said
she wanted to go to the States soon, and that she would
shove off when I had "gotten a good start with the G-mo"—
I'm to be a Chinese, a stooge that plugs the U.S. for anything and everything they want and then she fell in—"And

we're going to see that you are made a *full general!*" The hell
they are.

China has one friend, the U.S., a very generous one. Instead of making allowances for unexpected crises, the Chinese just abuse us for not doing more. They have gotten
away with bluff and abuse, and gotten apologies from the
President and Chief of Staff. Now they get hot over the
heavy bombers going to Egypt and present the "Three Minimum Demands"—three U.S. divisions in India, 500 combat
planes, and 5,000 tons a month [over the Hump], all by the
end of August! Utterly impossible, but they're so dumb, they
think we'll promise it. The alternative is that they will "make
other arrangements." "China cannot go on without help."
"The pro-Jap activity is very strong." Trying to throw a
scare into us. I think they are making a bad mistake. The
President's answer was quiet and dignified and promised
nothing.

Madame wanted me to transmit the clarification of the
500-plane point, *with recommendations*, and give her the
gist of the message. I take the stand that it's still an ultimatum from the Generalissimo to the President, and so beyond
my province. Took the occasion to explain my status as
(1) chief of staff for G-mo; (2) commanding general of
United States Army Forces of the China-Burma-India theater with responsibilities outside of China; (3) U.S. representative on war councils, presenting and maintaining U.S.
policy; (4) representative of President on all Lend-Lease
matters; and (5) a U.S. Army officer, sworn to uphold the
interests of the U.S.

If she doesn't get the point, she's dumber than I think
she is.

⁹ Chou Chih-jou and Mao Pang-chu, respectively the No. 1 and No. 2
men of the Chinese Air Force.

JULY 2   Paper work all a.m. John Liu [10] got the map [from the Chinese staff] with the divisions [of the China front marked] on it. The Bureau of Military Operations refused to give him a list of commanders.

JULY 3   Madame Empress [Madame Chiang] called for my report to Washington—and got it, without recommendations. She got hot on the phone and started to bawl me out, so I said I should like to see her. Kept me waiting till Tong got there; brought in Pearl Ch'en [Madame Chiang's secretary] and took down everything I said. Obviously mad *as hell*. She had snapped the whip and the stooge had not come across, and she'd reported to Chiang K'ai-shek that I had. My position: the whole thing was rigged; it was simply a clarification of the second of the *three minimum demands*, and so had passed beyond my province to comment on, till called on by my government to do so. I was called in and given the orders of Chiang K'ai-shek on the subject.

"And what would I recommend if asked?" I would study the question and recommend what was feasible and what would help win the war, if it turned out to be 800 or 1,500 planes. "But doesn't your position as chief of staff give you the right to speak up?" I repeated that I felt I was being given orders. I then showed her how the program tied in on the freight line, and what 5,000 tons [across the Hump] meant (304 planes, 275 crews, 3,400 officers and enlisted men on ground, five fields each end, each to take 50 transports). She began to get some light. (I took some of the onus; as a matter of fact I should have thrown the raw meat on the floor at the first.) But I told her I thought the G-mo wanted a soldier and not a rubber stamp or transmitting agency. And I also told her that at the first sign of lack of confidence, I wanted to go home. She had me dictate for the G-mo what I wanted to say about the message to the War Department, so I did. (I also told her the three demands had come out of a clear sky, with no opportunity for me to study or advise. Just a direct order from Chiang K'ai-shek.)

Developed gut ache and had it all night. Puked five times.

JULY 5   Now Currie [11] is coming out. They [the Chinese] asked for Harry Hopkins. They're off on the wrong foot again. Apparently, now that the stooge [Stilwell] won't come across, Soong is sending somebody that will.

Blood count showed worms. So I swallowed five doubtful-looking pills at noon. I knew there must be something the matter with me. Full list of "Medicine," 36 hours: spirit of peppermint; paregoric; sulfathiazole; cough syrup; vitamin pills; magnesium sulphate; luminol; hypoderme. *Feeling better!*

JULY 7   Broadcast at 9:00 p.m. Ho Ying-ch'in, 15 minutes of crap. J. W. Stilwell one minute.

[GENERAL STILWELL'S JULY 7 BROADCAST]   Five years ago today I went to Wan P'ing Hsien to find out what was going on in a clash between Japanese and Chinese troops reported there. I found that the Japanese were attacking the town and that, much to their surprise, the Chinese were putting up a spirited resistance. The defense of Lukouch'iao proved to be prophetic and symbolic; the Chinese defense has stood up, and now, after five years, it is a privilege to be here and pay tribute to the man who has carried the burden and gone through the test of battle—the

[10] Who had been appointed by the Chinese Army as Stilwell's Chinese aide.
[11] Lauchlin Currie, special administrative aide to President Roosevelt, later in charge of Lend-Lease for China.

Chinese soldier. To me the Chinese soldier best exemplifies the greatness of the Chinese people—their indomitable spirit, their uncomplaining loyalty, their honesty of purpose, their steadfast perseverance. He endures untold privations without a whimper, he follows wherever he is led, without question or hesitation, and it never occurs to his simple and straightforward mind that he is doing anything heroic. He asks for little, and always stands ready to give all. I feel it is a great honor, as a representative of the U.S. Army, to salute here today, the Chinese soldier.

JULY 8   Have been bombing Chiang K'ai-shek with memos on Kunming and reorganization and estimates, etc. He doesn't take the trouble to reply. Madame expects me to push all this stuff at him, but there seems to be no obligation on his part to even mention it. It is passed to the smart boys in the Chün ling pu [Bureau of Military Operations], of course, and I can imagine what they do with it. The "three demands" missed fire and the President's answer was very quiet and dignified. Maybe there will be a changed attitude in the U.S. If so, maybe I can force Chiang K'ai-shek's hand, and work in a scheme of reorganization and training.

JULY 10   Russki rumor: Yuan Liang [12] and party here with peace terms. Also a Jap, Kuroda: Chinese to go back to Nanking [the prewar capital of China]. Wang Ching-wei [13] to set up in north China. Japs keep Canton, Hangchow, Shanghai.

Possibilities. Sympathy here for the Nazis. Same type of government, same outlook, same gangsterism. The howl of "Beat Japan First" has two possible explanations—one, that if it is done, that lets China coast in without effort on her part: and two, that diversion of American effort to the Pacific would relieve Germany of worry about a second front, and perhaps enable her to get a decision from Russia. Chiang K'ai-shek would prefer to see Germany win than to end up with a powerful Russia at his door, backing up the Eighteenth Army Group [the Chinese Communist Army]. Which, by the way, has spread pretty well all over North China.

Well, well. This has angles. Our fool publicity "heroic resistance—five years' struggle" etc., etc. have set it up for Chiang K'ai-shek—he can say to us "Sorry, we've reached the limit: without help we can't go on." Accept the [Jap] offer and coast [along], telling us sub rosa he was just bowing to necessity.[14] Then, if we win, as he expects, he'll have it all handed to him. If we lose, he has salvaged something, although the Japs couldn't be trusted not to clean him up when they get through with the Russians. However, it would be harder to clean him up from the new position than from the present one. Chiang K'ai-shek can't get the material he needs anyway, so what's the difference till the war is over.

He risks two important things: (1) The definite loss of all supplies he was counting on from the U.S. and the big money that would be withdrawn and (2) the loss of the sympathy of the American people, who are with him while

[12] A Chinese politician of some fame in North China. He was a former mayor of Peking, and, during the war, reportedly aided the Japanese.

[13] The Chinese puppet installed by the Japanese as head of their satellite government in Central China.

[14] For more about the relations between the Japanese and Chiang K'ai-shek in the course of the war, see "Nazi-Soviet Relations 1939-1941" published by the U. S. State Department. Matsuoka, Japan's minister of Foreign Relations, told the Germans of his progress with Chiang K'ai-shek in the spring of 1941. "Matsuoka agreed with these ideas and cited the situation in China as an example. Chiang K'ai-shek, with whom he was in personal touch, who knew him and trusted him, was greatly alarmed as to the further increase of the influence of the Red Army in China."

he fights, but who won't back a quitter. These factors seem to outweigh all other considerations.

Gauss is positive they do. He has had assurances from highly placed officials that any talk of peace terms is bull and he snorts at the idea. I believe he is right and that they are trying to pull our leg again.

JULY 10, THE MANURE PILE: LETTER TO MRS. STILWELL This is the most dreary type of maneuvering I've ever done, trying to guide and influence a stubborn, ignorant, prejudiced, conceited despot who never hears the truth except from me and finds it hard to believe. I'm supposed to buck the inertia of this country all by myself and keep everything lovely by promise and persuasion. What a job. I'm exhausting the possibilities one by one and when I get to the bottom of the bucket, I'll tell 'em. Then they'll HAVE to do something.

JULY 15   Interpreters [for] Ramgarh ready. Artillery officers [for training] held up in War Ministry.

JULY 16   No answer from Chiang K'ai-shek to any of my memos sent during last month. No answer on request to see him, a week ago. Only action was appointing me commanding general of Chinese troops in India. Maybe they are ignoring me because I wouldn't get behind the ultimatum.

JULY 18   Long radio from Marshall. Chiang K'ai-shek wired T. V. Soong that I had "wired the American staff of CNAC to refuse transfer of two transport planes." A lie. Also that "Chiang K'ai-shek had to beg me for Lend-Lease materials already delivered to China." Another lie. (Don't I always ask *him*?) Some bastard is always trying to discredit me. Chiang K'ai-shek went on with a long drool about how I could not be in a dual status, or else I would be in a position to nullify his orders. Apparently he thinks that he tells me as chief of staff to get 5,000 tanks and I have to do it. F.D.R. gave it right back to him, and told him I was, under the law, the President's representative and had a different status from that of chief of staff. My statement that as [his] chief of staff my duties did not include procurement drew a blast that I "claim to be the President's representative to supervise and control Lend-Lease materials already delivered to China, and on the other hand refuse to secure war munitions to fight the common enemy." My point is that as chief of staff I can't be ordered to procure material. When munitions are needed, we should talk it over, see if there is duplication, and co-ordinate with Washington, where Soong is making all kinds of calls on the government. *So this is why they have ignored my existence for the past three weeks.*

JULY 19 Got Shang Chen in and gave him the memo on [retaking] Burma for transmittal to Peanut [Chiang K'ai-shek]. This is an attempt to give Peanut an out on his big demands, and show his willingness to co-operate. He can be ready with the only alternative the War Department can't ignore. It incidentally gives me a chance to stick a lever in. "O.K., do so and so with those divisions, to Stilwell's satisfaction, and we'll do it." It gets away from all this bickering over loot and attacks the main problem—BURMA.

Shang Chen was all for it and at once went after his aide to deliver it personally. Now maybe we'll see how they feel.

JULY 20 How it works. The Foo Hsing Corp. [a government-owned trading corporation with monopolistic charter powers] buys bristles locally at $1.40 U.S. a pound, sells them to us [the United States] at $3.40 U.S. a pound and kicks back 60 cents to the dealer. This leaves a little profit of $1.40 a pound for Foo Hsing and the gang who run it.

The [Chinese] government revenue is gone. No customs, no salt [tax], land tax collected way ahead. So how shall the Army be paid and fed? Answer: print money. The more they print, the less it's worth, *but*, the legal rate is pegged, so they buy from us, American gold, 20 to 1, when the rate should be at least 100 to 1.[15] And prices go up while the rate stands pat. Nothing is coming in, so prices on foreign luxuries are fantastic. Substitutes also rise in price. And so it goes. Then they print some more and the prices jump some more. The farmers can eat, but the government collects taxes in kind to feed the Army. This creates scarcity of food and so food prices jump up, etc., etc.

[LATER]   Usual paper work. At 6:00 got word that Currie was coming at 5:15. At 6:10 that he was coming at 6:00. Went to his house and waited till 8:00. Then ate his dinner with Hsü and the eunuch. Good chow too. Currie had gone to Gauss's.

The Chinese Air Force has been petted and favored in pay, uniform, prestige, quarters, etc., from the start. It was Madame's plaything and everybody in it is now spoiled. All the aviators affect the manners of a Fonck or von Richthofen, and let themselves be admired. But that's all. The pilots that went to the States are working hard to stay there, and go to schools or manufacturing plants, etc. If and when planes actually arrive, the only flying promises to be practice —at Chengtu. [600 miles from the front.]

———[16] back from Kweilin. Says I have a reputation for going after crooks, liars, and cowards, and insists I should go around and inspect the various fronts, throwing a scare into the boys as Chiang K'ai-shek's chief of staff. They wouldn't know I didn't have any real authority and would toe the line just by being inspected, for fear of a bad report. —— says for Christ's sake be patient. He really seems to believe I can work up enough influence to have a vital effect on the situation. Unfortunately, the Japs won't wait for twenty years while I do it.

JULY 21   Still hot. John Davies brought Currie at 10:00. He has Delhi-Belhi.[17] Very little hope on conditions in U.S., Australia, Europe, etc. He's mad at Soong. So am I. Soong planted the slur on me of running away. No hope for ground troops, in India. [Requires] too much tonnage. Just the Tenth Air Force and continued kidding. Swell outlook. Marshall says he can use me, however, so maybe all is not lost.

Currie said my blast to the press on Burma went big—a little truth for a change.

We pinned the Silver Star on Dorn at dinner. He was completely surprised.

JULY 23   Long talk with Currie. He did not dream the mess was as bad as it is. Primed him on the intriguing and lying, etc.

Churchill, in F.D.R.'s presence, told him to tell Peanut that England would invade Burma in near future. Currie

[15] This question of the pegged rate was to grow increasingly important during the war. The U.S. Army making purchases in China had to pay for its purchases in Chinese currency. This currency was sold to it by the Chinese government at 20 Chinese dollars for one dollar U.S. As the Chinese printed more and more paper the actual value dropped to 100, then 200, then 400 to 1. Prices rose accordingly and purchases by the U.S. Army in the field became extravagantly expensive. It cost $10,000 U.S., for example, in one instance, to build a single latrine at an airfield.
[16] A Chinese officer.
[17] Diarrhea.

had hardly gotten the good news announced when the wire from Wellington Koo came, saying that in view of the bad situation in Africa, they would have to reverse the announcement! So now where are we? Washington won't give us the troops. England announces she cannot invade. How can China do it alone?

JULY 24   Wrote up dope for Currie and took it down to him. He's getting educated. Talking about the iron hand in the velvet glove.

JULY 25   MURDER. Radio from George Marshall saying that Frank's [Roosevelt's] letter to Peanut and handed to Tommy [T. V. Soong] for transmission was never sent.[18] The damn fool: didn't he know he'd be caught? He should be called up, dressed down, and thrown out. Imagine an official of his position suppressing a message of such importance from Frank to Peanut. No wonder I am in the doghouse. And probably Peanut has been preening himself all this time that his message was unanswerable. (F.D.R.'s answer was dignified and strong and backed me up in no uncertain terms on every point. "It is therefore clearly not—repeat not—practicable for all of General Stilwell's duties to be subject to orders from you.") Caught Currie and gave him the dope. He'll ask Frank for authority to spring it. Then I'll be clear.

JULY 26   Radioed George that we're sunk unless we get tough. The wording of his radio was that the "message handed by Frank to Tommy for dispatch was *not* sent," and that there was another meeting, the "conversation centering about making tentative decisions on Lend-Lease matters here in Washington and then requesting your recommendations prior to final decision."

JULY 30   The egregious Mr. ———,[19] stooge for T. V. Soong, had the nerve to ask me if I had any difficulties with Chiang K'ai-shek. Ticked him off, and told him I could hardly accept him as an intermediary between the U.S. representative in China and the Chinese foreign minister. The bastard had the gall to think I would open up and spill my business to him. His association with [Soong] has made him think he's important.

AUGUST 1   To office and worked through some poison. SNAFU with Peanut. No answer on anything. He's having a hell of a time with his face.

OFFICE OF THE COMMANDING GENERAL, AMERICAN ARMY FORCES, CBI: LETTER TO MRS. STILWELL   Got some paper at last, so now you can see what a big shot I really am. Actually, it's all wind. This is just a side show, and I'm beginning to wonder if any life can ever be pumped into it. You can imagine the continuous struggle to overcome the inertia of centuries, and battle the jealousies of Chinese officialdom. That ought to be spelled Officialdumb. You know the type of gangster that gets to the top here, so I won't go further into my troubles. But it's a hell of a way to fight a war, from my point of view, and it makes me feel like a complete slacker. Now if I were in addition a slicker, I might make some headway.

AUGUST 3   ———[20] in, long talk. (Chiang K'ai-shek agrees on the Burma offensive.)

   Tipped him off about T. V. Soong, and he wasn't sur-

[18] See entry of July 18.
[19] A young American employed as an adviser to T. V. Soong's China Defense Supplies, the Chinese government purchasing agency in the United States.
[20] A Chinese friend of General Stilwell.

prised. Said there were too many liars around Chiang K'ai-shek—tramps like Yü Fei-p'eng. Same thing happened to Chennault. Chinese air service tried for years to discredit him and throw him out.—Asked if Peanut would ever agree to re-organize army. He said *Yes, he might*. Got talking about command, and he said it was all personal—that even Ho Ying-ch'in could not command the Janissaries (Chiang K'ai-shek's "students").[21] That's why Tu is so independent, of course. Hsüeh Yüeh [22] is the only tough guy in the Army —he tells them to obey the order or get their heads cut off. And if Chiang K'ai-shek writes him interfering messages, he howls for relief. He's a bastard, but it's what they need. (Chang Fa-kwei has made money and gone soft.) —— obviously knows what's up, and sympathizes; he also thinks it will iron out ultimately. (Ultimately is going to be too late.)

AUGUST 4   Chow at Huang Shan [23] with K'ungs, Chiang K'ai-sheks, Madame Sun, and Currie. Madame Sun [24] is the most simpatica of the three women, and probably the deepest. She is most responsive and likable, quiet and poised but misses nothing, would wear well.

Madame Chiang K'ai-shek is quick, intelligent; she's the executive. Wants to get things done. Wishes she were a man. Doesn't think deeply, but catches on in a hurry. Very frank and open, but strangely enough accepts without test reports and rumors that ought to be verified before action is taken. Impulsive to point of precipitation. Madame K'ung is pleasant but colorless; she doesn't give a damn what goes on. Well, so what the hell. Let other people worry about running the show.

Chiang K'ai-shek was late. He had been doing his evening prayers, which are not to be interrupted by anything. This is a new angle. Anyway, *he* takes it seriously, whether it's sincere or not. Maybe he is fortifying his intuition by communing with his Maker. He leans heavily on his supposed knowledge of psychology (Chinese psychology). How do you move a guy like that? How do you get his point of view? He can hurdle logic and reason by using his "intuition"; he dismisses proven principles and methods by saying that Chinese psychology is different; he jumps to a conclusion in keeping with a fancied resemblance to some former experience; and his obstinacy refuses discussion. He has lost all habit of discussion, in fact, because everybody around him is a Yes-man. No one dares tell him an unpleasant truth, because he gets mad. He's in a hell of a fix, and the best he can hope for is to maintain the present unsatisfactory balance of influence by fear and favor. He is not taking a single forward step, or doing anything concrete to improve the position of China, and so, incidentally, his own.

AUGUST 5   Shang Chen in. Chiang K'ai-shek told him the General Staff must arrange to keep me informed of the Order of Battle. Something has happened, apparently. Am I being taken back to Abraham's bosom, perchance? Asked him about the artillery. He said the *Chün cheng pu* [Bureau of Military Personnel] controlled it, and if the *Chün ling pu* [Bureau of Military Operations] got out any orders for it,

---

[21] General Stilwell refers here to the so-called Whampoa clique. The graduates of the Whampoa Military Academy, China's West Point, founded in 1924, were a tightly knit group of generals, fanatically loyal to the Generalissimo. These younger generals were sometimes referred to as Chiang's "students," for Chiang had been the founder and first principal of the academy.
[22] Chinese commander in Hunan province.
[23] The Generalissimo's summer residence on the south bank of the Yangtze.
[24] Widow of Sun Yat-sen, the founder of the Kuomintang.

the Chün cheng pu would very likely tell them to go to hell.
My God, it's even worse than I thought.

———— in, says the worst aspect of the Chinese setup is the
personal control of troops. Asked him why the Thirty-second
Army wasn't in the 30-division plan, and he just laughed.
"Oh, those are northern troops!"

*The diaries in this chapter and later chapters record Stil-
well's travels with no more than cold jottings of arrival and
take-off. It is important to grasp the nature of these travels,
for the jottings are meaningless unless the distances and
difficulties are understood.*

*Stilwell had two headquarters, Delhi and Chungking.
These were separated by about 2,100 miles of flight—roughly the equivalent of the distance from Pittsburgh to Los
Angeles. He made this trip almost as a commuting flight.
The usual route was from Chungking to Kunming (about
450 miles) over tablelands 6,000 to 10,000 feet high. He
would normally pause for inspections at Kunming, where
Chennault's air headquarters were located and where, in
1943 and 1944, almost all major American installations in
China were located. From Kunming, his normal route led
him 550 miles over the Hump—mountains lifting themselves to 17,000 feet in height—to the Assam bases of the
Hump command. During '42 and '43 the Hump was Jap-
patrolled. These bases—Chabua, Dinjan, Sookerating—were
usually his jumping-off places for inspection of the Ledo
Road or the north Burma front, which were within a few
hundred miles of upper Assam. From the Hump bases it was
another 1,100 miles to Delhi, where he negotiated with the
British. From Delhi he would usually make his minor inspections at the Ramgarh training center (500 miles away)
or the supply port of Karachi (700 miles farther). The ex-*

tremities of Stilwell's command actually spanned a larger distance than that from San Diego to Portland, Maine. Usually his pilot was Captain Emmet Theissen, his plane a beaten-up DC-3, and the terrain paddy field, jungle, and mountain without emergency fields, radio aids, or military security. When traveling, Stilwell and his crew flew night or day, good weather or foul.

AUGUST 7, KUNMING: LETTER TO MRS. STILWELL   I'm on my way to Delhi and got stuck here by bad weather. I've got about 12,000 [25] Chinese troops down there and we are making artillery [troops] out of them, using weapons in India that we can't get to China. I'm in command and this time I can shoot them up to the grade of major. I don't think I'll have to—they have been exceptionally well behaved. You can imagine what we hope to do with them ultimately.

Chungking has been an oven: it's a treat to get away from it and breathe some cool air. India will be hot, too, but you can get a cool drink down there. Also, I am escaping for a time from the poisonous atmosphere of "machines idiotes."

AUGUST 7   Off at 10:00. Currie was late of course. At Kunming, a band and guard turned out and I shoved Currie at it and stayed out. Was he bursting. Weather at Dinjan [26] bad. We're stuck.

AUGUST 8   Bacon for breakfast. Still raining. Got off at 10:00. Currie coming by CNAC. In clouds all way. Circled Dibrugarh and over Chabua. Enlisted men's lunch—alligator steak. Good fresh pineapple. Ate too much. Saw Jones, told him to rush weapons to Ramgarh. Off at 2:00 p.m.,

[25] Stilwell found later on arriving in India that only 9,000 Chinese troops had escaped to be concentrated at Ramgarh.
[26] One of the terminals on the Indian side of the Hump.

whole Ganges Valley flooded. Read and dozed. Slow trip
to Delhi: in at 1:00.

AUGUST 9   To bed at 2:00. Breakfast at 7:30.
    Gandhi arrested.

AUGUST 10   Saw Case and Currie. At 1:00 shoved off. Riots
in Delhi. Karachi [27] at 6:00. Circled and down at 6:30.

AUGUST 12   Off [from Karachi] at 9:30. Slept halfway.
Good look at Delhi. In at 2:00 p.m. Met Currie. He was sick
and looked like hell. To hotel and lunch at 3:00 p.m. Looked
over papers. Bissell, Ferris, Wheeler, and I talked till 10:30.

AUGUST 13   Papers, radios, papers.

AUGUST 15   Off at 9:30. We stopped over at Allahabad.
Heavy rain.

AUGUST 16   Off at 9:30. Ranchi at noon, to Ramgarh. Rode
around camp. Saw hospital, quarters, etc. Saw Sun [Li-jen].

Ramgarh was the name of a town in Bihar province in
India, a map mark set among rolling naked hills and arid
plains.
    Ramgarh was acre upon acre of sprawling one-story build-
ings and barracks of brick and tile construction that had
sheltered Italian prisoners from the African deserts.
    Ramgarh was an idea. The idea that Ramgarh framed was
that there was no mystery in the mechanics of Western war
which could not be taught Chinese. The British turned over
to Stilwell the field installations at Ramgarh as infantry,
artillery, and tank, training grounds. The British supplied
the food and the silver rupees with which to pay the troops.
The Americans brought in radios, signal equipment, rifles,
field pieces, tanks, trucks, and, most important of all, in-

structors. The Chinese flew over the Hump 66,000 soldiers to be taught the use of these tools.

Discipline and administration rested with Chinese officers. But technique and training were American responsibilities. Hundreds of Chinese student interpreters paired off with American instructors to teach Chinese soldiers all things from how to fix flat tires to how to load a mule with pack artillery. Friction developed on every level—from differing American and Chinese methods of using a rifle sling to the ultimate question of whose name was signed to basic orders—American or Chinese.

For the Americans, Ramgarh was Siberia, only one thin cut above jungle duty itself. Ramgarh was hot, dusty, itchy, far from anything green or pleasant. The food was bad and the barracks cramped. The movies were old and Red Cross hamburger parlors and recreation rooms mocked rather than relieved the loneliness and exhaustion of the GIs. The task of explaining American machines to Chinese soldiers whose tradition of tool handling went no deeper than a buffalo-drawn plow was exasperating and embittering; and to most Americans, unaware of its historic necessity, it seemed futile.

For the Chinese soldiers Ramgarh was a wonderland. They were fed, for the first time, as much food and meat as they could stuff into their hungry bodies. They gained an average of twenty pounds each in weight. They practiced on the ranges with live shells and real bullets. Hospitals doctored them for everything from malaria to foot ulcers. And most important of all—they were paid. Payment of troops was taken out of the hands of their commanding officers, who had previously received the division payroll and cut it

[27] By this time Karachi had become the major point of entry for American supplies.

into convenient morsels, and made directly on the parade ground into the hands of the individual soldier in hard cash. Between 1942 and 1944, four Chinese divisions were created and equipped here of an effectiveness never before known in Chinese history.

AUGUST 17   Heavy rain. Conference with head instructors all a.m.

AUGUST 18   Bissell's order out today—as commanding general Tenth Air Force.

Went to artillery range and two small-arms ranges in a.m., in p.m. did the combat ranges. Heavy rain.

AUGUST 19   Spent a.m. on artillery range: first firing, and they did well.

AUGUST 20   Left Ramgarh at 8:30, Dum Dum at 11:30. Sutherland met us. To Great Eastern Hotel. After good lunch, shopped. Williams and I to Kerwan for eye exam. Got new prescription. Cool in Calcutta.

To movie. Wallace Beery as a cavalry soldier. Lewis Stone with stomach sticking out. Why don't they catch such things? Wandered around looking for a sandwich. No luck. Back at midnight.

LETTER TO MRS. STILWELL   I have temporarily escaped from Chungking and its withering heat, and come down to India to cool off: and incidentally look over the setup. Flew to Delhi and then down to Ramgarh (also Karachi) where we are working on Chinese troops. They are going to be good and I have great hopes that this will be a demonstration that may prove something to certain dumb clucks who are now bucking me. Most of our staff are there acting as instructors, and everybody is enthusiastic. Came into Calcutta today to do some errands and get my glasses changed:

they have to be strengthened again. The doc surprised me by saying the right eye is clear and the other should be operated but no particular hurry. Just too bad not to see properly. Maybe I won't have to go around with a tin cup after all.

All North India is flooded and the railroads are having a terrible time. Added to the floods there are still enough "disturbances" to make travel precarious unless by plane. I prefer China to India, though it has its points. There were tigers on the artillery range [at Ramgarh] this week.

I radioed to ease my mind about you. A blank stretch of two months without a letter. What the hell do they do with the mail? Are our letters going only by planes that crash? Perhaps they are sending them by boat via Russia.

AUGUST 23, [RAMGARH]   9:00 a.m. talk to the Chinese troops. *In Chinese.*

Talked to all officers. (This a.m. ——[28] got a load off HIS mind. He says the Chinese Army is hopeless for the same reasons we do.) P.m. nap.

AUGUST 24   All a.m. on small-arms range. They are doing O.K., poor instruction in use of sling. But they hit the targets fairly well.

AUGUST 27   Off [from Ramgarh] at 8:30. Beautiful day. Quick trip to Delhi, 3½ hours. Saw Wavell, as usual, mumbly and indefinite.

Cooke, the inspector general, in: he has sure turned up the dirt on ——[29] & Co. Very loose financial manners. We'll throw the dirt in the lap of the Chief of Finance.

Cooke's disclosures: turned up a lot of irregular vouchers [of ——'s]. Ladies' fitted suitcases, lodging charged as of-

[28] A Chinese general, close friend of Stilwell.
[29] A general in the United States Army, whose activities were being investigated.

fice, jaundice campaign ribbons, booze parties. Cooke thought there should be a trial. (Someone charged a 200-rupee watch to me.) —— bought two rugs and had them cut up to carpet his plane. Retribution is catching up. —— had a Negro quartette flown to Delhi from Karachi for a party. British consternation when —— and ——[30] took their secretaries to Asmara. Thought, of course, they were males, etc., etc.

[UNDATED] ——[31] put up a poor mouth over his relief "humiliation." Couldn't serve under his junior. Luckily I had, and told him so. Then he was "a very sensitive man" and besides he had (1) a bad cold, (2) stomach trouble, (3) sinus, (4) sore throat, (5) intestinal germs, (6) exhaustion from overwork, etc., etc. Might never recover his full strength. Felt terribly abused. McNarney radioed him that the "chief abhors primadonnas," so thank God for that much. Bissell took over about August 12 and commenced straightening them out.

AUGUST 30, NEW DELHI: LETTER TO MRS. STILWELL   Been at Ramgarh at our training center and then in Calcutta. The Chinese troops are learning fast and I think will justify my contention that they are as good as anybody, when properly trained. The Limeys are watching us with considerable interest. It's something brand new to them to see colonels actually working. I worked up a Chinese speech and poured it on to the troops.

I have now arrived at the pinnacle of social success, having been entertained at lunch by the Viceroy himself. I am all in a dither over it. I took Dorn along and he has made some good remarks about it. Nobody dared open his trap at the table, so it was up to me and Vicey to keep the conversation going. They must be after something because Wavell also had me for lunch. He is not at all upstage, but he's not what you'd call animated—in fact he impresses me as being a tired old man. Very cordial and probably tied down with instructions from London.

I have run into a lot of poisonous paper work here but it's about polished off now and we'll start back for Chungking. Shoving off tomorrow for Dinjan, Kunming, and Chungking. There is a swarm of little bugs around the light and about two million of them are all over me. They bite just enough to be a nuisance, so in about a minute I'll scream and get under the mosquito net. It's an unequal fight. When I get to Chungking I hope to find some mail from you. What they've been doing with your letters I don't know, but if none are waiting for me I'm going to bust the Post Office Department wide open.

Make the most of Carmel and don't worry about me. I'm too busy to mope and I'm feeling O.K. again. And putting on some weight. If I could get some new teeth and eyes and some hair dye, I wouldn't look a day over seventy.

SEPTEMBER 1   News in, that Rommel jumped off Sunday. Poor Harold [Alexander].[32]

SEPTEMBER 3   Up at 5:00. Held up by bad weather. [We were] only plane flying in East India yesterday. Dinjan at 12:00. Cold and blustery to Kunming. (4:30) We suffered. I was in a dope for the last hour.

SEPTEMBER 4   Off from Kunming at 9:00. Chiu Lung P'o [Chungking] at noon. Warm. No change here. Got our new china out—broke the first cocktail glass.

[30] Another general in the U.S. Army.
[31] A U.S. Army general relieved of command.
[32] Alexander had been made British Middle Eastern commander after the Burma campaign.

SEPTEMBER 6   Office. Pushed papers around.

The fall of 1942 saw Stilwell settling down to the plodding tasks of administration: the reorganization of the Chinese Armies within China.

The four million men of the Chinese Army were a starved, sickly, underarmed, misled mass of peasant soldiers whose control and administration was shot through and through with politics, personal jealousies, and incompetence. It was a conscript army; for every soldier who died at the front, ten died of disease or deserted in the rear. The courage of its soldiery was never questioned; many of its individual officers were men of shining integrity—but as an instrument of war it had only a biological usefulness. It reacted, but could not act of itself.

Out of the three hundred-odd divisions of the Chinese Army Stilwell wanted to carve a number of the best, retrain, re-equip, and feed them. It was obviously impossible for America or for the limited American personnel in Asia to reform the entire Army—and the U.S. Army had decided that thirty divisions was the maximum they could effectively reorganize. Even before Pearl Harbor—in November, 1941— the Chinese had agreed to make available to the United States Army, for retraining, thirty divisions of their troops.

The delay and frustration attendant on the thirty-division program were composed of a host of tiny nagging frictions, no one of them important in itself. Considered as a unified chunk of history, however, the development of the thirty- division program floodlit the great gulf between the life of America and life under the Kuomintang.

The personalities in whom the great cleavage expressed itself were Chiang K'ai-shek and Ho Ying-ch'in, on the one hand, and General Stilwell, on the other. Again and again,

Stilwell records with exuberant delight that he has finally wrung assent to a program of action from Chiang; and then the weeks spin by while the promise grows sterile, is forgotten, and its execution becomes a wretched process of bargaining. It was almost a full year, from the promise of the fall of 1941 to the fall of 1942, before the thirty divisions of the program were even designated specifically. It was months after that before Stilwell could finally wring out of the Chinese staff the name of a commander to command these divisions. The Chinese readily assented to the shipment of troops to India for feeding, re-equipping, and training—but week after week went by while the Americans waited for the troops to be made physically available at the airports for transportation across the Hump.

Stilwell was insistent that the reconquest of Burma begin immediately. The thirty-division force which he hoped to establish in Kunming—and which was designated by the code name Yoke force—was one of the three vital units in the larger plan for reconquest. Once equipped, it was to strike down the Burma Road into Burma from the east, to effect a junction with the Ramgarh Chinese forces striking from India. Speed and efficiency of execution were necessary: but the Yoke program crawled ahead at the pace of a bullock cart.

Two forms of society were clashing: the mechanized, articulated, American system of command, responsibility and accountability—and the ancient habits of China which Chiang found himself powerless to alter. Chiang governed by fear and favor, by a political balancing of warlord against warlord, general against general, by a social balancing of landlord against peasant, patriotism against misery. Chiang could promise Americans on paper whatever they demanded.

To make these promises effective he had to overhaul his entire machinery of government and control. When Stilwell demanded over and over that commitments be fulfilled, Chiang, protesting violation of sovereignty, refused to reform his apparatus of government. American dignitary after dignitary flew to China for visits varying from a week to a month. Unanimously they were gratified by Chiang's willingness to agree; they left happy with his promises. Stilwell, they thought, trying to bring promise to execution, richly deserved his nickname "Vinegar Joe."

SEPTEMBER 7 John Liu [33] in for Chinese lesson. Willkie coming via Russia, cutting out India.

Saw Ho Ying-ch'in at 5:30. Pleasant enough. Invited him to Ramgarh. He bit. Nothing done on the 30-division plan.

SEPTEMBER 9 Chinese [lesson] with John Liu. Liu Fei [34] in to educate me: 2½ hours of pure crap. I'd like to push him off the dock. Exhausted with the effort. Nap. Walk. Movies. Madame is back and has summoned [me] to the presence!

Gems of thought by Liu Fei, No. 2 in the Board of Military Operations, a cadaverous, unkempt bird who needs a haircut. Takes himself seriously, very seriously. Never out of character, always the brilliant staff adviser, always in deep thought, every idea profound and thoroughly thought out. Knows everything. Nobody else knows anything. He says:

(1) The Burma offensive can be undertaken under three conditions, to wit:

    a. When the China front is quiet on both sides.

    b. When the China front is active on both sides.

    c. When the China front is active at a few points only.

(2) The object of the Chinese at present is:

    a. To maintain the status quo (complete quiet) .

    b. To "readjust their dispositions" and set up 2nd line reserves.

    c. To "prepare for the Counter Offensive."

(3) The Japs will put from 5 to 10 divisions in Burma. There must be 5 or 6 British and American divisions. Then 3 to 5 Chinese armies will *hold* 2 of the Jap divisions in the Lashio area, and the Americans and British will engage the other 3 to 8 Jap divisions.

(4) The Chinese *cannot attack*. They have no planes or guns. If the Chinese attack, the Japs can send 5 to 10 divisions and 300 to 500 planes to China and defeat them. Then all would be lost.

(5) The Chinese *will attack* when the international situation is favorable. This will be when the Japs are heavily engaged elsewhere.

(6) If the Chinese wait till the international situation is suitable, then everything will be all right, even if they are defeated. (Because, presumably, the Japs won't have enough strength to follow up.)

(7) "The Chinese will attack only if they are sure to win."

(8) The Communists are raising hell. One-third of the 49 armies in the north have to oppose them. They get in behind the Central Government troops and attack them. The Chinese can't cross the Yellow River because if they do, both the Japs [in front] and the Reds [in rear] will fight them.

(9) New and valuable conception of Liu Fei: the Jap occupation of Canton is a POINT. They have control of the

[83] Stilwell's Chinese aide also doubled in brass as Stilwell's Chinese teacher.

[84] Vice-Minister of Military Operations; Liu Fei later came to appreciate Stilwell greatly and at the end of their association was regarded by Stilwell with friendly tolerance.

sea, so we can't attack them. The Jap occupation of the
Yangtze is a LINE. They have ships and planes, so we can't
cut it. The Jap occupation of the north is an AREA. It is all
spread out, so we can't attack that, either.

SEPTEMBER 10   Conference with Madame. *She* went in to
Ti Hua [35] and did the dickering with the Sinkiang governor.
Got him back in the fold. [He] hadn't been out of his
yamen [courtyard] in six years. Heavily guarded. All [his]
servants wear two guns. Suspicious of poison, examines wine
corks before drinking, looks melons all over to see if they've
been needled. Ti Hua a dump. "Looks like a bedraggled old
tart," says Madame.

Chiang K'ai-shek stayed out, and Madame went in by
plane; she has her nerve with her. You've got to give her
credit.

Much impressed with Ramgarh training—"We must get
another 9,000 men down there right away." "Get after
Chiang K'ai-shek about that as soon as he comes." (Wants
to go down and see it.)

SEPTEMBER 12   *Department of Dirt.* The family life is occasionally enlivened by a few rounds of spirited in-fighting,
but this is spoken of only by a few intrepid souls in hushed
whispers in great confidence. Peanut has two sons [36]—one
(32) is a sort of district chief in Kiangsi, controlling six or
eight *hsien* [counties]. The other (24) is a major on Hu
Tsung-nan's staff. This one has the reputation of being a
pretty good egg. The other is also doing a fairly good job; he
apes Feng Yu-hsiang, and goes around dressed like a coolie
and popping in on *hsien* magistrates at inconvenient times.

SEPTEMBER 14, LETTER TO MRS. STILWELL   This censorship business occasionally has a laugh in it, although in

general it's too stupid to be humorous about. A bird here sent a trunk home and mailed a list of contents—shoes, old pants, this and that, and one wooden Buddha. The censor cut out the word "Buddha." You see this lad's wife could have reasoned that he must be somewhere in a Buddhist country and she might have told someone that there were Americans in the Far East and of course this would have tipped it off to the Japs that we are hot on their trail. If you get a better example than this one, let me know. Censorship is necessary, but it's a pain in the neck conducted that way. —— is still hot but not nearly as bad as it was when I left for ——. (Now isn't that interesting? Yet it's the approved manner, although I have broadcast from here in Chungking and the newspapers in India had several notices about my trip. I'd better change the subject.)

We have been marking time. The Peanut is out of town, and of course the machinery of the government has shut down. A one-man dog is a grand institution but a one-man government is something else. If I last through this job, and get back to Carmel, it will be as an old man of eighty and you'll have to push me around in a wheelbarrow. I'm getting used to being pushed around. I'm off to a meeting with La Grande Dame—and hope to get something settled.

SEPTEMBER 16   No word from G-mo. Lo Cho-ying back with his plan for 45,000 [Chinese troops] in India.

[85] Capital of Sinkiang province, Chinese Turkestan. Sinkiang is the westernmost of all Chinese provinces, lying beyond the Great Wall, on the border of Russia. Under the governor Sheng Shih-tsai, it had been almost autonomous for nine years, and in closest association with the Soviet Union. When Sheng decided to break with the Soviet Union, and return his allegiance to the Central Government, it was Madame Chiang who flew to Ti Hua, his capital, to conclude the negotiations that led to the re-establishment of the Central Government's authority.

[86] Chiang Ching-kuo, the elder; Chiang Wei-kuo, the younger, both of them sons of Chiang K'ai-shek by earlier mates.

SEPTEMBER 17   Rain. Session at War Ministry. Usual slop. Japs pulling out detachments. P.m. walk.

SEPTEMBER 18   5:30 to Ho Ying-ch'in. Everything agreed to. Why not, for Christ's sake? We're just giving them everything. Ho had not informed himself.

SEPTEMBER 21   Dinner at Chiang K'ai-shek's. They stood us up for ten days after Peanut got back from the northwest. Luckily, we had had a preliminary discussion with Ho Ying-ch'in, and when business came up, we polished it off in ten minutes. Everything [of India training plan] approved. Reinforcements for Ramgarh O.K. We can pick our men, too. That's the way it goes—you worry yourself sick for weeks, and struggle around, and then suddenly it all crystallizes in a moment. The thing that sold Chiang K'ai-shek was the photographs [of Ramgarh]. That was a brilliant idea—he could actually see what was going on. Apparently, he was much pleased with it. Why shouldn't he be, the little jackass? We are doing our damnedest to help him, and he makes his approval look like a tremendous concession. This attitude has its effect, too; after being blocked and double-crossed endlessly, to finally get the "go" signal gives such a feeling of relief that you are almost grateful to the very guy you are trying to help, in spite of himself. We got an O.K. on the CNAC contract, the pooling of parts, both pursuit and transport, and the Ramgarh increase. We nailed him to the statement that all transports must be used exclusively for the prosecution of the war.

For the first time I carried on a conversation with the G-mo in Chinese without any help.

SEPTEMBER 22   Piddled with papers. Nap. Lo's dinner. About twenty-five. Wine flowed freely. Hollington Tong emerged as champion drinker. Dorn and "Ironside" Hsiao out. Heinrich out. Several other casualties.

SEPTEMBER 23 Went over the *Chih hui pu* [37] setup with John Liu. It looks tricky. Letter of instructions for Lo so as to tie him up. Office. Back in p.m. Double-header movie.

Swallow your pride and persist. My going to Ho Ying-ch'in has borne fruit on several points. I'll try him on the 30-division plan and see how that works.

SEPTEMBER 24 Talk with Lo Cho-ying and lucky we did. Neither Yang nor Li [of the Chinese General Staff] had told him anything. What a staff. [They were] afraid to get him a copy of the [Ramgarh] staff organization because he turns out to be No. 2 [under Stilwell as commander in chief]. Maybe waiting to get him committed [to assignment] and so cinch their own jobs. Anyway, he didn't know [his subordinate position] and when he read it,[38] the effervescence went right out of him. He was counting on the old by-pass game—I to be *ts'an mou chang* [chief of staff] again. I told him what I wanted done and gave him a letter of instructions, which ties him up the way we want. . . . Also told him I'd have some officers for the staff myself. Blow No. 1.

Blow No. 2 was the pay. He wanted me to put the 450,000 rupees in his hand. When he found he'd have to account for it, he squirmed and tried out the old "Chinese method" (lump payment to commanding generals) . But I said I was a bystander; if he, Lo, wanted any change, he could get the Chinese government to confer with the British.[39] Now

[37] Administrative Command. Here Stilwell is speaking of the Administrative Command framework for the Ramgarh training command.
[38] Stilwell's letter of the previous day.
[39] Who were in charge of the financial details for payment of Chinese troops in rupees in India.

he'll have to submit a statement of strength by grade.

If we hadn't had this talk, there would have been one hell of a mess down there. He would have insisted on command, and pushed out orders, and generally raised hell.

Busy with Lo and forgot Ho [Ying-ch'in]. An hour late for the bull session. *Item.* Ho tells me there are only 3,000 Japs in Hanoi [French Indo-China] and none north of there. And it never enters his fat head to go down there and get them. He is the chief of staff of the Chinese Army, and yet a golden opportunity like that is passed up. But he gives lots of thought to sticking his long nose into our business and asking for details on tonnage, etc., carried by our planes. If he would put ten per cent of his attention on his own rotten machine, he'd make some progress.

Idea. Why not use their own methods on them?

But whom shall we work on? Let's go over the possibilities. No use fooling with small spuds. Where is the influence? The court at Chungking is the milieu—outside, though trusted, the boys have no hand in making the big decision. Hu Tsung-nan, Chu Shao-liang,[40] etc., etc., are trusted executives, but they don't handle the daily business and make the plans. Who does? For information, Handlebars,[41] of course. Fully trusted and supreme in his line.

In political matters, the Tailor,[42] although Peanut has taken over his job in the Executive Yuan and made him assistant. The handling of dough is cut and dried and purely routine. ("Purely" is not exactly the word.)

For confidential secretarial work, paymaster to visiting firemen of their "expenses," scanning of personnel, etc., Ho Yao-tsu.

For military affairs, the Blocking Back [Ho Ying-ch'in]. Not only the local Stimson, but also head of *Chün cheng pu* [Board of Administration] which controls the transport board. Military education and ability, a joke, and so, very susceptible to clever suggestion. He gets it from the *Chün ling pu* [Bureau of Military Operations]—not from the *pu chang* (bureau chief), Hsü Yung-ch'ang, who is pretty much of a figurehead, but from Liu Fei, our garbage man Adonis, who needs a haircut. This guy wields a big influence; he is the *ne plus ultra* of the Chinese military "mind"—the analyst *par excellence.* He make inaction a virtue by proving conclusively the impossibility of action—a military ascetic. But he produces the kind of stuff they love (point, line, area) and he works 24 hours a day at it. A one, two, three, four boy. Everything ticketed. Everything full of false assumptions, and mistakes of fact, and twisted viewpoints, but so assured as to cover the contradictions and absurdities. He overawes the Big Boys, who won't take the time to do the pick and shovel work. A hell of a bad influence. His colleague, Lin Wei, has been sent to the bushes, and he reigns alone.

The real list narrows down to a few chosen boon companions. Of course, the skirts [43] have their influence, but it's limited; for big decisions they don't figure. And that's what really governs this country.

SEPTEMBER 25 ———[44] back from Yang Kai.[45] Usual graft and corruption. Each of seven *hsien* [counties] furnishes 8,000 workers. Actually about half show up. Each man works a month and is then released. They get (presumably) $5 a day (about a pound of rice). (Chiang K'ai-shek gave a bonus of $50 each to about 15,000 of them.) Each worker

[40] Field generals, also provincial politicos.
[41] Admiral Yang, the mustached chief of Chinese intelligence.
[42] H. H. K'ung.
[43] Mesdames Chiang and K'ung.
[44] A Chinese official.
[45] At Yang Kai, the U.S. Army had contracted for the construction of a heavy bomber field.

gets at the start (maybe) $70—for a hat and raincoat ($40),
use of shelter ($20), medicines ($10). All paving is *pao
kung* [crushed stone]. Stone masons get $20 or $25 a day
(maybe). Contractors underpay their help, steal trees, or
buy them at low prices. *Lao pai hsing* [the common peo-
ple] very dissatisfied. They desert in droves; why not, if they
can't eat? The ground is condemned at $3,000 a *mou* [1/6
of an acre]; its market value is $4,000 or $5,000. No arrangement yet for making payment. ——— says the top gang
must be knocking down a lot of jack.

Fuss over getting Willkie into China.

SEPTEMBER 26   Radio from George Marshall about Three
Demands.[46] Asks for recommendations. Worked at it.

SEPTEMBER 27   Rainy. P.m. nap. Wavell says O.K. on increase [in Chinese troops] at Ramgarh.
    Better news at Stalingrad.

At last. Answer [from Washington] to Three Demands
—scaled down. 265 combat planes. 100 transports. No
ground troops. Tonnage to be built up to 5,000 if, as, and
when. "Appreciate your co-operation." "Will assist at Ramgarh." It amounts to doing *nothing* more than at present.
I suppose I am to kid them into reorganizing the Army.
    [Forces for the] Burma [offensive] will be the Ramgarh
Detachment, the Tenth Air Force, the Yünnan mob, and
a "limited British detachment." In other words, what we've
got. How very generous. Oh, yes, a guy from Operations
will come out and show us how to do it.

SEPTEMBER 28   This may be a red-letter day. Went to see
Ho Ying-ch'in this afternoon and put the bee on him about
the 30-division plan. "Just [to] justify shipments." "War

Department asking questions." "Embarrassed how to answer." "American psychology—help those who make a fight out of it." "If China gets busy, we can have anything; if not, they'll shut down on us." Well, it apparently went over. He'll see me again on Wednesday. (Time to make some arrangements.) I suggested help in training, filling [units] up to strength, concentration in groups, equipment, etc.

Then I got a look beneath the curtain. The Central Government can't be too free with the troops under the *Chan Chu's*,[47] but they have 10 *chun* [armies] of their own. These can be pushed around, at will, and are undoubtedly the units that will be on the 30-division list. So that's promising —once we get a start on this, they can hardly stop, especially with the Ramgarh experiment going well. (Maybe it will pay to swallow my pride and swap horses, but I don't care how we do it, just so we arrive.)

SEPTEMBER 29, LETTER TO MRS. STILWELL   Just rereading the Feast of Letters. Boy did I get some letters. I've read it all three or four times already and it helps greatly to offset the manure pile. Letters postmarked in May and from then on into August. I envied Ben's experience at La Jolla spearing fish. The African grass seems to have gotten out of control. I don't know what you can do about it except cut tunnels through it when it gets a little higher. Every time I see a picture of Garry, I think, "That lovely Dog." I wonder if he'll remember me when I turn up with my white beard and a crick in my back? Perhaps I have a distinctive scent: I've heard of generals who stink.

[46] Chiang's June request for 500 planes, three American divisions, and 5,000 tons monthly over the Hump.
[47] War Areas. Control of the Chinese Armies by the Central Government was very loose. War area commanders conducted themselves almost as independent satraps, and the troops at their disposal for defense of their war areas were considered almost as private property.

I'm keeping one eye (the only one) peeled for a radio telling me of Nance's acquisition. Al [48] has sure been educating the Pacific coast in the art of painting. I hope the boobs loosen up enough to buy, instead of just saying, "How delicate."

My letters must be dull as dishwater. I could pep them up but it would just be a field day for the censor. Of course, I was prepared for many things out here—the manner of doing business, the intrigue, the obstacles. But when you really get behind the scenes, it's still a shock, if you get me. There seems to be a little progress, which you will see publicized in the States pretty soon. If I can develop the idea further, something may come of it. Anyway, I've done my damnedest and that's all I can do, win or lose.

Everybody is well here. One or two want to go where they think the show is a more spectacular one. They can go: I'll get along with the deck-hands who stick and see it through. It makes an interesting study of human nature.

The heat is over. We'll be wearing wool in a few days. The winter weather here is filthy—rain, fog, mud, and slime continuously. Better than the terrible muggy heat of the past few months.

We made Dorn a full colonel tonight. Bergin called us to attention at dinner, read out the order, pinned an eagle on him, swore him in, and then kissed him. I put the other eagle on him after sticking it into his shoulder. Sort of surprised him.

Just go along the way you have been and you'll break all records.

LETTER TO BEN   That was a grand letter you wrote me: if you don't turn out to be a snake charmer or a landscape gardener, you might try being an author. "Uncle Ben's col-

umn" in the newspapers ought to go big. You could tell
all the dumbbells in the U.S.—and there are a lot of them—
many things about birds and bugs and fish and snakes that
they never knew. "Natural History for morons who don't
take time to see what they are looking at." "How to keep
African Grass from inundating the Home."

It must have been great fun getting under the water and
swimming around spearing fish. But kind of tricky. I'm
afraid I'd spear myself as often as I did the fish. And if I
get home with a wooden leg, I'd have a hell of a time sub-
merging. On second thought I'll stay on the beach and
you can go out and get the fish. I can remember when I was
15—oh yes, I can—and I thought I was pretty hot. The principal did too; he thought I was hot enough to fire.

SEPTEMBER 30   Fixed October 21 to begin move to Dinjan.[49] Indications of British obstruction. Radio to George
Marshall about it. Radio to Sibert to make another official
request on Wavell. Those bastards will sabotage this scheme
yet.

OCTOBER 2   Fourth clear day. P.m. to *Chiu Lung P'o* [air-
field]. At 3:50 Willkie arrived. He looked tired out. Mob
rushed him.

—— arrived with mail and news. Washington is just
what we've thought, one big mess. This theater kaput. No
help coming.

General impression, pessimistic. Major strategic effort
not in Pacific. Henry [Stimson] sympathetic, but no offer of
help. Chief of Staff says no ground troops. McCloy [assist-
ant secretary of war] noncommittal.

[48] Alison, one of the Stilwell daughters, who had just given an exhibition
of her paintings.
[49] The movement of Chinese troops across the Hump by air.

LETTER TO MRS. STILWELL   Just a few photos to show you
I *did* get rid of the jaundice. This is the fourth consecutive
day of sunshine, which is a world's record for this dump at
this time of year. Bombing always stops September 1, and
the mantle of fog, murk, mud, and muck takes charge till
April, but something is screwy this year, and it becomes an
open invitation to the Japs to come up and see us. We have
a dugout handy, however, and also a little surprise waiting,
out at the airfield. The reception committee is standing by.

Willkie arrives this afternoon and he has a full schedule
for his visit. He has to go to lunch, tea, and dinner every
day he is here. They are going to drag him around to see
schools and factories and girl scouts and sewing circles and
arsenals and keep him well insulated from pollution by
Americans. The idea is to get him so exhausted and keep
him so torpid with food and drink that his faculties will be
dulled and he'll be stuffed with the right doctrines.

Paul Jones is to be turned loose on October 12 and come
up here where I can haze him personally. I want somebody
around that appreciates the family. I mean thoroughly and
vocally, and certainly Paul is both thorough and vocal. Paul
makes good wherever you put him—running a railroad, ware-
housing supplies, driving coolies, or repairing trucks. I wish
I had a hundred like him.

Take a look out the window and give me by telepathy an
idea of the patio, and flowers, and fish pool and lawn, the
trees, the ocean, Point Lobos, the air, the sun, the waves,
the beach, the rocks. It's lucky we can't see the future.

OCTOBER 4   Lo Cho-ying shoved off [for India].

OCTOBER 5   Lo went to Peanut to kick on command but
got nowhere. That's somepin.

Saw Willkie at 2:30. Nothin'. He didn't ask a question.

Completely sold on Chiang K'ai-shek and Madame. Advised me to put it on with a trowel. To hell with that stuff.

Troubles of a Peanut dictator. At first the Peanut thought that military and political functions could not be separated, so he combined the authority under the military commanders. Now he finds that it makes the boys too powerful, and he's been trying for over a year to shake them loose, without success. In Hupeh, *Ch'en Ch'eng* (governor and commander in chief); in Hunan, *Hsüeh Yüeh* (governor and commander in chief); in Honan, *Wei Li-huang* (same); in Kansu, *Chu Shao-liang* (same); in Shansi, *Yen Hsi-shan*, etc., in Chekiang, *Ku Chu-t'ung* (same); in Yünnan, *Lung Yun* (same).[50]

The way it works is by threat. The Peanut wants to shake Hsüeh Yüeh loose. If he pulls out troops, Hsüeh squawks, "I cannot be responsible for the security of my area," and he might even arrange for a Jap reaction. The understrappers are told to pressurize, and a flood of protest reaches various officials of the Central Government. They then tell the Peanut the opposition is very strong, and that forcing the issue might cause dirty work. So the Peanut lays off and waits. The plain fact is that he doesn't dare to take vigorous action—they are sure to be sulky and they may gang up. His best cards are the air force, the artillery, and the ten armies whose training is under the Central Government.

Why doesn't the little dummy realize that his only hope is the 30-division plan, and the creation of a separate, efficient, well-equipped, and well-trained force?

Willkie is being thoroughly immersed in soft soap, adulation, and flattery. All the "front-line fighters" are "inspired

[50] Names of Chinese provinces along the war front in which the commanding general was also the civil governor.

by his presence." "Victory has been brought closer," etc., etc., etc.

OCTOBER 6   Barrett [51] back from Ch'ü Hsien. It was even worse than we thought. A bitched-up action at Ch'ü Hsien, buggered completely by the Generalissimo, and then orders to retreat, which were thoroughly carried out. The "reconquest" was merely reoccupation after the Japs had gone, allowing plenty of time to make sure. Halt at Ch'ü Hsien, because the Japs are still at Kin Hua, moving loot out. The Japs took out all metals, rails, cooking pots, etc., and destroyed about half the buildings in the area. Crops perhaps not ruined, although the water was let out of the paddy fields. Ch'ü Hsien airfield cut by deep ditches at 40-foot intervals, across the field. There was no fighting at all, except one little action to the southwest of Ch'ü Hsien. The Japs used about thirty or forty old planes to bomb and strafe the roads. All the artillery was lost at Ch'ü Hsien. There were no communications, and orders never reached the units on time. Ku Chu-t'ung [the Chinese commander in chief] was fifty or more miles in rear, and never went up. The division commanders—same.

Peanut "directed operations" from Chungking, with the usual brilliant result. The whole thing was a mess. Peanut ordered two armies to hide in the mountains and attack on flank when the Japs passed. The Jap simply blocked the exit roads and went on. The chüeh chan [critical contest] was to be at Ch'ü Hsien. Two divisions deployed on the north and east of the town and, just as they were ready to fight, Peanut ordered them to withdraw. The Japs attacked at the same time, and then there was chaos. Two armies in rear of Ch'ü Hsien did nothing.

The troops had only the poorest equipment. No medical

attention. No transport. Many sick. Most recruits were conscripts, delivered tied up.

Conscription is a scandal. Only the unfortunates without money or influence are grabbed. Many men of military age are kept in the middle schools.[52] One example [of such a student], 26 years old, married, three children, *but son of a pao chang.*[53]

Ku [the commander in chief] lives, with his wife and children, in a big villa many miles from the front, and never leaves the place. The junior officers are pretty good; the men are good; even the division commanders will do. *But* someone has got to push them up front, and Peanut *must* keep his goddam hands off.

OCTOBER 7   Willkie off, thank God. On Pai Shih Yi trip he hardly spoke to me. Utterly indifferent.

Hsieh Yu-lan showed up. "Got a piece of bad news (wife died) and a piece of good news (getting married on October 10) ." Still giggling and cheerful.

[51] Colonel David Dean Barrett, then U.S. military attaché in China. He had visited the eastern front to survey the Chekiang campaign of 1942. The Japanese, startled by the Doolittle raid, in April, had invaded East China and destroyed all usable airfields, particularly the large bomber field at Ch'ü Hsien. After completing their work, they had withdrawn. Barrett's account was the first U.S. official report on the action.
[52] Equivalent of American high schools. Students or graduates of middle schools were exempt from conscription, and attendance at a middle school was a favorite method of beating the draft.
[53] A local official.

Chapter 5

ALL THE ALLIES AGREED that the Burma campaign would begin in mid-February of 1943. The fall, then, was to be a period of high preparation on both sides of the Burma wedge and Stilwell took it on himself to urge both his reluctant allies to activity.

In India, Stilwell's particular project was the training of the Chinese combat force—the X force—at Ramgarh. He had, with some difficulty, persuaded Chiang to fly 45,000 troops from China over the Hump for training at Ramgarh and eventual use on the north India-north Burma border. He soon found, however, that the British viewed this increase with distaste. A quick trip from Chungking to New Delhi was necessary to goad Wavell into approval of the increase in China forces in India. With some help from Washington, Stilwell won British acceptance of the Chinese training project and their promise to commit seven British Indian divisions to the attack on the Japanese in south Burma.

In China, Ho Ying-ch'in and the staff of the Chinese Army promised the necessary divisions for the Yoke force and finally put the divisional designations on paper. From Washington, the combined chiefs of staff informed Stilwell that he could expect, for all practical purposes, no increase in equipment or supplies for his projected offensive. Undismayed, however, he urged the project on.

OCTOBER 8   Rain. Conference at War Ministry, usual crap.

OCTOBER 9   Talk with Ch'en Ch'eng (commander in chief of sixth war zone) . Asked him about training and ability of officers and enlisted men. Confirms my opinion: Junior officers O.K., division commanders wobbly, all need training in the offensive. Ch'en seems a likable sort of guy. Commanded center at Shanghai, and defense of Hankow.

OCTOBER 10   Last night gloomy wire from Ferris [1] about Ramgarh. Arch [Wavell] has approved [the increase in Chinese troops], but [the] viceroy has referred it to London. "Civil government has last word," says Hartley. So they are determined to bitch it. Sent George a hot radio, asking for help. Otherwise, [it will] sabotage all our work, enrage the Chinese, jeopardize all future co-operation, and generally bugger the show. We have some rights, after what we've put in over here. Do they pay any attention to them? No—politics [British]. "Can't have the dirty Chinks"; Long-range policy: fear of Chinese-Indian co-operation; fear of independent operation; or what not.

[1] Stilwell's deputy chief of staff in India.

Anyway, Chiang K'ai-shek will get hot and perhaps pull out the whole show. If he does, we have labored in vain. Maybe George can save it.

OCTOBER 11   Date with Peanut at noon. Ordered me to dinner on Wednesday, so we have to cancel Ho and K'ung. He was quite blithe and cheerful. (Resting his teeth.) Rotten interpreter. Shang Chen helped out. Told him about Wavell and Ramgarh obstruction.

OCTOBER 12   Office a.m. and p.m. Dinner for Ch'ien Ta-chün, Shang Chen, Liu Fei, and Admiral Yang. Movie. Liu Fei ran true to form. Left to take his yao [medicine].

OCTOBER 14   Shang Chen in with plan for offensive against Burma. Peanut had changed 10 to 15 divisions to 15 to 20 divisions! Looks good.
    Dinner with Peanut. Peanut said, "Giving you full authority in India. Be sure and keep strict discipline."

OCTOBER 15   Off [for India] at 10:00 a.m. J. L. Huang also.[2] Threw off two interpreters to take him. Kunming at 1:00. Lunch. Long squabble after getting Huang out of bathtub at 5:00 p.m.; the bastard sorely tried my patience.

OCTOBER 16   Off at 7:00. Over the Hump, at 20,000 feet. Arrive Ranchi at 6:00. Guard of honor at Ramgarh and *hsien pings* [military police]. Tea first. Long conference with our gang. Got things settled.

OCTOBER 17   Got Lo [Cho-ying] and told him what the score is. He took it. An hour and a quarter of it. John Liu translated and we got it straight. Off at 12:15. Bumpy ride to Delhi. 4:15. 5:30 with Ferris to see Wavell. A lot of bull and crying about this and that. [He] made it plain we [the Ramgarh training project] are not welcome. All sorts of difficulties—railroad, roads, water, food, transport, etc. Will hinder Indian Army development. If we get trucks, it will reduce his tonnage. (He is down [short] 11,000!! trucks.) He has been kept in the dark, no request has been made, the number has not been definitely stated. In fact, it makes him tired.

Well, to hell with the old fool. We have just smoked them out. They don't want Chinese troops participating in the re-taking of Burma. That's all. (It's O.K. for U.S. troops to be in England, though.) Discouraging encounter, after my labors to get the Chinese going.

OCTOBER 18 Good letter from George Marshall. Office till 11:00. Bissell, Ferris, and I to GHQ. (Wavell, Hartley, Peirse.) Wavell made it plain [that the] Chinese [are] not welcome. No room, or transport, or supplies, or anything. His plan [for Burma campaign]. Three divisions to Chindwin. One division at Chittagong. Limited advance. Possible landing at Akyab. (Bare possibility Rangoon.) Conflicting statements. Yesterday 11,000 trucks short. Now, 33,000. Indian Army 1¼ million. Anything he turns over to us comes off *his* troops. General attitude of rebuff for Chinese. But, he wants our air force under him. I told him how it would work.

[UNDATED] Limeys getting nasty about Ramgarh: Wavell must have a formal request—for the Viceroy! How many [Chinese] troops [to come], and what for. WHAT FOR? My God! I told them to help our allies retake Burma. They are making it difficult; they don't want to be beholden to the Chinese for anything. Same old stuff, like closing the Burma Road and refusing troops. They appear to learn nothing.

[2] J. L. Huang, president of the Chinese Officers' Moral Endeavor Association, a close personal friend of the Generalissimo.

[UNDATED]   Conferences in New Delhi. *First day:* obstruction and difficulties. British short 11,000 trucks, no animals available, railroad congested. Two hundred [troops] a day from China upper limit. Camp couldn't accommodate more than 600! Any supplies would come from Wavell's troops. Etc., etc. They were sore at having any Chinese in India at all.

Second day: same story. Now short 33,000 trucks, railroad could only move 200 a day. Animals impossible etc., etc.

Third day: remarkable change. They must have gotten the word from London. Now they can move 400 a day. They can get some animals. And trucks. They will give us a sector at Ledo. They will supply us. But they want [to command] the Tenth Air Force. They won't get it.

Now they find they can move the Chinese up [to the north Burma front] in time to go in. Everything is lovely again, so obviously George has turned on the heat. Wavell's plan fits in fairly well with mine. He insists on command of Ramgarh force. That's O.K.; we are in a separate slot and will work off to a junction with the Yünnan gang. No mention of unified command, and no mention of Yünnan force. I let it ride.

Joint planning committee to set [it] up and we sit in on it. Junior officers are O.K. and working with us. Another pass at Tenth Air Force, but we brushed them off.

George Marshall assures help [to Burma campaign] if Egypt going well. All available bombers.

Talk with Viceroy. Very pleasant, but fishing for dope on probable Chinese action after the war. Told him a few characteristics of the Chinese. He said we could be sure of one thing—any Indian government set up by the Indians would *not* be representative or democratic.

OCTOBER 21, LETTER TO MRS. STILWELL   4:00 p.m. and
I feel as if I had been through the wringer. This is the fourth
day of continuous conferences and paper pushing, from early dawn to dewy eve and on to murky midnight, and I'm
fed up. I'm in no shape to write even a note, but I don't
know when I'll get another chance. In general we're getting
along—our Limey friends are sometimes a bit difficult, but
there are some good eggs among them. It is no fun bucking
two nationalities to get at the Japs, but George Marshall is
backing up the line in grand shape and maybe something
will come out of the struggle.

We had a big party last night. I had Archie [Wavell] on
my right and the chief justice on my left. The British don't
quite know how to take me—I catch them looking me over
occasionally with a speculative glint in their eyes. Some of
them that I had thought most hidebound and icy prove to
have a good deal of my point of view and take delight in
watching me stick the prod into the Most High.

Pinky is going strong—mad at lots of people. I imagine
Joe is on his way and I've asked for Ernie.[8]

[UNDATED] LETTER TO MRS. STILWELL   Our training school
for the Chinese troops is going in grand style. The boys are
learning fast. They get good chow, medical attention, efficient instruction, AND their pay, as well as movies, athletics,
etc. They love it; as you know, Chinese troops have never
experienced such treatment. They'll be good. The Peanut is,
I believe, quite impressed. Unless he is terribly dumb, he
will want to go on with this kind of business.

Bergin is a mainstay, Powell is doing fine work. Arnold
has blossomed, Paul is a dynamo. Pinky keeps up a healthy
hate for all hypocrites and stuffed shirts.

[8] Colonel Ernest Easterbrook, General Stilwell's son-in-law.

OCTOBER 22   Office. Rush all a.m. Jam at Kunming. Troops not there.[4] Frantic wires to get after Ho Ying-ch'in.

OCTOBER 31   Good trip to Dinjan. Got in about 5:00. Chinese troops coming in regularly.

NOVEMBER 1   Up at 3:00, at field at 4:00. Nobody woke the aviators. Left engine wouldn't start. Off [across Hump] about 5:00. 17,000 feet—cold as hell—5° below zero outside. Me in shorts. Near Kunming, lost the bearing and wandered around in the soup. Theissen had gone way east of Kunming to clear the mountains. Might have been nasty. Had lunch. Everything going nicely. Left at 1:00. Quick trip. In [to Chungking] at 3:15. To house and unpacked. Nothing changed.

NOVEMBER 2   Saw Ho Ying-ch'in at 2:00. Gave him the dope. No decisions of course. Threw the scare at him about preparations. He couldn't comprehend the problem at all. Hadn't given it a thought. No decision on anything. Wants *me* to recommend about pay. I'm to see Peanut. Then he'll talk with him.

NOVEMBER 3   Conference: Peanut, May [Madame Chiang], T. V. Soong, Shang [Chen], and I. Reported on conferences with Wavell. Series of surprises. (1) I can fire Lo any time. This was repeated by Chiang K'ai-shek. (2) I can order the *chang kuan pu* (commander in chief's office) to do anything in making preparations. (3) Chiang K'ai-shek will put in 15 divisions on Yünnan side, exclusive of Indo-China border defense, and be ready [for Burma offensive] by February 15. (4) He will put his available artillery with them. (5) Madame proposed that I pick the divisions and name the commanding generals (after my remark that 15 were plenty if properly led and good troops) .

Chiang K'ai-shek said O.K. (6) I command the Ramgarh gang. (The question was asked, would I be under Wavell? and if so, would it be O.K.? Yes.) (7) Unified command. My suggestion—Chiang K'ai-shek command. No, he could not, but could he accept and delegate me as chief of staff to take over? No: I told them Wavell would not accept. Well, said Chiang K'ai-shek, form a staff—one Limey, one American, one Chinese, and put me on top. No; Wavell again. I said if Slim [5] could command the Limeys it would work fine.

Peanut said, "Naval and air domination must be assured," or he wouldn't move.

Something has happened. If they mean what they said, it's grand. The biggest step forward we have taken. (Ho Ying-ch'in? T. V. Soong? Did George tell Soong they would not sidetrack me? Did I scare them with the list of things that must be done? In this connection, they had talked it over, obviously, and proposed replacing Lo with a man of less rank who knew more about modern weapons.)

(8) Chiang K'ai-shek said *another* [Chinese] division should go to India. I told him British might object, but after a while it could probably be done.

NOVEMBER 4   11:00 a.m. saw T. V. Soong. If he does half of what he promises, we'll get somewhere. Madame will now fade out and I deal with T. V. Wants a list of good commanding officers. Apparently ready to back me. What's the game? But who cares, if we get going?

---

[4] The 45,000 troops promised by the Chinese government for flight to India for training were scheduled for air embarkation across the Hump from Kunming; they had not arrived as promised.

[5] Lieutenant General William Joseph Slim, a British officer in India whom Stilwell respected enormously. Slim was later to co-operate closely with Stilwell in the 1944 campaign.

NOVEMBER 5   British have the Huns on the run in Egypt.
Wrote up synopsis for Soong.

NOVEMBER 8, LETTER TO MRS. STILWELL   Usual rush. Papers, radios, conferences, and this and that. No one knows
the back history and ramifications of any question that
comes up. However, things in general are looking up and
the right people are beginning to listen.

NOVEMBER 9   Good news from Africa. Landings at Algiers
—Oran and Casablanca. Good effect here. Rommel catching hell, Italians all surrendering.

NOVEMBER 10   Big powwow with the Brain Trust of the
Chün ling pu [Board of Operations] Liu Fei, Lin Wei,
Ch'en, Pao, and Wang. Long spiel by Liu on estimate of
the situation. He figures 800 Jap planes and 16 divisions
available in Indo-China, Siam, and Burma. Possible 8 divisions in Burma. British with 7 divisions handle 4 [divisions]
and we with 5 armies handle 4 to 5. (Ramgarh force not
counted in.) (At present 150 Jap planes in Burma, 400 in
Siam, 250 in Indo-China.)
   Well, this begins to look like something. Actually accept-
ing an offensive operation. Actually assigning the troops, re-
ducing number of divisions, filling to strength, adding weapons, and attaching artillery. Actually thinking of getting
after the SOS, contemplating command for me. Any one of
these items would have meant a month of struggle a little
while back.

NOVEMBER 13   (Knock wood.) Word came—Joe [6] coming. Joe in at 2:30. Talked. (He did, I mean.)

NOVEMBER 16, LETTER TO MRS. STILWELL   Joe's here! Hooray! He came in with General Wheeler [7] (never travels with

anything less than a major general) and started right in talking. The first night I fell asleep at midnight and at breakfast he reproached me for not being attentive. He brought a grand envelope of letters and I've had a feast of reading. Which I will repeat tomorrow, pretending the mail has just come in. Thanks to all of you for taking time and trouble to "cheer up the meal" for Ole Pap. Joe was apparently relieved to find that I was not yet a hopeless wreck or living skeleton. The socks were delivered promptly and are gorgeous. If they will prevent cold feet you've done something for your country.

I am still shoveling plenty of fertilizer and much of my time is spent on "affaires empoisonnantes." Unwanted visitors, inspectors and others, keep arriving to make life miserable and waste our time, but I am learning patience and let them bounce off and go home and tell their tales. George C. Marshall continues to back me and if he didn't I would have tossed in my hand long ago.

NOVEMBER 18 Everybody excited over Solomons fight. A.m. to Chiu Lung Po to see Snow White[8] off. Just the family out there. Madame Sun included. Said goodbye and beat it.

7:00 p.m. Chow at Pai Chung-hsi's. What a gathering!
Pai Chung-hsi, Deputy Chief of Staff
Li Tsung-jen, Changkuan (commander in chief) 6th war zone
Ch'en Ch'eng, Changkuan (commander in chief) 5th war zone

---

[6] General Stilwell's son, Lieutenant Colonel Joseph W. Stilwell, Jr.
[7] Major General, later Lt. General Raymond Wheeler, commander of the SOS in the CBI theater.
[8] Snow White is code for Madame Chiang K'ai-shek, who was departing for the U.S.A.

Yü Han-mou, Changkuan (commander in chief) 4th war
  zone
Chu Shao-liang, Changkuan (commander in chief) 8th
  war zone
Huang Shao-hsiung, Governor Chekiang
(Hsüeh Yüeh) ABSENT, Changkuan (commander in chief)
  9th war zone
Fighting each other like cats and dogs a few years back.
Yü Han-mou, the traitor to Pai and Li. Ch'en Ch'eng, on
Chiang K'ai-shek's side in '36.[9] All polite and merry and
perfect gentlemen. Li had a gag about a worm that turned
into a weed in summer. Pai had one about a fish that jumped
out of the water and turned into a bird. Only one place
where this happens—a lake in Kwangsi.

NOVEMBER 19   We're rolling.
    We have now gotten both the Limeys and the Chinese
committed, and working at it. If we can keep a fire lit under
Wavell and horn in on command and training on this side,
the job is in a fair way to get done, bejesus. And since everybody said it was impossible, naturally I'm pulling for it hard.

NOVEMBER 21   Murder will out. Teevy [T. V. Soong] let
it slip today that "Gong" [10] had his orders from Peanut during the Burma fracas. This came out in connection with an
analysis of Gong's character, in which I said he did not control his subordinates. Teevy clicked at once; he knew the
reasons. My criticism of interference with the field commander obviously got under the skin of the Most High. They
have talked it over, and it has come out on other occasions.
    Ominous stuff from India. Limeys thinking on limited
lines. Their objective is a joke—Arakan Hills, Chin Hills, and
Kalewa. Then they will harass the Jap Line of Communication. The Admiral knew nothing, so there goes the Bay of

Bengal. The RAF can't say they will do anything, either. On the whole, they want to dig in in north Burma, and wait till next fall before going after it seriously.

NOVEMBER 26 White in with sad tale of Paoshan front. Sickness, no food, no strength. Bad communications, etc. Williams in and talked at length. Sutherland appeared.

From George Marshall: For our "war," we are graciously allotted (1) the Lend-Lease stuff we already have, (2) the personnel for training, (3) some engineer equipment, how much not known, the (4) "increasing effectiveness of the ferry line." My God. So that's the support we get to put on a campaign. I wonder what they gave them in Africa. Am I to comfort the Chinese with this prospect? This is for the "support of the Chinese Army," and I'll be God-damned if I can tell whether they're laughing at me, or whether they can possibly be that dumb.

LETTER TO MRS. STILWELL This is Thanksgiving Day and I received a most appropriate message right on time. You know I have a little job to do over here, so I asked for a few tools to do it with. I have tried it once without any tools at all and it didn't work, so I reminded our folks of some promises and made what I thought was a very modest request. You should have seen the answer—I believe you would have helped me to bite the radiator. Peanut and I are on a raft, with one sandwich between us, and the rescue ship is heading away from the scene. They are too busy elsewhere for small fry like us, so we can go right ahead developing our characters and working on that shoestring I had presented

[9] In 1936, Pai Chung-hsi and Li Tsung-jen had led an uprising against Chiang K'ai-shek, accusing him of appeasing Japan. Yü Han-mou had betrayed Pai and Li and gone over to Chiang K'ai-shek; Ch'en Ch'eng also had fought against them.

[10] Kan Li-ch'u, commander in chief Sixth Army.

to me. I'll feel better tomorrow with Thanksgiving behind me and Christmas ahead.

Peanut's gang is more and more friendly and I find them even respectful if you get what I mean. They begin to think maybe we have something. The sourballs of a few months back have come around and are now playing on our team. This is all to the good, if my maternal grandfather's people[11] would only co-operate wholeheartedly. Believe it or not, I have almost as many headaches from them as from Peanut's crowd. This is proving to be as lousy a job as was ever invented. All we can do is keep on swinging.

NOVEMBER 29 ——— says attitude of military gang toward me has changed radically. Now they "understand" me. He thinks the Ramgarh experiment will rejuvenate the Chinese service. Now we have Ho [Ying-ch'in] with us (ostensibly at least), Liu Fei friendly, the ordnance asking me for orders, divisions being consolidated, artillery being made available, the SOS taking advice, and the Chinese agreeing to an *offensive!* If I could have seen this four months ago, I would have slept better. If we can continue and enlarge the Ramgarh school, we'll strengthen our grip on the Army, and with U.S. instructors planted in the Y force,[12] maybe we can get action. The only sour note now is Lo, who may command the Y force. I'll make a fight on that, but win or lose, we are a long way along the road. A success in Burma will put it over.

NOVEMBER 30   Saturation point? Teevy cautioned me this a.m. about pushing too hard. He said Chiang K'ai-shek might resent being pressed because of feeling that he had already done a great deal and would take it as critical if much more were demanded. Teevy thinks that great progress has been made and that we'd do well to let well enough alone for a while. He has been talking with Ch'en Ch'eng about Army matters in general, and wants me to get closer to Ch'en [Ch'eng], Hsüeh [Yüeh], and Hu [Tsung-nan]. (An indication of what he thinks of future developments.) Spoke of Ho's maladministration, as if it were well known. Said it was known in the Chinese Army that I was the only one that had any faith in it.

DECEMBER 1 The month opened auspiciously, anyway. Teevy in. Peanut agrees to carry the ball, in person. Lo will have the Y force, but it won't hurt, under the circumstances, and the responsibility will be where it belongs. Now I can breathe easily, and we can get the whip cracked. Peanut pleased at proposal to keep Ramgarh going (for artillery, armored force, machine guns, trench mortars, etc.).

Saw Ho Ying-ch'in and gave him the dope. American instructors will be welcomed. He will get out orders for artillery moves. He will get the staff for the *chih hui pu* [administrative command] (about the tenth time he has promised).

Political stuff. Teevy goes to Yünnan to see Dragon Cloud [13] and line him up. Commentary on Central government control there. Peanut not at all sure of him. *Sui shih* [at the same time] Teevy sees the Frog consul and offers a welcome and asylum to any French troops who may decide to come over [from Indo-China]. (French want me to broadcast to Indo-China a message of cheer and help.)

Teevy will reassure the Limeys on his way out [to the U.S.A.], as to Chinese intentions after the war. Especially as to Burma.

[11] The British.
[12] The thirty Chinese divisions gathered in Yünnan.
[13] English translation of "Lung Yun," name of governor of Yünnan province where the 30 divisions of the Yoke force were to be concentrated.

DECEMBER 2   Doot's[14] birthday. A rainy, windy night just like December 2, 1916, at West Point, when I went for the nurse. A.m. office. P.m. nap. Dorn woke me up at 5:30.

DECEMBER 5   [General Stilwell is here jotting down a few notes on information and communiques published by the British in Indian papers.]

LIMEY STUFF: "Mr. Churchill's speech greatly encouraged the American people." (The complacent!!!!)

"Allied planes . . . ." (All were U.S., of course.)

"British planes—with certain allied units . . . ." (This is the formula when any Limey units participate.)

Unimportant: ("The Russian attacks at S—— continued.")

Important: ("Our fighter planes made a sweep over the Channel, driving off a German reconnaissance plane. Near misses were scored on a barge near Boulogne.")

"A devastating raid was carried out on Shwebo. Disregarding heavy (i.e., two guns) antiaircraft fire, our bombers dropped their loads squarely in the target area. Bombs were seen to strike the runway. All of our planes returned."

"Bombs were seen to strike the east bank of the Irrawaddy" (!)

"Heavy explosions were heard as our bombs struck the airfield."

"The masterly conduct of the withdrawal from Burma was one of the bright spots of the war."

"General Alexander's motto is attack! Attack! And then attack again!"

(U.S. attack on Naples.) "Allied bombers—It is not yet known whether American units participated." The snooty bastards.

Item: *Attlee in House of Commons says: "We are sending all the help possible to China!"*

"Three buildings at Gangaw were hit in an offensive sweep by Blenheims."

DECEMBER 6   10:30 meeting at *Wei yuan hui* [National Military Council]. All the big pool-balls present—Ho, Liu Fei, gang of *Chün ling pu* [Bureau of Military Operations] boobies, hangers-on. The big table was full. *We actually did business.* They asked a lot of questions about organization, supply, command, etc. Ho and Liu seemed to be on my side throughout. "How will command be exercised?" They're asking *me* now! "What is your opinion on so-and-so?" "Can this be done?" Etc., etc. And they agree at once to *all* my suggestions. Most satisfactory meeting I have attended.

Early in December, Stilwell's plans for a spring offensive were shaken.

General Wavell in India decided that the Burma offensive was much too difficult a project to undertake at the time. Stilwell flew from Chungking to Delhi to reinstill him with confidence; but the trip was only partially successful. Wavell insisted on cutting the limits of the objectives previously agreed on; and on diminishing the number of British-Indian troops promised.

Returning to China, Stilwell found that delay was gnawing at all the preparatory target dates. The promises made by the Chinese staff were still far from implementation and the date of attack—now postponed till March 1—was drawing closer. He attacked those responsible for the delay with passion and urgency. He urged Washington to add its pressure to his protests.

On January 8, Stilwell received the news that he had

14 General Stilwell's daughter.

feared: Chiang K'ai-shek, he was told, had wired Roosevelt declaring that Chinese forces would not fight in Burma that spring. Such messages were to become typical of the Chiang-Stilwell relationship: Chiang's protests were made not directly to Stilwell, his chief of staff, but through Washington to Roosevelt. Stilwell was to learn of them third-hand, through roundabout channels.

Chiang's stand made a spring offensive in 1943 impossible; he had the support of the British. Stilwell accepted the decision and set about organizing his forces for a fall offensive instead.

DECEMBER 7   Archie [Wavell] asks Ferris if he (Ferris!) will agree to "eliminate" the proposed X-Y operation! [15]

Previously he had asked Ferris if the Peanut hadn't been pushed into it.

DECEMBER 8   Wavell weaseling. War Department welshing. Chinese playing ball.

LETTER TO MRS. STILWELL   Life is all ups and downs. Just as I think we have things going nicely I get a smack in the snout or a kick in the pants that puts more gray hairs on me. Just had such a billet-doux from the Brain Trust and I'm relaxing by dropping you a line. "The voice of one crying in the manure pile." Sometimes I get my head out and think "Boy! this is going fine!" and at that precise moment our own people dump another wheelbarrow load on me and throw in a hand grenade for good measure.

Saw *Tortilla Flat* last night, with its glimpses of Monterey and the bay and coast and was tempted to pack my musette and take off. The dogs got me—I like dogs, after 59 years of contact with human beings.

DECEMBER 9   T. V. back from Yünnan, T. V. will stick around till this operation jells. Will go to India if I say the word. Gave him the artillery dope, and the hard word about getting a move on.

Ho Ying-ch'in. Poured the artillery plan all over him. He didn't know a thing about it. Chief of staff of the Chinese Army! God save the mark. And this morning I got a long letter from him telling me some boxes had been broken, and also a *bottle of iodine!* Explained the procedure he would like us to follow in similar cases.

This guy is [ex officio] a combined Henry L. Stimson, George C. Marshall, and political power, and he worries about a bottle of iodine. He pays no attention whatever to the preparations of the Chinese Army for a vital campaign, but gets eloquent because a bottle of iodine is spilled in India. The colossal ignorance and indifference of responsible officials is simply amazing. And Peanut is called a great man! There must be tremendous cohesion in the Chinese people for them to survive the terrible neglect and maladministration of their so-called "leaders."

LETTER TO MRS. STILWELL   Don't know where I'll be for Christmas—maybe back here, maybe in India. It doesn't matter a bit, because I won't be in Carmel. If I can get some cream and some whisky I'm going to make an eggnog and drink a bucketful or at least enough to get partially stupefied. Then we'll organize a game of rummy and gamble for 50 cents—and a big time on the 25th. Don't waste any sympathy on me: I'm getting along O.K. and there are those among the Chinese who think Ole Pappy is not so bad.

DECEMBER 17, [DELHI] At 11:00 to GHQ and had a two-hour session with Wavell and his gang. Just whining about

15 X-Y was abbreviated code for the Burma plan. In effect Wavell was asking Stilwell's deputy if he would agree to the cancellation of the Chinese attack on north Burma.

difficulties. No advance from Akyab. Everything indefinite. Crap. P.m. office. Papers. 5:30 nap.

DECEMBER 20   Radio from George Marshall saying Currie had been in to "eat his words" and acknowledge his error! George and Henry surprised at "remarkable progress" we have made in getting Peanut to move.

New industry in Chengtu. Due to superior quality and market price [for fertilizer] of pig manure—a factory has been set up to make imitation of same. The workmen are equipped with bamboo pipes through which human manure is pushed; it goes through a mold, and mixed with a little dirt of suitable color, comes out looking just like the real article.

[These undated notes summarize General Stilwell's conclusions after his December 13-22 trip across the Hump.]

Back from India—Delhi, Ramgarh, Delhi, Dinjan, Chungking.

ADMIRAL SOMERVELLE [Royal Navy]: No hope of naval action in Bay of Bengal. No cruisers. Only three subs and some destroyers. Will not venture near coast. Might raid with destroyers if Jap convoy located.

BUMBLE WAVELL: Everything is very difficult. "Administrative difficulties." Can't supply the boys during monsoon. Japs have the road net on interior lines. He has already started the Akyab venture without notice to me. Objective— occupy and hold Akyab; use airfield to operate against lower Burma by air. Remainder of plan—17th and 23rd [Divisions] from Imphal on Kalewa. Reach and hold line of Chindwin. *Make raids east of river* (i.e., patrols) . Original 7-division plan now down to 3. Very skeptical about Chinese action of Y force. Wants to wait till November, 1943, before doing anything serious. Has directive to prepare for major offensive then, 22 divisions, against lower Burma and Malaya.

STAFF: Extremely pessimistic and obstructionist. Helping with material, but misrepresenting capabilities of railroad, roads, etc. Winterton playing ball.

Meanwhile, in China:

Ho Ying-ch'in tells me the time is too short to reorganize and concentrate the troops in time. Typical tactics—deliberately delay, and then plead lack of time as an excuse.

DECEMBER 23 Gave T. V. the blast. A frank statement of maladministration that will ruin the project [the Burma offensive]. Naming names including the Peanut, and using veiled threats of the inevitable consequences. Demanded a commander [for Yoke force] and some action. War Ministry must be energized and Peanut must go to bat. Teevy says he'll work on the Peanut.

DECEMBER 25 I hear sub rosa that Peanut has ordered Ch'en Ch'eng to Yünnan to command Yoke force.

Xmas party for Ho Ying-ch'in. I really believe they enjoyed it. Completely changed atmosphere compared to a few months back. Now very friendly. Even Liu Fei acts human. Gave him my picture. Imagine his asking for it! Joe makes a hit with all of them. He busts right ahead with his bum Chinese and gets the idea across somehow. He fills a big gap in the social struggle. At Chiang K'ai-shek's party Ho Ying-ch'in went and got Joe to introduce him to Peanut, and then, realizing that Peanut and son, and *Shih* [Stilwell] and son were there, he pushed us into a group and got the photographers busy on us. Ho Ying-ch'in, mind you!

JANUARY 3, 1943   Ch'en [Ch'eng] O.K. [for Yoke force] and has authority.

Commanding general for New First Army [16] still not decided on. Ch'en Ch'eng has not yet arrived.

The obstructioneers have been busy in the War Ministry. They delayed and delayed till X-Y [the Burma offensive] is damn near impossible, and now of course the excuse is that there isn't time to put it on. Peanut screams that the British Navy hasn't appeared and the Limeys will use only three divisions instead of seven. The Limeys squawk that it "can't be done," and look on me as a crazy man, as well as a god-dam meddler stirring up trouble. If anything goes wrong, I am sure to be the goat. Both Chinese and Limeys want to sit tight and let the Americans clean up the Japs.

It is becoming apparent that we must get rid of the Main Dodo.[17] Luckily, Teevy takes to the idea, and now says he's going to do it, substituting therefor the Little Fellow [18] from down the river. This would be all to the good, and we are encouraging the idea. If it could be done now, we could get going, but it will take time. Teevy claims the Peanut really means business, and I have been painting a dark picture of consequences in case he doesn't. If we can depend on the Peanut to say "Go," and on the Little Lad [Ch'en Ch'eng] to push the boys ahead, and if the Limeys will do their bit, we can put it over.

Dorn has been talking very frankly to Teevy lately and the latter is our big hope in handling the Peanut. (These talks confirm all our suspicions about where the block is and what should be done to remove it.)

Our batch of staff officers [for Ramgarh], furnished by War Ministry, goes down [to India] on January 6. What a farce! From August to January getting us a few officers! And all the time *such* good friends.

JANUARY 4, LETTER TO MRS. STILWELL   This damn climate is depressing and leaves me inarticulate. Cleave [19] put me to bed with a cold last week and babied me through the holiday parties, thank God. He even sent the Chinese nurse over to rub my back. Boy, did I have fun. Everybody kept peeking in to see what I was up to, however, so you'll probably hear some grand stories. We had an air alarm one day and you would have thought the world was coming to an end, the way Cleave fluttered, trying to drag me to a dugout. I knew nothing would happen, but to save a battle I dressed and went out and sat by the dugout in the sun. It was the only sunshine we've had in a month and it made me homesick. That made it three different kinds—the cold, the homesick feeling, and the sick-of-shoveling-manure feeling. Well, I've come out of it now, and I'm beginning to snap at everybody again, so I must be well.—Our routine is as usual, battling away at inertia and obstruction, and trying to be patient. You can realize what it means—a struggle for every toe hold and every man's hand against us. The Jews had to make bricks without straw: I wonder if they could have done it without even the mud? My worst time is the early morning, when I think of puttering around in our own kitchen getting breakfast. Well, there are compensations, even for that. I can remember the cold feelings in the lower bowels in the summer and fall of 1940, when all the news was terrible, and each day worse than the one before. At least now we can see the out, and Russians have crashed through in such grand style that we don't have to worry about everything going to hell. I can at least look forward to having a few breakfasts in

[16] The first Chinese divisions trained at Ramgarh were organized into an army designated as the New First Army.
[17] Ho Ying-ch'in.
[18] Ch'en Ch'eng.
[19] Stilwell's doctor.

peace, if I can stand the racket another year. Pinky is as usual. He hates everybody's guts, and it's very refreshing. We've been designing an "Order of the Rat" to be hung from a double cross for the ones who ran out on us. The fancy boys fall down. I'll take deck-hands from now on. How wise we were to build the Carmel house. I'll always be thankful for that and it's a grand feeling to know that you are all there with Garry to look after you.

Social note: Last night I had dinner with T. V. Soong. Chinese food and damn good, though he insisted it was just *pien fan* [casual food]. The pièce de résistance was the cook's specialty and he was so proud of it that he peeked in to see how we took it. It was fried, in rings about the size of a thumb ring. Nice brown crackly skin and chewy on the inside. I had swallowed one and was enjoying the second when I asked T. V. what it was. "That's tripe. You know, the *gut*. The end of the big gut in the pig." In other words, fried pig bowel. Roast sphincter. Well, now I've bitten a pig's backside. All I've got to do now is take a bite out of a skunk and I'll be fully qualified as a dietary specialist. When our Thanksgiving goose came on the table, his head and neck were sticking out stiff and straight at a rakish angle, his eyes had a surprised look in them and there was an electric light in his mouth. The boys had stuck a flashlight down his throat and produced a most novel and elegant effect. No, he did not have a tail light but I expect to see one on the next big occasion.

You know about Chinese plumbing. Well, my bathroom is right over Powell's bed and the drain pipe is hung on his ceiling. The pipe developed a hole about the size of a dime, so that when the handle was pulled upstairs, Powell had to leap for his life. A brand-new brigadier general, too, has his dignity to think about. Luckily, Powell used to be a pole vaulter, but in his palmiest days he never made a quicker start.

Every trip from India to China I get a shock. In India the natives are depressed, dejected, hopelessly poor, ragged, dirty, underfed, skinny, sick, unsmiling, apathetic. In China they have their heads up, they are bright, cheerful, laughing and joking, well fed, relatively clean, independent, going about their business, appear to have an object in life. India is hopeless.

When a Hindu is cremated, the nearest male relative has to crack the skull open so it won't burst when the fire gets hot.

JANUARY 8 *Black Friday.* T. V. gave Dorn the Peanut's answer to F.D.R. (Afraid to see me with it on account of probable blowup.)

Peanut says he won't fight. "The Japs will fight desperately. They have had time to prepare. Our supply lines are not good. The British force is inadequate. We risk defeat. Failure in Burma would be disastrous. A combined land- and seaborne operation is necessary. We can use the time by making an air offensive, for which *I* guarantee results out of all proportion to the force used," etc., etc.

Of course, next fall the Japs won't fight; they will have had no more time to dig in; our supply lines will be perfected; the British force will be "adequate." There is no more assurance that he will do anything then than that he will do it now.

What a break for the Limeys. Just what they wanted. Now they will quit, and the Chinese will quit, and the goddam Americans can go ahead and fight. Chennault's blatting has put us in a spot; he's talked so much about what he can do that now they're going to let him do it. Unless we

get tough and nail the G-mo down *now*, he'll get out of hand
for good. I warned George before getting Peanut's message
off, and have prepared an ultimatum for the Peanut, to be
sent from Washington if George agrees. If we can get the
War Department to be tough enough, and threaten to get
out—lock, stock, and barrel—we may gain enough to offset
this weaseling. But if they don't get tough, we put ourselves
in Peanut's hands for good.

JANUARY 9   Rumors that Madame's mission [in the
United States], whatever it was, has failed. What the hell
is up?

JANUARY 10   F.D.R. comes back at Peanut. "Why didn't
you wait? I told you I was about to dicker with Churchill.
For Christ's sake, hold your horses."

Dorn tipped off T. V. about my set of conditions for
Peanut. T. V. said for God's sake make it in form of agree-
ment for *him* to sign. The Peanut would blow up. T. V. is
quite frank with us. Feels he has done a great deal for
Chiang K'ai-shek, and gotten little for his pains. Thinks
Peanut is beginning to see the necessity of an efficient, pow-
erful Army. Told him [Chiang] that I was the only Amer-
ican who had consistently backed the Chinese as soldiers.
Has been dinging at him every day along the lines. Today
Peanut sent hurry-up call for Ch'en Ch'eng.

Told T. V. that Tu [Yü-ming] would have to go. Gave
him the dope on Tu, and T. V. promised he would get his
scalp. The idiot has been dickering with Lung Yün, and
T. V. knows it. —— wrote up the data on Tu and gave it
to him. Maybe we'll get our revenge on the little bastard
after all.

JANUARY 11   Madame [Chiang] has sent an S.O.S. to
T. V. [from Washington] to come and help her. She has

apparently bogged down. The rumor here is that she has "failed her mission," whatever it was.

JANUARY 14, LETTER TO MRS. STILWELL   This is one of the "mark time" intervals. The only progress I am making is straight up and down, and when I start to bite the radiator, some jackass comes in and tells me I must be patient. You had better be prepared for a soured old pickle, if I ever get through with this shoveling.

> Pappy's done his bit,
> He shoveled all the ———,
> He's just a sap,
> He took the rap,
> The wringer got his tit.

> Pappy's now a wreck,
> He got it in the neck,
> He took a ride,
> They tanned his hide,
> They worked a phoney deck.

> Pappy's sore and lame,
> He'll never be the same,
> So yank the dub,
> Put in a sub,
> And let him play the game.

There are times I need a strait jacket. Ordinary straightforward shooting and killing would be a relief, and I prefer associating with soldiers and sleeping on the ground to this bickering and dickering that I've gotten into. However, we are making progress and if I don't explode, we may arrive. Something has happened to May's [Madame Chiang] trip. She had apparently planned a Queen Marie tour of the

States, turning on the charm all over the place, and keeping the suckers in line. Now she's howling for help, so maybe the higher-ups are getting hep and are putting on the lid.

JANUARY 16   Ch'en Ch'eng due tomorrow. A.m. office. Dorn caught three guys at my desk yesterday.

General Wang in for 300,000 gallons of gas and six transports for Chinese Air Force. "The G-mo desires it." T. V. at 4:00. He says "Pay no attention to it." Ch'en [Ch'eng] due [in Chungking] tomorrow. Not hot for the job. On arrival at No. 3 Dorn met me. Surprise. Staff lined up. Joe pinned the Distinguished Service Cross on me. We all had a drink.

JANUARY 17   ———[20] in. The old story. "Stick it out, for the sake of the 400,000,000." Ho's gang tried to short-circuit me in Washington. Couldn't do it. So now they play it here by delay and obstruction. They tell people not to come and see me at No. 3, implying that it won't be healthy for them if they do. Their only thought is to hold on to their jobs.

——— says: The G-mo *does not know* how rotten the Army is, because nobody dares to tell him. Everybody is watching the Ramgarh experiment. It *must* succeed. More troops should be sent to India, a few thousands at a time. The Communists *cannot* compromise; if they give up their military organization, they'll be massacred.

[20] A Chinese general.

Chapter 6

SOLDIERING is a profession which, at every level, swings wildly from the ecstasy of adventure to the bottomless depths of boredom.

The first five months of 1943 were, for the CBI command, a period of waiting. The fronts were quiet. All along the thousands of miles of trench, foxhole, and jungle outpost that Stilwell commanded, the troops rested. In China, the armies of Chiang K'ai-shek held their lines against Japanese and Communists; in Burma, the jungles insulated the Japanese from the Allies, preventing contact. Fitful American air raids darted out from their deep West China bases to hit at Japanese-held ports.

All men seemed trapped in an endless expanse of drudgery that stretched across the future as far ahead as the imagination could reach. Across the Hump, drudgery was the quality of flight—over the mountains in ramshackle planes, deposit two tons in China, come back for more, back again, 30—60—90 missions with the Japanese and the monsoons waiting. And only 3,000 tons a month getting to China. In the jungle, drudgery was sweat and labor—dynamite the

187

trees, clear the undergrowth, move the dirt, bulldoze that trace over the hills. And no one knowing whether the Ledo Road being built east from the Indian border would ever get to China, when or how the Japanese would be driven from the trace that the map projected through the heart of enemy territory. In India, drudgery was supply and training: Americans teaching Chinese how to pack a howitzer, how to build a sanitary camp, how to handle wounded, how to sight a battery of American 75s. Over and over again in the heat, each word, each phrase of instruction repeated twice by a Chinese interpreter to peasant soldiers lost and tongueless in a strange land.

For Stilwell, the commander, drudgery was negotiation, drudgery was Delhi and Chungking, the same arguments repeated endlessly until a commander's authority was reduced to the status of a housewife's nagging.

Stilwell was preoccupied with his training projects: In India at Ramgarh, the work went well; but the larger training program of the Y force in China at Kunming was just beginning.

The Yoke force plunged Stilwell into the complexities of Chinese politics. The governor of Yünnan hated Chiang K'ai-shek; his enthusiasm for 30 divisions of Chiang's troops in his province was nakedly forced. Ch'en Ch'eng, who had been nominated commander of the Yoke force, was an old rival of Ho Ying-ch'in, the Chinese chief of staff. Ho's attitude to the development of Yoke strength was colored by this rivalry. The gathering of the troops, long promised to Stilwell, was infinitely slow in getting under way.

As Stilwell goaded Chiang to the performance of his commitments, Chiang grew not only bitter but less sure of the strategy. Why open Burma? Why wait for land communications? Why not urge America to double and redouble the air transport system over the Hump, and pour supplies into the Chinese Army at large for an offensive at a much later day, and into Chennault's Fourteenth Air Force for direct continued assault on Japanese coastal positions?

The theory that underlay Chiang's irritation was a simple one: what China needed, above all, was arms. Let the arms be flown in, and the Chinese would know best how and where to use them along their long front. Stilwell's insistence that the use of modern arms was not merely a matter of mechanical know-how, but a matter of discipline, training and military organization, met Chiang's theory head on. It was impossible, felt Stilwell, to graft American instruments of war on the ancient doctrines of the Chinese Army and government and win a modern war.

The struggle gradually narrowed itself to distribution of Hump tonnage. The CBI theater in global strategy was a pauper's theater, and Stilwell bitterly pressed Washington for more and more material to strengthen it. Within the theater, however, he was accused by every subordinate commander of niggardliness as he tried to satisfy the Yoke force, Chennault's air force, and the Chinese staff with morsels from the three-way split of Hump supplies.

In Major General Chennault, commander of the U.S. Fourteenth Air Force, Chiang K'ai-shek found an American who agreed with him on strategy and tonnage distribution. The conflict within China echoed as far as Washington. In May, a cable from Chiang to Roosevelt resulted in the summoning of both Chennault and Stilwell to Washington to present the opposing points of view.

JANUARY 18   Conference. T. V. Soong and Ch'en Ch'eng. Latter seems reasonable. Definitely will be in command. Spoke nicely of U.S. help. Agrees on direct action and no red tape. If Ch'en proves amenable, we can now accomplish something—if the goddam desk-sitters will mind their own business and keep their noses out of ours.

JANUARY 19   Conference. Gave Ch'en Ch'eng the program and proposed courses [for the Yoke force training center]. G-mo has indicated general agreement.

Office. P.m. nap. 7:30 to Russian embassy for movies. Excellent. *A Day of War.* June 13, '42. Taken by 160 cameramen. Also views of Stalingrad—recent. The Russians are O.K. Victor Hu there.

What a fight the Russians have made. The nation has obviously found itself. Twenty years of work and struggle. Results: tough physique; unity of purpose; pride in their accomplishments; determination to win. Stalin's decision—*three days* after the war started—to move half of Moscow's heavy industry to the east. (June 25) Leningrad actually exporting munitions to other fronts. Rugged young soldiers. Tough women. Every last man, woman, and child in the war effort.

Compare it with the Chinese cesspool. A gang of thugs with the one idea of perpetuating themselves and their machine. Money, influence, and position the only considerations of the leaders. Intrigue, double-crossing, lying reports. Hands out for anything they can get; their only idea to let someone else do the fighting; false propaganda on their "heroic struggle"; indifference of "leaders" to their men. Cowardice rampant, squeeze paramount, smuggling above duty, colossal ignorance and stupidity of staff, total inability to control factions and cliques, continued oppression of masses. The only factor that saves them is the dumb compliance of the *lao pai hsing* [the common people]. The "intellectuals" and the rich send their precious brats to the [United] States, and the farmer boys go out and get killed —without care, training, or leadership. And we are maneuvered into the position of having to support this rotten regime and glorify its figurehead, the all-wise great patriot and soldier—Peanut. My God.

JANUARY 20 & 21   Conference. Ch'en Ch'eng and T. V. (Soong).

Ch'en Ch'eng of course has to protect himself. He gives up his cushy province and zone and takes a job [the Yoke force] he must succeed at. If he fails, his enemies will romp all over him; he'll be through. Ho Ying-ch'in will block and undermine him if he's not extremely careful. He must be sure of his ground, sure that Peanut will support him, and he must line up everybody he can on his side. He's going slow, necessarily. Of course, I have to go over the whole damn story once more, and sell him the idea. He doesn't know about Ramgarh, he doesn't know me, he doesn't know what we can do for him. Even if he understands, he doesn't know he can depend on us. Instead of stepping into a fine command, he's walking into a trap that can be sprung on him unless he sees to it that he has his enemies tied up. Ho Ying-ch'in realizes that if Ch'en succeeds, he'll be the big name, and Ho will slide down into the discard. So Ho will accept the failure of the effort with great equanimity and will perhaps actively try to sabotage it. A fine kettle of fish. And Ch'en knows I'm responsible for pushing him into it. He might very well hate me for it.

JANUARY 20   Lend-Lease figures, to December, '42. England, $3,450; Russia, $900; China, $120; all others $51—in MILLIONS! (Add for England 400 million for shipping.)

JANUARY 23   Oh Christ. Ho Ying-ch'in is trying to push T. V. Soong out of the play. In one way it's good, it indicates that we are getting along too fast to suit him, and he feels he must make a fight. [Ho] told G-mo I had said I did not want to deal with T. V. Latter is much worried.

At his [T. V.'s] tea this p.m., Ho again spoke to him and said he and I had arrived at several agreements and [were] even in complete accord. In other words, he is telling T. V. to lay off. Wrote a letter for T. V., thanking him for his help and telling him I was putting it through to Marshall and Stimson. Ho smells a rat in the Ch'en Ch'eng appointment and is going to block us if he can.

This week has been a bitch. All this walla-walla over and over the same old stuff, pushing and pulling and worrying, has got me fagged out.

Bond [1] for CNAC put up $150,000 gold to some Chinese concern. It wasn't paid; explanation being that it had been banked in Rangoon. Bond put on pressure, and finally the Chinese manager came to him and said that if Bond would bring three planeloads of cargo to Chungking from Calcutta, the manager would pay him regular cargo rates, *and* give him his $150,000 besides!

JANUARY 24   Q. What's the matter with training in the Chinese Army? The Chinese start any analysis with the broadest general statement, then they deduce other things from that and so on down. In considering the Army, they begin with the War Ministry and General Staff, and go on through war zones, *chi t'uan chüns* [group armies] to *chüns* [armies] and *shihs* [divisions], but by that time they have exhausted the topic and stop. What the hell, all the important people are in—*shih changs* [divisional commanders] and up. The rest is easy; grab some recruits and get the graft organized.

The Chinese fix up the roof first, with the necessary minimum of supports and foundations. Nobody can see what's underground anyway, so why fool with it? We take a hell of a lot of pains with the foundation and groundwork, and figure the house will stand up.

Tripoli taken. Russians take Salsk. Guadalcanal not yet cleaned. Elsewhere quiet.

Indications of interest in CBI. Arnold and Somervell [2] coming with Dill [General Sir John Dill]. Second priority now, only behind Africa. Maybe it will open up.

LETTER TO MRS. STILWELL   Ole Pappy has been over the barrel and in the wringer for a solid week but this morning I begin to see light. I am frayed all around the edges and if this has to be fought out all over again, I'll be fit subject for a sanitarium.

The other day as I reached the house, Dorn was at the gate all dressed up, with the staff lined up inside. They lined me up and Joe pinned a medal on me, and then we all went inside and drank whisky.[3] All but me, I still don't like it. I don't know who was behind this business, but I have strong suspicions. The whole thing was bunk, pumped up out of

---

[1] William L. Bond, the American general manager of the China National Aviation Company, later vice-president of Pan American Airways.
[2] General H. H. Arnold of the U.S. Air Forces; Lieutenant General Brehon Somervell.
[3] See page 186, Chapter 5.

a very minor incident, and entirely undeserved. On that account it is embarrassing, but luckily time moves on and such things are soon forgotten.

We are pinched for personnel and everybody is doing double duty. Do you know that this theater of war is the size of the U.S.? Chungking is at Washington, and Karachi is at San Francisco. A trip from here to Delhi is like one from New York to Denver. And we have to hop over the Japs on the way. And the communications aren't developed quite as well as in the U.S.

JANUARY 26   Dinner with Chiang, apparently in my honor, to congratulate me on being decorated. Very simple food and little ritual or ceremony, but oh! the atmosphere. In the presence of the Most High no one dares to make a remark or venture an opinion. The hushed silence continues till a Pearl of Wisdom is dropped, or some brash foreigner asks if the melons came from Hami. You can see from the rigid postures and strained expressions that the sweat is running down the boys' backs. If addressed at all, the recipient of the honor answers briefly in a low respectful tone. No argument, no questions: just poker face and icy dignity. The merry throng was entertained by a movie that we sent over and which nobody understood. There was a lot of kissing and swapping of wives and at this point it was my turn to sweat. What crude barbarians we must still appear to them. There was a short training film on motors, introduced by a shot of a review of the 7th Division. I made some face by announcing it as my outfit.[4] I think I am making progress. If all goes well now, something will have been done that the wise guys said was impossible.

Lights out. Regular thing to save coal. Back to candles, and I've got to save my eyes.

JANUARY 27 F.D.R. at Casablanca.

JANUARY 29 Arnold and Somervell will be in Delhi to-morrow instead of next week. "Can I make it?" Christ, no. Can't they read a map?[5] "Important conference with Wavell and Dill." If they don't come to Chungking, the Peanut will be furious.

JANUARY 30 The Battle of the Mud still continues. These people are hard to help, I have to keep thinking that there are 399,900,000 of them worth helping or I wouldn't be able to stick it out with the other 100,000. Even in the Gang there are bright spots and understanding exceptions who encourage me to stick it out and come back for more. This trip may give me a chance to get my blood pressure down. Having a conference with Chiang at 5:00. I hope he had a good lunch. The destinies of nations sometimes depend on small factors. What a laugh it is to see the continual adulation and glorifying of small potatoes whose reputation grows in spite of what they do rather than because of it.

Date with G-mo at 5:00. He was sour as a pickle. Never one word of gratitude to the U.S. Just what he can get out of us.

FEBRUARY 1 Up at 5:00. Shoved off [for India from Kunming] in C-47 at 7:00. Got up but 100-mile wind held us and we turned back. Changed to C-87[6] and left at 10:00. Up to 23,000 and made it. Arrived Delhi at 10:30. Waiting dinner for us. Arnold and Somervell here. No other planes over the Hump today.

[4] General Stilwell had activated and commanded the 7th Division.
[5] It is 2100 miles from Chungking to Delhi.
[6] The C-87 was a transport-type plane converted from the B-24 bomber.

[UNDATED   Résumé by General Stilwell of Arnold-Somer-vell-Dill visit]

Conferences in New Delhi. Back and forth on plans. Tentative decision. Then Arnold and Dill came up [to Chungking]. Peanut retired to Berchtesgaden Huang Shan, so we went over. Arnold and Dill had their eyes opened. Arnold said, "You ought to have a laurel wreath." After arranging for 137 transports and a heavy bomber group [for Chinese] Arnold thought he had done pretty well. Peanut said he was much disappointed in conference. (Now he wants 500 planes, 10,000 tons [a month], and Chennault independent. Last June, 500, 5,000 tons, and three U.S. divisions.) Arnold said, "I'll be God-damned if I take any such message back to the President." He was well fed up.

At last conference, I pinned Peanut on whether or not he would attack next fall, in case conditions limited naval support. He got mad as hell and said, "Didn't I say I would?" [7] He sent word by T. V. that I had embarrassed him publicly. He can go to hell; I have him on that point. Arnold and Dill got a faint idea of conditions here and it made them sick.

FEBRUARY 10   Off at 8: 30. Ranchi at 10: 00.

FEBRUARY 11   Tactical classes [at Ramgarh] in the a.m. P.m. long session with Boatner.

FEBRUARY 12   General impression here [Ramgarh] great progress. Over the hump now. Personality troubles continue, but not so bad.

FEBRUARY 15   5,000 troops lined up for T. V. They looked good. He's off at last. 2: 00 p.m. to delousing of new recruits. Evening, conferences.

FEBRUARY 17   Up at 5:00. Off at 7:30. Slept most of the way. Cold. In [Delhi] at 11:30. Bissell blatted all the way in.

MARCH 4, CHUNGKING   ——[8] in. He confirms *all* my most pessimistic opinions. Peanut is really no dictator. He issues an order. Everybody bows and says "sure." But nobody does anything. He knows all about the smuggling and the rottenness, but he hasn't the power to cure it. Ho Ying-ch'in proposed Liu Ch'ih [garrison commander of Chungking garrison] instead of Ch'en Ch'eng for Yoke [command] and the Peanut bawled him out. "What! Would you make a joke out of a serious situation? Would you play politics in such a crisis?" Ho knows all about the rotten conditions, too, but he can't do anything. Lung Yün [governor of Yünnan] is not so bad; he just wants to be let alone in Yünnan. His Sixtieth Army can't be moved—they would refuse to obey the order. Opium traffic in Yünnan still enormous. Guarded by soldiers. Big stocks of hoarded gas, cloth, and other commodities. Gang of rascals around Lung Yün. They are loyal because of the money hookup and he trusts them rather than the Central Government which wants to get his graft away from him. The Yünnan people are suspicious not only of us, but of outside Chinese as well. What saved China was not the fighting by the Army, but the size of the country and lack of communications. We can get our way in Yünnan, but only by going slow. The Chinese Red Cross is a racket. Stealing and sale of medicines is rampant. The Army gets nothing. Malnutrition and sickness is ruining the army; the higher-ups steal the soldiers' food. A pretty picture.

[7] See entry, eleven months later, December 15, 1943.
[8] A distinguished Chinese.

MARCH 6   Chinese military spokesman: "Tali—March 6. After being subjected to furious Chinese counterattacks resulting in heavy casualties, the Jap troops on the west bank of the Nu River [upper reaches of the Salween] have started a general retreat. Many strategic points have been recovered by the Chinese." Utterly false. Jap patrols withdrawing after a reconnaissance. Typical of most Chinese reports.

MARCH 12-18   Took Ch'en Ch'eng to Kunming. Lung Yün did not meet him. Several conferences with Ch'en Ch'eng, who is doing exactly what he agreed to in Chungking. Training is U.S. pigeon;[9] discipline and administration is Chinese. Tu Yü-ming is handling all arrangements for school for Ch'en Ch'eng and in spite of my fears, is doing it as agreed. For the first time since arriving, I feel we are getting real co-operation. Ch'en Ch'eng has decision and appreciates what we are trying to do.

All arrangements made to begin schools on April 1. First infantry class will be Fifth Army, because of difficulty of getting students from outlying units.

FAILURES BY CHINA [Chinese promises]:
Consolidation of divisions [promised] by January 31. Not started.
All units [of 30-division Y force] move [to Yünnan] by January 31. Only two armies started.
No funds allotted for roads.
No action on use of land [for training ranges].
Lung Yün [governor of Yünnan] refused to obey any order from War Department.
All divisions under strength.
No action on Sixtieth Army.

MARCH 10   MIDSUMMER NIGHT'S DREAM   Statement by [Chinese] military spokesman at Chungking:

Jap strength (1937 to date)	6,576,000
Enemy killed	642,647
Enemy wounded	1,286,982
Enemy captured	21,314

MARCH 16   The Japs put out Chinese casualties for 1942 as follows:

Killed	642,657
Wounded	1,287,682
Captured	21,314

Pretty even fight!

MARCH 21, LETTER TO MRS. STILWELL   I did not write on March 19 because I wanted to let that terrible date ooze by.[10] Now it's over and I can look forward to being seventy. Actually, I am no more creaky than I was last week and I can still go up the 65 steps at the office faster than most. Slowing down but not stopped yet. This is the First Day of Beautiful Spring. Dorn, Bergin and I took a walk.

Lyric to Spring

I welcomed the Spring in romantic Chungking,
I walked in her beautiful bowers.
In the light of the moon, in the sunshine at noon,
I savored the fragrance of flowers.

(Not to speak of the slush, or the muck and the mush
That covers the streets and alleys.
Or the reek of the swill, as it seeps down the hill,—
Or the odor of pig in the valleys.)

The sunset and dawn, and the dew on the lawn,
And the blossoms in colors so rare.

[9] China-coast slang: "pidgin" or "pigeon," meaning responsibility.
[10] Stilwell's sixtieth birthday.

The jasmine in bloom, the magnolia's perfume,
The magic of Spring's in the air.

(The garbage is rich, as it rots in the ditch,
And the honey-carts scatter pollution,
The effluvium rank, from the crap in the tank,
Is the stink of its scummy solution.)

Aromatic Chungking, where I welcomed the Spring,
In a mixture of beauty and stenches,
Of flowers and birds, with a sprinkling of turds,
And of bow-legged Szechuan wenches.

Take me back to the Coast, to the place I love most,
Get me out of this odorous sewer.
I'm in ——— to my neck, but I'm quitting, by heck!
And I'll nevermore shovel manure.

MARCH 23 V FOR VICTORY A great load rolled off today. The picture is just as we thought—all units sadly depleted. (List of shortages below.) *But*—they say that orders are out for [recruit] fillers to report. All drafts start by end of April and should join units by end of May. Total, 133,000. A ghastly situation, but curable if they mean business. The astonishing thing is that orders are out.

Shortages in Y force (as of December, January, and February).

2nd Reserve Division—short 8,000 men. 71st Army, Divisions 36, 87, 88—short 9,437 men. 93rd Army has not moved—short 20,000 men. 2nd Army, Divisions 9, 76, N33 —short 17,381 men. 53rd Army, Divisions 166, 130—short 4,120 men. 6th Army, Divisions N28, N39, 93—short 13,500 men. 52nd Army, Divisions 2, 25, 195—short 7,733 men. 54th Army, Divisions 14, 50, 198—short 9,806 men. 60th Army, Divisions 182, 184—short 4,765 men. 5th Army,

Divisions 49, 96, 200—short 20,140 men. 8th Army, Divisions Honorary 1st, 82, 51—short 7,167 men. 74th Army has not moved, Divisions 57, 58—short 11,215 men. Total 133,264.

MARCH 24 Honeymoon continues. Dorn saw the Table-of-Organization boys and everything is just the way we want it. No question or anything. One hundred per cent agreement. If this keeps up, we'll be in a daze. Pai Chung-hsi reported in yesterday, offering to help. *He* wants to see Ramgarh now. Is it too good to last? Ho making speeches about Ramgarh and how wonderful it is!

[Editorial note: At the end of March, General Stilwell left on a long survey of his Indian installations. His notes thereafter are scattered. The following jottings are his résumé.]

APRIL 18 At Delhi, the Tagap Ga [11] affair broke loose. Took Boatner,[12] Cannon, etc., up. Wheeler calling for 25 binoculars, barbed wire, and 15 days' U.S. rations for 32 men. Panic at Miao, and general air of hysteria. Boatner got it under control. Wheeler was radioing that the situation was "desperate," and that four determined assaults had been made on the position and they might have to retire. I asked about casualties, and they turned out to be one killed and two wounded. Got the boys calmed down, and stopped the stupid demands. A typical SOS and Leavenworth map war. Eckert [13] hadn't even read the reports carefully. He figured this was a "co-ordinated attack by ground

[11] A small Allied outpost in North Burma, held by Chinese troops under American command; in the spring of 1943, the first Chinese troops had been moved from Ramgarh to the North Burma front where they were activated under American command as the Chinese New First Army.
[12] Brigadier General Hayden Boatner.
[13] The American Commander.

and air on the base." The "battle" at Miao, for which they
had alerted the whole command, turned out to be one
man of the Sadiya Elephant Transport Company, who was
wounded by the Chinese company at Miao. Colonel Tizey
could not "comply with the *request*" to defend north of
Khalak Ga, and Wheeler very properly had him relieved.
The affair was a feeler by about 200 Japs and Kachins.
When the Chinese stood firm, they skirmished around and
then withdrew. It was a good thing I caught this early—
Eckert was pulling in other British forces and we'd have
been in a mess shortly.

Arrowsmith doing fairly well with the road,[14] but no ball
of fire. Road standing up well. Poor command in 823rd and
45th (U.S.) Engineer battalions. Chinese 10th Engineers
doing good work.

British reneging on labor for airfield.[15] Indian Tea Plant-
ers Association ordered to raise more tea, quality no matter
—just tea. The U.S. can go without coffee, but the Limeys
must have their tea. Rushed to Delhi to squawk to Wavell,
and we got action. In two days, 5,000 were at work on each
airfield. Meanwhile, Alexander was sitting on his hands.
Told him to get the boys flying, and he did.

Famous letter from Roosevelt to George Marshall. [Re-
ferring to Chiang K'ai-shek]—"[he] came up the hard way
to accomplish in a few years what it took us 200 years to attain. . . . One cannot speak sternly or exact commitments
from a man like that, as if he were a *tribal chieftain*."

Then orders came for Chennault to have 1,500 out
of 4,000 tons [total monthly delivery of Hump airline in
China] for his war. Then he gets a separate Air Service
Command. Then he is to control the ATC by orders of

Arnold, speaking for the President, and giving it to me verbally through Glenn [Chennault's chief of staff]!

Wavell has a grievance. 18,000 of "his" trucks are in U.S. ports, and the goddam Americans won't ship them to him. Furthermore, if he doesn't get 180,000 tons a month, he just can't jump off [for a fall Burma offensive]. He only got 60,000 tons in March, and it's a bloody crime.[16] He's gone to London to squawk. "Can't" is his best word. Everything is so goddam "difficult" that it's practically impossible. This is ominous. If he can contemplate further delay now, we're sunk.

Ch'en Ch'eng is a joy. That was an inspiration, getting him.

Then the famous call to Washington. Peanut radioed Roosevelt that he and Chennault had been cooking up a plan that Chennault must come and tell him about. George [Marshall] tipped me off. I suggested that he call me, Bissell, and Chennault in, [he] saying he was going to anyway. Roosevelt crossed Bissell off, and George told me to bring one of Bissell's staff. Then I taxed Chennault with the matter, and he knew nothing about it. No new plan and no visit to Washington. So Peanut is just talking about Chennault's "6-months-to-drive-the-Japs-out-of-China" plan. I arranged for priority air travel, but luckily did not alert Win [Mrs. Stilwell]. Will see Peanut on Monday (4/19) and the thing may calm down. Must be in Washington by end of month, as George Marshall leaves soon after.

[14] The Ledo Road. Construction of a road from India to north Burma had begun in the spring of 1943. Starting from Ledo in Assam it was to run to Myitkyina as soon as combat troops had driven the Japanese back from the road trace.

[15] The chief source of labor in north Assam were the workers on the British tea plantations.

[16] The Chinese theater at this time got about 3,000 tons.

[This undated paper is General Stilwell's brief summary of the May, 1943, Washington conference in which he participated.]

WASHINGTON   Continual concessions have confirmed Chiang K'ai-shek in the opinion that all he needs to do is yell and we'll cave in. As we are doing. F.D.R. had decided on an air effort in China before we reached Washington. This suited the British, who want no part of a fight for Burma. Why should they fight to build up China, if we can be euchered into bearing the brunt of the war against Japan? They'll get Burma back at the peace table anyway.

Nobody was interested in the humdrum work of building a ground force but me. Chennault promised to drive the Japs right out of China in six months, so why not give him the stuff to do it? It was the short cut to victory.

My point was that China was on the verge of collapse economically. That we could not afford to wait another year. That Yünnan was indispensable and that a force had to be built up to hold it. That if the Japs took Yünnan, the recapture of Burma would be meaningless. That any increased air offensive that stung the Japs enough would bring a strong reaction that would wreck everything and put China out of the war. Witness the Chekiang campaign, brought on by the Jap belief that Tokyo was bombed from bases there. That the first essential step was to get a ground force capable of seizing and holding airbases, and opening communications to China from the outside world. Overruled. Churchill's idea was, so he said, that China *must* be helped, and the only way to do it within the next few months was by air.

At the same time they decided on Saucy [17] they made it practically impossible for me to prepare the Y force, and then ordered it used in an offensive. But British reluctance caused the wording of the directive to be so loose that it would be up to the commander as to what he could do. He could go the limit or he could quit at any time. With Wavell in command, failure was inevitable; he had nothing to offer at any meeting except protestations that the thing was impossible, hopeless, impractical. Churchill even spoke of it as silly. The Limeys all wanted to wait another year. After the Akyab fiasco, the four Jap divisions in Burma have them scared to death.

The inevitable conclusion was that Churchill has Roosevelt in his pocket. That they are looking for an easy way, a short cut for England, and no attention must be diverted from the Continent at any cost. The Limeys are not interested in the war in the Pacific, and with the President hypnotized they are sitting pretty.

Roosevelt wouldn't let me speak my piece. I interrupted twice, but Churchill kept pulling away from the subject, and it was impossible.

So everything was thrown to the air offensive. F.D.R. pulled 7,000 tons [monthly over the Hump] out of the air when told that 10,000 was impossible, and ordered that tonnage for July. First 4,750 [tons] for air [Fourteenth Air Force], then 2,250 for ground. They will do the Japs some damage but at the same time will so weaken the ground effort that it may fail. Then what the hell use is it to knock down a few Jap planes.

Farewell lunch. Mr. Churchill: "Mr. President, I cannot but believe that an all-wise Providence has draped these great events, at this critical period of the world's history, about your personality and your high office." And Frank lapped it up.

[17] Code name for a Burma offensive in the fall.

Henry Stimson and George Marshall were understanding. The War Department was O.K. Even the air was a bit fed up on Chennault. But what's the use when the World's Greatest Strategist is against you.

Unsatisfactory as the Washington conference had been, it set a target date for new action, and slowly the wheels began to turn in China.

On returning, Stilwell found that his first duty was to defend the organizational integrity of the Yoke project. During Stilwell's absence the Japanese had launched a drive from their Central China bases on the gorge barriers of the Yangtze that guard Chungking. This Japanese campaign had terrified Chungking. Although it was learned later that the campaign had been a foraging raid for the Japanese divisions, it had cost the Chinese tens of thousands of casualties.

Ho Ying-ch'in and Chiang K'ai-shek wished to divert the painfully accumulated supplies of the Yoke force to support of the general front in China. Stilwell, fully aware of the general strangulation of supplies in China, insisted that the only alternative to progressive starvation was to break the Japanese blockade; and the only way to break the blockade was to keep on equipping and training the Yoke force for the great campaign.

The great campaign was embodied in a series of proposals Stilwell had brought back, generally known as the Saucy plan. It was simply the old three-pronged drive into Burma, embellished with more naval strength in south Burma, and adorned with the promise of use of American and British Commando groups. Chiang after some delay accepted the Saucy proposals.

JUNE 16   Ho Ying-ch'in: "We don't need to widen the Burma Road. It's O.K. Anyway, the Burma operation will probably fail, so what's the use? The Japs are on interior lines with good communications; they can concentrate against us rapidly. If we attack at Paoshan and Ledo, by the time our troops reach Myitkyina they will be all tired out, and then the Japs can defeat us, because we will not have any reserves to send up. The first push might succeed, but then the Japs would send more troops to Burma and we could not hold them. It is this second fight that would be disastrous. What should be done is to have the British and Americans take Rangoon; then the Japs could not get in and we could crush them."

Ho's argument that nothing should be done to make it possible to win, because we will probably fail with things as they are, is typically Chinese. His naïve suggestions that the British and Americans should take Rangoon shows how much he is prepared to push the Paoshan operation.

JUNE 18, LETTER TO MRS. STILWELL   Back again on the manure pile after that wonderful trip home. The world's greatest anticlimax. You gave me a perfect send-off, for which I bless you. Whatever happens to me I am 'way ahead of fate. "Better an hour in Carmel than a cycle of Cathay." The trip back was smooth and uneventful. The plane that passed ours over the Bay of Biscay was shot down. But ours wasn't. The plane that landed just ahead of us at Cairo crashed. But ours didn't. Back to find Chiang same as ever— a grasping, bigoted, ungrateful little rattlesnake. This place was in a dither during the Ichang affair. He had the wind up in a big way, to the point of throwing teapots and vases at visitors.

JUNE 19, LETTER TO MRS. STILWELL   You must be laughing about today's news that Wavell is to be pushed upstairs and the Auk [General Sir Claude Auchinleck] replace him.

If they give the Auk a free hand and real authority, things will look up.

Now the 22nd. What stopped me I don't remember. We are in the doldrums waiting for a peanut "brain" to function. "The mountain labored and brought forth a mouse," but this product will probably be a skunk. It's hell to be plumped back into this cesspool after having had a breath of fresh air. There is no change in the high command and the wrestling match continues. I've got to pin a medal on Chiang and it will make me want to throw up.

JUNE 21   Yü Ta-wei [18] worried about raw materials. Total [quantity of] 7.92 [caliber bullets] left in depots: 40 million.[19] (10 million used at Ichang.) Without raw material, arsenals will close down. Crisis in November, unless we can bring stuff in. If Japs repeat [Ichang threat], Peanut will respond to threat and divert stuff from Yoke. But [says Chiang] "don't bring any troops down from Shensi; we must watch those devils the Communists."

—— says to build up a stock [of munitions] at Chungking so Peanut won't be tempted to wreck Yoke, but of course that means tonnage, and to do it we have to deny Yoke an equal tonnage of much-needed weapons. The situation is critical and will remain so. Any Jap threat will put the Peanut in an uproar, and if they are wise they will repeat their attempt, for this if for no other reason. And if they seriously want to gum the game, they can attack Kunming or Chungking, or both, with five divisions on either line and finish the matter. If we sting them badly enough in the air, they are almost sure to try it.

Seventy thousand replacements diverted from the Yoke on account of Ichang. Last year 56 per cent [of recruits] arrived at their units; the rest died or deserted on the way.

Can we expect a better result this year? The Peanut's promise of picked men for India is so much wind. 68 per cent [of the replacements offered were] rejected, mainly for trachoma and skin disease, in last batch of 1,800.

JUNE 25 Conference with Ho. Amazing. Peanut has not discussed the Combined Chiefs of Staff proposals [20] with Ho! And Ho says Liu Fei knows nothing about them. Obviously, no one in War Ministry has seen them if Ho hasn't. So with whom did the Peanut take counsel? With the cook, perchance, or his old pal, God. This tops everything. The little squirt, on his own initiative, will decide the fate of nations.

JUNE 28 Letter [from] Ho Ying-ch'in. This is colossal. He asks us to turn over to the War Minister [21] the antitank weapons and ammunition of the Y force. Ho, chief of staff, would deliberately weaken the already scant resources of Yoke and scatter the proceeds in the sixth war zone. Of course, it's because Peanut has had a scare,[22] but it shows their conception of preparations to fight on the other front.[23] Words fail on this one; not only does he fail utterly in his own duty, but beyond that he obstructs all my efforts to build them up, and crowns it by trying to take away what we have so painfully accumulated.

I gave him [Chiang K'ai-shek] the dope,[24] two weeks ago. I'm told he'll answer today. Then he says, "Where's the

[18] Director of arsenals for the Chinese government.
[19] This was the total supply of bullets in depots for all the Chinese Armies at the time. Perhaps as much more was actually in the hands of troops. It averaged out to a supply of twenty bullets per man.
[20] Saucy proposals.
[21] Ho Ying-ch'in himself.
[22] The Japanese thrust at Ichang.
[23] The Yünnan-Burma front.
[24] On the Saucy plan for the Burma invasion as decided at Washington.

translation?" So Shang Chen and I rush back and get the paper and Shang goes back with it and translates. And the Peanut says, "Well, that sounds O.K. But exactly how much navy is to be furnished? The important part of this operation is the navy. There is no use of attacking Burma unless the Bay of Bengal is secured."

So —— comes back and tells me and I write a letter with a long list of battleships and heavy cruisers and light cruisers and aircraft carriers, and destroyers, etc., and explain the word "adequate" for the seventh time. And —— goes back for the third time to try and explain.

This is going beyond all bounds. This insect, this stink in the nostrils, superciliously inquires what we will do, who are breaking our backs to help him, supplying everything— troops, equipment, planes, medical, signal, motor services, setting up his goddam SOS, training his lousy troops, buck- ing his bastardly chief of staff, and general staff, and he the Jovian Dictator, who starves his troops and who is the world's greatest ignoramus, picks flaws in our preparations and hems and haws about the navy, God save us.

JULY 5   Still [Chiang K'ai-shek] does not answer the Presi- dent: (1) Saucy. (2) Date.[25] (3) Stratemeyer.[26] Last two are recent, of course. . . . But No. 1! Since June 16 and the world burning up. . . .

Recent rumor here to effect that the Reds have been told they can "co-operate" . . . or else. The "else" being that he [Chiang] will attack them in September. Chou En-lai has left for Yenan. Reds reported to have asked for freedom of speech and no coercion to join the Kuomintang. Ha, Ha. How can he, the Great Democrat, answer that? This whole thing seems farfetched, unless the slippery little bastard is deliberately setting up a stop on Saucy. He is quite capable of doing it and reporting that he is too involved against the Reds to join the party in Burma.

JULY 6   Conference with Tseng Yang-fu (minister of communications), Kohloss, McCammon, Edwards, and I. We're asking these bastards for Christ's sake to supply a lousy 1,200 broken-down trucks for their own damn army [27] and we stand ready with 22,000 on the other side. And will they do it? No, they won't. They'll think it over and yen chiu [study] and shang liang [consider] and propose four-way shifts, and grabs from the troops and hire of commercials, etc., etc. But the money to run them? Oh, that's k'un nan [difficult]. "General Stilwell must convince the Generalissimo." Let General Stilwell do it. "How about the traffic?" Well, nominally, that's under the engineer. But actually it's under a special bureau and Tai Li [chief of the Chinese Secret Police] controls it. Another pretty kettle of fish. Of course he controls it, and takes graft off it in large hunks.

So we're right where we started. Trucks, but no money. Then the road. No hurry; we can do it in three months, or even two and a half. Maybe we'll have more labor. After the airfields are finished. Maybe in August we can begin. . . .

JULY 7   Decoration [28] of Peanut, Ho, Shang, and Yü. Peanut was half an hour late. He was ill at ease during the performance. I read the Chinese citation and made my speech in Chinese. Madame present, and full of herself and

[25] Target date for beginning of Burma campaign.
[26] Whether he would consent to the appointment of Major General George Stratemeyer as air commander of all aviation units in China, Burma, and India.
[27] For the Burma offensive, to move troops in Yünnan into position.
[28] The U.S. government at this time instructed General Stilwell to decorate Chiang K'ai-shek as chief commander of the Legion of Merit, the highest possible decoration that the U.S. government can give to a foreigner.

what she's going to get out of the President. Said he had promised two divisions. Everybody anywhere near Peanut turned to stone. Ho sat there like a graven image, and never opened his trap.

JULY 8   Another shock. ——— found out today that Tseng Yang-fu did not know what he was talking about at our conference. Had not been to his office and had not seen his people. Everything had already been arranged as per Ho Ying-ch'in's scheme. My God. This truck business is endless. We are now going to take the [Chinese] War Department's scheme and start at last.

JULY 12   RED-LETTER DAY   The answer came from Peanut to the Combined Chiefs of Staff Saucy proposals. In *writing*. And *signed*. After a year of constant struggle, we have finally nailed him down. He is committed, in writing, to the attack on Burma. What corruption, intrigue, obstruction, delay, double-crossing, hate, jealousy and skulduggery we have had to wade through. What a cesspool. . . . What bigotry and ignorance and black ingratitude. Holy Christ, I was just about at the end of my rope.

With Chiang's acceptance of the plan, the Allies set up the Southeast Asia Command (SEAC) for the conquest of Burma. SEAC's commander was to be Lord Louis Mountbatten, its deputy commander was to be Stilwell.

The broad outlines of the campaign had been set, the basic decisions made. Beneath the level of high policy, however, the old struggle and old frustrations continued. By the end of September the friction between Stilwell and Chiang was nearing one of its periodic climaxes.

[UNDATED]   EXAMPLES OF DELAY, ETC., ETC.

   1.   30th Division: Promised positively in Kunming by

May 20. Postponed to June. Postponed to July. On July 12, only 1,200 men had left [for Kunming].

2. The 200 men promised for the 155s [at Ramgarh]. All but 65 rejected by Chinese doctors; 30 more by U.S. doctors; 35 went to India.

3. 4,500 replacements for 22nd and 38th [Divisions in India]. Promised early in spring. By March. Not one has appeared up to July 12.

4. Replacements for Y force. 132,000 started, months late, and 70,000 diverted to Hupeh.

5. Units of Y force. All to be in position by March 1 at latest. Not in yet.

6. Heavy trench mortars for west front . . . 23 promised with probability of 21 more. Now . . . July 12 . . . none on west front.

7. Labor regiments to report in June. Now . . . July 12 . . . no sign of them.

8. For airfields $500,000,000 or a billion [Chinese dollars]. O.K. For the Burma Road after months of struggle $8 million, where $200 million is needed.

9. Animals. Refused to buy them when we asked because too expensive. One mule, [then] 12,000 [Chinese dollars]. Now . . . July . . . the price is 40,000. Solution is to buy smaller number with same amount.

10. Attempts to steal payroll at Ramgarh. The "lump sum" [29] stunt. Constant agitation. Lo Cho-ying got away with 100,000 rupees a month. Split in Chungking of course; he's now in War Ministry.

[29] The U.S. Army insisted that the soldiers at Ramgarh be paid individually and by public roll call. The Chinese constantly agitated that the soldiers' pay be turned over in a lump sum to the commanding officer of the units involved. This was the traditional channel of theft in the Chinese Army, and the U.S. Army refused.

11.   War Ministry interference in command and organization at Ramgarh. Constant fight.

[UNDATED   These are General Stilwell's notes of a conversation with a Chinese of cabinet rank.]

—— ON PEANUT   "He wants to be a moral potentate, a
religious leader, a philosopher. But he has no education!
How ridiculous this is. If he had four years of college education, he might understand conditions in the modern world
but the picture we see clearly is dark to him. He simply does
not understand. If he did, conditions would be better, because he wants to do right. No one tells him the truth . . .
no one. He will not listen to anything unpleasant, so nobody tells him anything but pleasant things. It is impossible
to reason with him . . . one could with Sun Yat-sen . . .
but this man! He flies into a rage if anyone argues against
him. Everyone avoids rocks and gets around knotty problems by devious means. He does not know what is going on.
He writes orders by the thousand . . . like snowflakes . . .
and everybody says "yes, yes" and he never knows what has
been done. He is afraid of the crowd and what people will
say, so he tries to stop them talking. This is very foolish. It
is like trying to stop the sound of a rattlesnake's rattle while
leaving the poison in his fangs. There is no reason for him
to fear anything. Let them talk. He does not need to fear the
Communists, either. He should use them.

"Education is China's only hope and this takes a long
time. Europe has been working through the process for centuries; China has had only about fifty years and is working
on an imported civilization, not a domestic one. Very few
people know what it is all about. The mass of the people
know only that Japan is fighting China.

"The Peanut, fifty years ago, would have been an acceptable leader, but his lack of education handicaps him under modern conditions. Even now there is no better one in sight. His successor would undoubtedly be a military man, and there is no one who could do any better. There are some who seem capable in their present positions, but if they had to formulate national policy, they could not do it. The only way out is to have patience and make progress slowly."

After the war, there will be a great deal of trouble in China. Peanut knows only what goes on immediately around him, and the country is so big that he will not be able to control it. Obstinate, pigheaded, ignorant, intolerant, arbitrary, unreasonable, illogical, ungrateful, grasping.

JULY 14, LETTER TO MRS. STILWELL   This last time up I pinned a medal on Chiang and you can imagine my feelings. It was very formal and I read him the citation in Chinese and then made a few remarks to him, also in Chinese, about the meaning and importance of the decoration. He was seated and not at all at ease. When I grabbed his coat and pinned it on, he jumped as if he was afraid I was going to stab him. On July 12 I passed a milestone. Got a decision in writing which eases my worries and responsibility no end. The buck is now passed and the boys can no longer block me out with impunity. It's a grand feeling after a solid year of struggle. Somehow or other things look better all around. Maybe we'll get out of the sewer after all.

[UNDATED.   General Stilwell flew to India on July 14 and remained there till September 1. His following notes summarize the stay of six weeks.]

[UNDATED] KASHMIR: LETTER TO MRS. STILWELL   Snuck off to Kashmir for three days, 4,000 feet up in the hills from the "Vale." What a bust. Kashmir is overadvertised, of course: the Jhelum is full of mud, the houseboats are jammed in like Coney Island cottages, the place is dirty and full of flies. Gulmarg is a Limey attempt to reproduce the home-side touch. Polo, tennis, dancing, golf, and tea. Dress for dinner and keep up the jolly old prestige. It rained all the time and was generally miserable, but at least it was a change and the trees were grand. Spruce, pine, fir, etc.

THE WÊN CASE This moon-faced s.o.b. Brigadier General Wên, deputy chief of staff at Ramgarh, had big ideas. A graduate of Leavenworth, get-rich-quick course. Always concerned with the Big Picture. Utterly ignorant of basic requirements. Always writing long reports. "It's pretty good, but we must make it perfect" kind-of-stuff. Crazy ideas about Antiaircraft and Antitank and Chemical Warfare Service detachments in all units, [from] battalions up. Smart guy with sly criticisms of Americans and American methods. Took Cheng T'ung-kuo, that moron, under his wing and figured on moving right in on us. Kept agitating for the Army special units. Well, he went too far. Put four Wêns [i.e., his own men] in various jobs without reference to Bergin.[30] Threw Lin Wên-shih in the clink for a fancied personal slight. Put a Wên[31] in radio room and suppressed radios. Asked for ten Military Academy graduates for the staff without reference to me or to Bergin. Recommended himself over my signature for the Ch'ing T'ien Pai Jih Chang.[32] Asked in my name for relief of Wu Ch'u-chang and suppressed answer to cover the move.

So I tied a can to him. Relieved him as deputy chief of staff and made him Kao-chi Ts'an-mow.[33] This is a Chinese fa tzu [method] for easing 'em out quietly. The whole chih hui pu [command] was tickled to death. They threw their hats up and cheered. Wên came over and squawked and pleaded. When Bergin asked him for the missing radios, he just blubbered. I then got out an order about the dignity of the Chinese officer's commission and some other crap, telling one and all, by God, that they had better get down to business and stop all this nonsense.

Got Ayers going on motor transport and he is turning up all sorts of mismanagement. He's a roving inspector, with orders to nose in everywhere.

Threw Colonel ———[34] and his nurse girl friend out. She to Karachi, he to Calcutta. He had to make a display of his love affairs.

At Chabua [35] the mess is gradually straightening out. Alexander is mired in, but struggling. The overpromoted air corps is sunk when it comes to administration and management. Just a bunch of aerial chauffeurs. Bawled out ———; he had let the contractor tear out brick walks, just laid, to get bricks for new buildings! Alexander has 3,000 men and 750 pilots and still they can't get going. The C-46 [36] is full of bugs. Carburetor ices up. We have lost six over the Hump and the boys' morale is lower and lower. John Davies was in one, with a very mediocre crew, and had to jump out in Naga country. They were lucky. Now Alexander thinks the C-87 is the thing. A while back only the C-46 would do.

[30] Brigadier General William E. Bergin was administrative commander of Ramgarh training center.
[31] One of General Wên's henchmen.
[32] A Chinese military decoration.
[33] A staff officer, senior grade.
[34] An American officer.
[35] Chabua by late 1943 was the largest of the Hump terminals in India, and was headquarters of the Hump Command.
[36] The Curtiss Commando—a two-motored plane which later became the Hump mainstay.

And the DC-3 was no good at all. As a matter of fact, it has the best record over the Hump. June, about 3,400 tons. July 4,500 tons. August . . . ?? They were to hit 7,000 in July and 10,000 in September. The Air Transport Command record to date is pretty sad. The CNAC has made them look like amateurs.

LEDO BASE   The roads in the base are good, but the road [37] itself has been standing still. "General" Arrowsmith commands from his château, Glenn is in the hospital, York is out on location, and God knows who is running the road. I got York and talked to him and then sent Wheeler a hot radio. Arrowsmith is a sulky, indifferent bird, who can't see that this is the chance of a lifetime. You wouldn't catch him out in the mud, pushing. No, he's the Big Shot at the base, directing. "Where is So-and-so?" "Oh, he's my section engineer in charge of roads in the base," etc., etc. Wheeler at once yanked Arrowsmith to Delhi and proposes to use Strong. I don't know. At any rate, he'll be better than Arrowsmith.

SCORE:
   U.S.   1 Brigadier General relieved
              1 Colonel relieved
              2 Colonels bawled out
              1 Brigadier General bawled out
   Chinese 1 Brigadier General relieved
              1 Army Commander bawled out

AUGUST   The East Asia Command is set up. India, Burma, Singapore, Malaya, Sumatra, and Ceylon, with Lord Louis Mountbatten at the top. I am deputy and have to kid the Peanut into using the boys. But George is leaving me in command of all U.S. troops, air and ground. The command setup is a Chinese puzzle, with Wavell, Auk [Auchinleck],

Mountbatten, Peanut, Alexander and me interwoven and mixed beyond recognition. Stepchild [38] will be put on but late, probably. However, they are coming to their senses on tonnage for ground troops, and the air will have to step down. Louis will have a mixed staff with Wedemeyer on our side. It looks like business now. George has read the riot act to T. V. and maybe Peanut will come across.

SEPTEMBER 2, CHUNGKING   Victory! Got the list of the SECOND THIRTY.[39] That commits them to [the] training scheme. Subject to change, of course, but what a struggle that has been. A year ago, when we were wallowing in the mire, it wouldn't have seemed possible. If the Japs let us alone, we may put it over.

Victory AGAIN. Radio from George Marshall on U.S. [combat] units for Stepchild. Only 3,000 but the entering wedge. Can we use them! And how!

SEPTEMBER 4   The Chungking "military spokesman" comes out with a lot of crap. "The Japs have put three and a half divisions into Burma recently, and are feverishly preparing for the Allied counterattack." "The Japs have put 100,000 men into French Indo-China," etc. This looks like an inspired statement to give the Peanut an out in the coming pressure for action. "They are too strong." "We haven't the weapons." "What we need is planes," etc., etc. The same old crap.

N.B.   When I started in over here, I said to myself that the only safe policy for a deck-hand of my caliber was to go

[37] The Ledo Road into Burma, which was to link with the Burma Road.
[38] Code for a phase of the Burma offensive.
[39] The Chinese were to concentrate thirty more divisions in East China, near Kweilin, to be known as the Z force; it was to be a training command which would ultimately become a tactical command similar to the Y force at Kunming.

straight down the middle of the road. With a one-track mind, I couldn't afford to get away from the main objective and try to pick daisies. There could be no attempted short cuts by playing politics—my throat would have been cut on the first détour. I had to be plain John Doe and live like a goldfish. In that way, I could concentrate on what was ahead and would not have to worry about the lies I had told the day before.

It was a good policy. I never had to worry about the spies that Tai Li and the Kuomintang put in my house, even when I caught them going through my papers. Rubber heels and a quick, unexpected return did the trick. I never had to worry as to what to tell the G-mo. I could see his "advisers" chewing their nails and shivering, and laugh at it. All I had for him was the truth, pleasant or unpleasant, as the case might be. It frequently made him mad as hell, and for a long time he must have been suspicious because I was the only one he was getting it from. And there must have been a lot of people telling him I was a liar. It was necessary for them to do so, because I was getting after such things as false reports, cowardice, neglect of duty, smuggling, stealing, and similar irregularities. And I could prove enough of them to convince him that in those cases, at least, it was true.

The G-mo thought that by making me his joint chief of staff I would accept without question any order he chose to give me. He is that dumb. He could never understand that I had another status as U.S. representative on councils, another as commanding general of U.S. troops, another as Lend-Lease watchdog.

It made him mad as hell to find that I would not simply pass out Lend-Lease stuff on his order, and that I would stand between him and the abuse of U.S. troops. He might get sore, but he could get nothing on me, and that was a comforting thought. I could say anything I pleased and go away secure in my own mind that the crowd of Yes-men, parasites, idolaters, and sycophants around him could not break it down. How could they, if it was true?

After finding that I would not obey his slightest wish, like the crowd he was accustomed to, he tried to reduce my importance and prestige by ignoring me and anything I was connected with, including his own army. It is hard to imagine that he would do this, but I believe it an added reason to two others that mainly actuated him: (1) that it would be risky to have an efficient trained unit under the command of a possible rival, and (2) that his policy is to suck in U.S. air power and sit back while they fight his war.

The continued delay and obstruction in getting training done must have been due to his fear of a challenge to his authority, as well as to his belief that air power is decisive and there is no use putting any time on ground troops. Otherwise, he could not complacently take the terrible risk of leaving his army in its deplorable condition and his southern frontier open to an attack which would be fatal to China and to him. The only other possible reason is that he really thought the Army was in excellent shape and only in need of weapons to make it formidable. It is hard to imagine a military man as dumb as this, but he appeared convinced in 1942 before the Burma campaign that the Fifth and Sixth Armies were the flower of his troops. The 55th Division, the 96th, the N28th, N29th, 93rd. Kan Li-ch'u! Tu Yü-ming! Yü Fei-p'eng. My God.

To ignore your chief of staff completely [may] be good practice, but I doubt it. Over a period of a year and a half, I submitted memos and studies on various subjects to him. He never deigned to discuss any of them. It was impossible

to argue with him. He would simply pass down the decision
—always "No." And that ended it. The All-Wise had decided. Finish. He must have thought me a queer bird to
stick along on these conditions. But I had my mission and
gradually, painfully, and slowly I got a foothold that he
couldn't shake. American efficiency, sincerity, and honesty
began to be proven and respect for us and our methods began to spread through the Chinese Army. A small group of
Chinese officers of character realized the chance we were
offering of revitalizing the Army and kept telling me to hang
on, be patient, and for God's sake not quit. [This paper
unfinished.]

SEPTEMBER 7   Colonel Earthworm Ch'en has been figuring tonnage. He says, "You know there are times when a
3-ton truck weighs as much as a 20-ton tank." This bird
is the executive for the war minister. McCammon said,
"Now, if you have a 2,000-pound cow, and she stands on one
foot on a bridge, how much will she weigh?" Ch'en's idea
was that she would weigh 500 pounds. (Calculations for a
troop movement.)

Chapter 7

HIGH ON A MOUND on the northern shoulder of Chungking stood the squat, stone mansion of Chiang K'ai-shek and Madame Chiang. A few hundred yards away, across the crest of a gentle ridge was the residence of Dr. K'ung, China's prime minister, and Madame K'ung. Madame K'ung and Madame Chiang were sisters. Their brother, T. V. Soong, was China's foreign minister. He lived half a mile down the road. Half a mile beyond lived General Stilwell.

The next episode of Stilwell's stay in China unfolded itself back and forth between these houses. The fabulous Soong family—which included not only Dr. T. V. Soong and Mesdames Chiang and K'ung, but also Madame Sun Yat-sen, widow of the founder of the Republic—conducted itself frequently as if war and politics were a family affair.

In November, Mesdames Chiang and K'ung, in womanly fashion, interested themselves in the increasing bitterness between Chiang and Stilwell. Stilwell refers to them in his notes as May (Madame Chiang K'ai-shek, for Mei-ling Soong) and Ella or Sis (Madame K'ung, for Ai-ling Soong).

The sisters decided to take Stilwell under their wing and foster friendship and light.

Their intervention in Stilwell's behalf may have stemmed from an itch for high politics; or out of family rifts and feuds still unknown, or out of the most sincere devotion to the cause of Allied unity. Whatever their motives, their sudden sponsorship of Stilwell was successful—and came at a most propitious moment: Chiang had decided to demand Stilwell's relief from command and had so informed both Mountbatten and the U.S. government.

SEPTEMBER 13 (3:00 P.M.)   Summoned to audience at Hsin K'ai Ssŭ[1] with May [Madame Chiang] and Sis [Madame K'ung]. "Why haven't you been to see me?" etc., etc. Apparently T. V. has told them they had better get behind me and co-operate, as result of General Marshall's prodding.

[They were] alarmed about state of preparations and hot to do something about it. Gave them the low-down on conditions in the Army and they were appalled. Told them about blocks and delays and who was responsible.

Remedy? Make May [Madame Chiang] minister of war. Specifically—*men*—unity of *command*—reduce number of divisions. Feed 'em. Went over all our trials and tribulations. Suggested northwest[2] as source of drafts [for more men].

May craves action. [She] told Sis [Madame K'ung] to move to town so we could meet at her place. I am reported to be anti-Chinese. Sis said she didn't know how I had the patience to carry on. We signed an offensive and defensive alliance. Whatever the cause, they mean business now and maybe we can get somewhere.

———[3] says, "He [Chiang] thinks he is the Lord Incarnate. Actually he is an obstinate little ass."

(Never mind when they lie about you. The time to worry is when they begin to tell the truth.)

SEPTEMBER 14   I am reported to have called Yü Fei-p'eng "that bandit." The interpreter softened it a bit but Ch'en Ch'eng is said to have told the Peanut. If he did, whom can I trust? (Even if I did, the Peanut knew I felt that way because I had already told him myself.) I am also being spoken of as anti-Chinese! There are leaks in Washington or else we are making progress more than I thought. The wonks are yapping.

SEPTEMBER 17, LETTER TO MRS. STILWELL   Today, letters written by you, etc., dated February and postmarked Miami, March 16, reached me. I'll be damned if that isn't about the record for this war. Where the hell it has been in the meantime I don't know and can't guess unless it was torpedoed and they have since raised the ship and started all over again. That's what makes the troops boiling mad. Our boys had a fight yesterday in north Burma and put it over. Just a skirmish, but the training is proving out. This is the third little engagement in our favor. Maybe we'll do something when the time comes, even though the Limeys *do* think it's impossible.

[1] The Generalissimo's residence in Chungking.
[2] General Stilwell here refers to the approximately twenty divisions of government troops, stationed in the northwest, blockading the Communists.
[3] A Chinese Government official.

SEPTEMBER 17 Ch'en Ch'eng. Talk about plans. He is worried about the French Indo-China frontier. Wants to block off by threat of attack from Kwangsi. Sound idea. Only two [Chinese] divisions there now. We need two more armies.

Ch'en Ch'eng is as disgusted as I am over replacements, etc. I told him I was pushing for unified command [of Burma operations]. He says "of course." "Put somebody in command—me or somebody else."

Asked him about a commanding general for the second thirty. He said Li Tsung-jen or Hsüeh Yüeh. Surprising. Neither one is in his clique. Ch'en Ch'eng is all right.

SEPTEMBER 18 Lunch and conference with May [Madame Chiang]. A very good act she puts on, plus being serious about action. She craves action, wishes she'd been a man, and abominates Ho Ying-ch'in and his gang. Told her my experience with him. He has apparently laughed her off, because she's a woman, and she was furious: "Why in God's name that goddam old fool doesn't do something, I don't know." "They are like a lot of ostriches with their heads in the sand and their bottoms sticking out. How I would like to take a big club and go after them!" "Why can't they see the importance of this thing?" "We should put everything aside and concentrate on the Army." "What good will politics and the youth movement do us if we lose?"

I am being accused now of various crimes. Such as signing memos to G-mo as "Lieut. Gen., U.S.A." instead of "Chief of Staff for G-mo." Campaign appears to be on—I being the stumbling block. Meanwhile, Peanut sits in holy grandeur and lets it all rock along.

SEPTEMBER 20 Turned out at 10:00 p.m. to go to K'ung's. May and Ella [Madame K'ung]. They had been working on the Peanut. Ella gave him the works this p.m. Told him the gang had been lying about me. Explained the chief of staff stuff and why I signed as "Lieut. Gen., U.S.A." They had put over the Kweilin site on Ho,[4] whom May calls "the unmentionable." Ho was furious. May made a speech today at the People's Political Council meeting and bawled out critics of people who were doing their stuff. "Don't criticize till you know mistakes are being made. Don't criticize out of jealousy." Looking directly at Ho. She enjoyed it. They both say that Ho must go, but I don't see how they are going to do it.

May and Ella have sworn in as fellow conspirators and are talking frankly. They are convinced that I mean business and they will play ball. And all the time the Peanut sits on his golden throne and lets us struggle. He's afraid to take action . . . that's the only explanation.

SEPTEMBER 25 Went to Hsin K'ai Ssŭ to see Ella and May. Went over my memo on command . . . tanks, trench mortars, and Boatner's status. Took out my offer-threat to stand aside. Also the word "face." They thought it most reasonable and right and are going after the Peanut on it. In fact they have already.

I get more and more the idea that these two intelligent dames have (1) been told by T. V. Soong to get behind the U.S. effort and that (2) the family, less Peanut, realizes the gravity of the situation. Peanut looks less and less like a dictator and more and more like a political straddler. He actually has little power except the reputation built up around him, and the family realize it. If he could make himself obeyed, why all this monkey business with Lung

[4] General Ho Ying-ch'in had wanted the Z force to be concentrated at Liuchow; General Stilwell had wanted them concentrated at Kweilin.

Yün and troop movement and replacements. Ho Ying-ch'in looks to me like the rat who is gnawing away the foundations and the Peanut may be secretly afraid of him. Then, again, the Peanut is even more whimsical and flighty than even I had thought. May [Madame Chiang K'ai-shek] keeps letting it out that he is very hard to handle, that you have to catch him at the proper moment, that he forms opinions on little evidence, that "they" are telling him all sorts of stuff about me. For instance that I am "haughty" and "anti-Chinese" and sign as a U.S. officer and say the Chinese are no good and look on them with contempt, etc. A whispering campaign.

SEPTEMBER 28 Saw Ella and May. It seems that Ella made Peanut fight at Ichang. He was *pu-yao-chin* [it's unimportant] this and *pu-yao-chin* that. She told him *pu-yao-chin* hell. "You've got to make 'em fight, and not only not give ground any more but get back what they've lost." May says that without her insistence the Great Man would have kept on pulling out and God knows where we'd be now.

More of my crimes have come to light. I won't permit the Chinese officers to approach the British. I moved a unit without any notice to the division commander and told them to get a move on or they wouldn't get any rice. I removed Wên without notice to G-mo, etc., etc. Many other tales have been told. May says Wei-kuo [5] will come back and tell a lot of nasty tales to the G-mo but she will anticipate it and will demand chapter and verse. Both Ella and May have been using the arguments I have given them. Ella says you have to watch Peanut to catch him in the right mood. It is a highly technical business, apparently. But they will work at it.

They are both sold on a new minister of war. How they

hate the "unmentionable" [Ho Ying-ch'in]. The only way to handle him is to tell him he is the most wonderful man in the world. A terribly conceited little monkey. They are all for my reforms, reduction of units, reorganization, training and efficiency.

May let out that she has a hell of a life with the Peanut: no one else will tell him the truth so she is constantly at him with the disagreeable news. It can't be easy to live with the crabbed little bastard and see everything balled up. She will take a trip to India and make some pep talks to the troops. Also line up the officers and give them hell.

OCTOBER 2   Dirty work at Kunming. Colonel Clarke, Limey assistant military attaché, and Hsien Wu, whoever he is, overheard telling each other that Peanut and Auchinleck have both asked for my relief, for not co-operating! Clarke later told —— that the lack of co-operation in the command was all due to me and I couldn't even get along with my own air force. The Limeys are up to their usual tricks.

OCTOBER 3   Long talk with Yü Ta-wei. He emphasized psychology and personal acquaintance. No doubt he's right. Apparently recommending that I cozy up to Ho Ying-ch'in. He says there is no cause to be pessimistic. Feels that Burma will be tough, but possible. This is a great change from the last year when he felt it was hopeless.

2:00 p.m. Saw Ho—about Kweilin, etc. Told him I had to justify requisition for second 30 [division]. Could I state definitely that they are designated and will be trained, reorganized, and grouped for action? He said Yes, except that they could not be grouped in one place. They would be used

[5] Chiang Wei-kuo. The youngest son of the Generalissimo, who was taking a course of U.S. training at Ramgarh. Chiang Wei-kuo is the son of a previous mate of Chiang K'ai-shek. Madame Chiang is his stepmother.

to attack Ichang and Hankow. I said I meant only a general area, and that Hunan and Kiangsi would cover the bill. He said this would be all right. So that's one more step. Actually two groups of 30 each in sight and an objective for each. Actually training one and beginning to train the other.

OCTOBER 7-15   To India to meet Louis [Mountbatten] and confer with Somervell [6] and Wheeler. Louis is a good egg . . . full of enthusiasm and also of disgust with inertia and conservatism. He and the Auk are not hitting it off any too well. Louis is hot for the "one happy family" idea, and is very cordial and friendly. Came back [to Chungking] ahead of him. On October 14, at Chabua found the Japs had at last begun to attack our transports [on the Hump]. Four lost today (14th). We'll have to go to night flying. Shoved off at 7:30 on the 15th, with four P-40s as escort, and reached Chungking same afternoon.

OCTOBER 15, LETTER TO MRS. STILWELL   Louis [Mountbatten] has just arrived in town, and there is a tremendous flutter and fuss and rushing to and fro. You can imagine our difficulty out here, associated as we are with people whose policy is totally different from ours. We'll be judged by the company we keep and I don't like it. Now I'm expected to get the Chinese to play ball and like it and if I don't it's all my fault. I've had twenty months of this now and the first burst of enthusiasm is beginning to pall slightly. If things don't look up in the next few months, I'll be tempted to ask for a division or a regiment or even a squad, somewhere else, where the mental wear and tear is less.

Louis did not get in after all. It was just a couple of other fellas. This makes twice that a large and (self) important group of dignitaries has taken the two-hour ride to the field and stood around in the mud waiting for his Lordship.

Won't they love him if it happens again. I'm having fun these days, looking on. Somebody else is responsible and it's a grand feeling.

[UNDATED] Louis [Mountbatten] arrived [in Chungking] on Saturday, October 16. Met him at airport, later at Grimsdale's lunch, which was a mess. All the tramps in town were there . . . Liu Ch'ih, Yü Fei-p'eng, and all.

Long talk with Louis later, then back to house with Somervell, where he gave me the news: THE G-MO SAYS I MUST BE RELIEVED. The reason is that I have "lost the confidence of the troops." He was quite emphatic about it and so I guess that's that. (Somervell says that President Roosevelt has asked George to relieve me more than once, because I "can't get along." Nice backing.)

The real reason is hard to guess. It may be with me out, nobody else will push the campaign. Neither the Limeys nor the Peanut wants to do it, so everything will be jake. Or it may be just the suspicious, jealous Oriental mind, listening to lies and thinking that it won't do to let a damned foreigner gain any more influence. Or he may be afraid to let the thing grow and upset the equilibrium of mediocrity through which he retains control.

———[7] says I have gone too fast and have used T. V. and Madame. This antagonizes Ho and gang. What I should have done was to go slowly and spread it out over twenty-five years, I suppose.

OCTOBER 17 Mountbatten called and we had a long talk. He is burned up. Feels the double-cross himself, because he'll have to work with a brand-new man. Wants me to wait over and break him in.

[6] General Brehon Somervell.
[7] A Chinese.

Somervell came in and said Ho Ying-ch'in had been to Peanut to ask why. Peanut hauled out the old Ch'en Ch'eng report on "Yü Fei-p'eng the bandit," and Ho said he didn't think that was of much importance.

————[8] just couldn't believe that Ch'en would repeat such stuff to the G-mo.

T. V. Soong is sure that Peanut won't change his mind, and says that Louis will get a "good" Chinese general to advise him. Won't that be hot! T. V. also says "any corps commander" from the Southwest Pacific will be O.K.

(6:00 p.m.) New angle. I am so damned arrogant that I roused the resentment of the troops. This attitude might even cause trouble between China and the U.S. and disturb our cordial relations. This was the result of Somervell's talk with Peanut, this afternoon . . . Peanut, T. V., Madame, Somervell and Shang Chen.

(10:00 p.m.) May called me over at 8:00. Ella [Madame K'ung] was there. They are a pair of fighters, all right, and Ella said there was still a chance to pull the fat out of the fire. I was noncommittal and calm and told them I did not want to stay where I was not wanted. They talked "China" and duty, etc., and asked me to be big enough to stick it out. Ella said if we put this over my position would be much stronger than before. "Your star is rising." What they wanted was for me to see Peanut and tell him I had only one aim, the good of China, that if I had made mistakes it was from misunderstanding and not intent, and that I was ready to co-operate fully. I hesitated a long time, but they made it so strong that I finally said O.K. and May said we'd go right now. Went over and put on the act, the Peanut doing his best to appear conciliatory. He made two points: (1) That I understand the duties of the commander in chief and the chief of staff. (2) That I avoid any superiority complex. This was all balderdash, but I listened politely and Peanut said that under those conditions we could go on working harmoniously again.

Now, why was Ella [Madame K'ung] so sure it would come out O.K.? This p.m. she had attacked the Peanut and he had turned his back and left the room. A hell of an insult but she just waited and he came back. Both she and May went to bat for me. Maybe they got him half turned around as they claimed, ready for me to complete the act. And maybe the Peanut realized finally what a stink would be raised and decided to reverse himself, using them to raise a smoke screen. A good way to partially save his face, although he has lost a lot beyond redemption. This will make him mad at his misinformers. "They" have been upset at the most unexpected time. As Ella put it, they had us down to the last trench and we made a brilliant comeback. She says I will be immensely stronger and they will be flabbergasted to find they can't push me out. But it is suspicious that Ella was so sure it would come out all right, if I made the advances. As if the thing had been arranged.

At any rate, this fuss is over. The next may be just around the corner. May said everybody expected her to divorce the Peanut within a year after their marriage. Both Ella and May reiterated that they had put the family jewels on me, and would continue to back me up. All through this mess I have felt as free as air—no regrets and no self-blame. A grand and glorious feeling.

OCTOBER 18 (33rd [Wedding] Anniversary)   Here's a hunch. T. V.??* Is he the troublemaker? If Roosevelt has the dope that I am disturbing relations, where did he get it? Ans:—Only from T. V. So T. V. wants me relieved. Why?

---

* A Chinese friend of Stilwell.

Because I am working with Madame Chiang and she is
for the G-mo and that crabs T. V.'s ambitions.

Maybe that's why Ella and May won't tell me; why they
warned me about Ch'en Ch'eng, T. V.'s man; and why
they want K'ung built up. I'll watch for confirmation of this.

OCTOBER 21   Well, well, it was T. V. He told Somervell
in Delhi it was coming off. He had it all set up with the
G-mo, when May and Ella heard of it. At once there was
a hell of a fight. Ella finally told me yesterday that I didn't
know the half of it but ultimately would. Said she had to
choose between "her own flesh and blood" [T. V.] and the
good of China. Gave me a lot of slop on their size-up of me.
Regrets we did not get together a year ago. Good advice in
re Chennault. Pull his teeth and give him no ground for
complaint, so he can't cry to the Generalissimo. Says we
have stopped Peanut in full career and turned him around
180 degrees. Considers it a big victory. Says my position is
greatly improved and that no further attacks will be made
. . . positive about this, so I suppose T. V. got a good swat.

The Peanut is now affable again. Impressed by my presentation [at Mountbatten-Somervell conference] of Chinese
participation [in projected Burma attack]!! Ordered Ho to
be cordial to me. Ho and Liu Fei at the [Mountbatten-
Somervell] conference but Peanut had me present the facts
on Chinese participation in Champion.[9] What a gag. Neither Ho nor Liu could tell you what troops are in Yünnan,—
Minister and Vice-Minister of War.

OCTOBER 18-19-20   The conference at Huang Shan. Happy
family stuff. Dicky [Mountbatten] was superenthusiastic
about mixing us all up.[10]

The Chinese politeness has fooled Dicky. He thinks they
will do everything. The one big thing accomplished was

that Peanut agreed to unified command. A formula was reached on boundaries. Neither Chinese nor Southeast Asia Command could invade Siam and/or French Indo-China without prejudice. Next step is [to make a] plan. I go to India [Delhi] and bring back proposals.

T. V. showed up at ferry and went to Huang Shan [for the Mountbatten conference]. There was a fight there and he was told [by Chiang K'ai-shek] to be sick and go home.[11]

OCTOBER 21, LETTER TO MRS. STILWELL   I'm off for the other end of the line after a big walla-walla. An attempt has been made by certain elements here to grease the skids and gently put me on them. It was all set but our side rallied and went after them, and we won the game in the last minute of play. It has been a nasty damn experience and I was on the point of telling them to go to hell, but now it's all smoothed over and I am assured that not only will such a thing not be repeated but that my position is stronger than it was. If you all weren't playing the game as you are, Ole Pappy would just have to step outside and shoot himself. As it is all I have to do is remember what I'm coming home to.

OCTOBER 24, LETTER TO MRS. STILWELL   I couldn't resist writing you from my office in the Southeast Asia Command Headquarters. How do you like our stationery? It's about all we've got so far. Everyone is "conferring," looking serious and important, and "thinking in big numbers." Being as I'm just a deck-hand, I don't get it but am trying to be

[9] Unidentified war plan.
[10] Mountbatten wished to establish an Allied High Command, in which Britons, Americans and Chinese would function in one compact staff; such a staff would parallel Eisenhower's staff in the Mediterranean.
[11] This argument with the Generalissimo marked the beginning of a fall from power for T. V. Soong that lasted almost a year.

inconspicuous, which I find very simple, and I am waiting till I'm spoken to. Louis [Mountbatten] is a good egg.

What gets me is the enormous setup considered necessary to launch a relatively small operation and the tremendous fuss and blah that is going on. Everybody that has been detailed to the staff is either "high-powered" or "a damn good fella," so you can see how submerged I'll be. I must be some good though, the plan I handed in a week ago on a piece of scratch paper is now coming out via the "planning staff" as the real McCoy. One of my troubles seems to be that I can't say 2 and 2 are 4 in a sufficiently ponderous and pontifical manner and can't think up a thousand words to use in saying it. I'm just fed to the gills with delay, pretense, inaction, dumbness. Also with intrigue, maneuvering, double-crossing and obstruction. I will be happy when the real shooting starts: it will be a welcome relief from bickering and recrimination and throat cutting. Garry grows in my estimation every day.

The reconciliation of Chiang and Stilwell took place on the eve of the great mid-war conferences. Cairo and Teheran were about to convene and China, for the first time, was to be represented in Allied councils by Chiang, in person.

Brigadier General Patrick Hurley was sent as Roosevelt's personal emissary to Chungking to arrange the final details of the Cairo conference. And Stilwell, high in Chiang's favor now, found that the Generalissimo expected him to accompany the Chinese delegation to Cairo to present China's military case, to fit the last pieces together for the Burma offensive which had been brewing for so long.

NOVEMBER 3, CHUNGKING   Back again, but no proposals. Al Wedemeyer hasn't got going yet. [Wedemeyer:] "General Marshall told me to go over there and get that operation

put on. He said to me that he was giving me a good commander—Louis—and that he expected results. And if they
wouldn't fight, he would pull me out, and put [me] somewhere else." "Where they can make good use of my talents
and ability." The young man sure does appreciate himself.
Gave him my idea of the tactical plan, and now he's giving
it back to me as his.

NOVEMBER 5 Conference with May and Ella. May calls
me Uncle Joe now. Gave them the dope and they insisted
on a prompt report to the Peanut. They will do anything I
propose, and back it to the Peanut. Shift armies, use complete units for replacements . . . anything. Want me to
go to Cairo and leave Ho Ying-ch'in behind. Agree on plans
to put China right with the powers.

NOVEMBER 6 Reconciliation Day! Love Feast Day! Morning—office, haircut and papers. Afternoon, call from Ella.
    May sick. . . . Saw Ella at 4:30. She went over to
[Chiang K'ai-shek's] to prepare the ground and I followed at
5:00. The rattlesnake was affable as hell. 50,000 men [for
replacements]? Sure, they'll be there. The only thing is to
get some gas to move them. He will even feed his troops.
Extra rations? Sure, just talk it over with Ho. Anything else?
No? "Well, then, officially I request you to make the report
for China at Cairo." (Two parts—Champion and after.)
"See Lin Wei and get the dope."
    Ella had told me he was in a jubilant state of mind and
ready to be very friendly. Well, if I hadn't heard him rattle
his tail, I might have been taken in. Mistake! Last time he
didn't rattle at all—just struck.
    Later—8:00 p.m. Ella called on phone and said Peanut
was much pleased over the conference, which was "the most
satisfactory we had ever had." "Not only pleased but

happy." Said I was "beaming." For Christ's sake! What's going on? Is this a love feast or is he just nuts?

NOVEMBER 7   Yü Ta-wei [12] in. [I asked] "How about your promise of 12,000 rifles by August and 5,000 more by December?" He squirmed and alibied. "No raw materials." Nuts.

Saw Ho Ying-ch'in. The 50,000 men [promised the day before] has shrunk to 25,000 trained and the rest recruits. While we were talking, the 25,000 became 20,000 and then when pushed to state what units they were, and when and where available, the 20,000 became eighteen battalions which at full strength will be 14,000. Maybe 12,000 will show up, and 11,000 arrive!

Then saw Lin Wei. Same picture. As to eats [for troops], very difficult. Solution will be fixed price for Army, i.e., confiscation [from peasants].

BAD NEWS: Ch'en Ch'eng sicker than thought. A substitute will go in [to command Yoke force], and it will probably be Wei Li-huang.[13] The Y force needs a pusher, and I doubt if this is it.

NOVEMBER 10   Hurley [14] talked with Louis [Mountbatten], who is after my scalp. I stand between him and dominance in China and he wants to get rid of me. Hurley warned him about my standing in the U.S. and told him that he could expect plenty of trouble, and that if he got me, I would go after him. Said that I had kept China in the war at a very critical period, and was considered in the U.S. as the "Savior of China." (My God!) Pat laid it on thick. He says he is in my corner. Does not believe that F.D.R. has been after me, but thinks he is very changeable and *could* be almost any time. . . . This confirms Merrill's hint about "our little playmates." What a sweet gang of crooks we are playing with. The old doublecross is going strong. Louis is playing the "Empah" game and won't take chances. All he wants is something that can be labeled a victory, and if the Chinese can be left to take it on the nose, so much the worse for them—and me. Louis is working up the "controversy" between me and Chennault and spoke of it to Hurley. Apparently, the idea is to judge me, take the part of my subordinate, and kick me out. Hurley asked him right out if he were by any chance following the old British game of "divide and rule."

Hurley spoke of the trek out of Burma and said I had rung the bell by my statement. Then he overdid it by saying it reminded him of Marshal Ney with his rear guard. My God did I squirm.

NOVEMBER 11   It *is* Wei Li-huang.[15] Shang Chen brought him in this a.m. to report. He was very respectful!! In fact, all the boys are showing more respect lately. (Tu Yü-ming was in yesterday and quite concerned about delays in Fifth Army instruction. He has put the 49th, 96th and 200th Divisions on same basis as other infantry divisions, and segregated his mechanized units.) I told Wei what I expected of him and he promised to be a good boy and get busy. He has to jump in without his own staff and take what he finds.

Shang Chen goes to the U.S. as head of the Military Mission. I am pretty sure this was on my recommendation.

NOVEMBER 12   Dinner at Peanut's. Hurley and I talked to Peanut till 11:40. Pat gave him the low-down. (1) The U.S.

[12] Director of Chinese Army arsenals.
[13] Wei was later to become a good friend of General Stilwell.
[14] Brigadier General, later Major General, Patrick J. Hurley, who had flown to China to make preparatory arrangements for the Cairo conference.
[15] To succeed Ch'en Ch'eng as head of the Yoke force.

policy is to maintain Britain as a first-class power. (2) The U.S. is against any form of imperialism, including the British. (3) We believe democracy will win. (F.D.R. is for dilly-dally, Hurley for speaking out.) (4) We believe in striking Japan at home, not at Singapore. (5) We believe in a free, strong, democratic China, predominant in Asia.

NOVEMBER 13   Saw Ella and May. They talked about Ho and possible successor. May proposes Shang Chen for secretary of war in place of "unmentionable" [Ho Ying-ch'in]. I put in a heavy plug for him. May and Ella reminded me they had promised to can Ho if I could be patient. Wouldn't that be somepin. Six months ago it was only a wild dream that we could can "the unmentionable."

They had been yapping at Peanut about his "brilliant generals" in connection with my proposals. Asked him why some of his wonders hadn't done it. Cracked about Liu Fei and his presentation at Huang Shan [Somervell-Mountbatten conference], when he said certain units had from 200 to 270,000 men in them. Hooted him for his "accurate and highly qualified technical" assistants. They had been after him in a big way.

Peanut accepts, or in his words, "will appoint" a U.S. commander for Chinese-American force in China after the Pacific is opened. Another impossibility six months ago.

Ramgarh lore. On October 10, 1943, the New First Army commander reviewed the troops . . . on a horse. An orderly led the horse around with a rope. And the dumb photographer missed the picture.

F.D.R. must be given credit for broad-mindedness in using political opponents, in common cause. Knox, Stimson, Hurley, etc.

NOVEMBER 14 —— in from Peanut. Ho Ying-ch'in had been raked over the coals for delay of replacements. He squawked about alcohol and gas and refrained from telling Peanut I had promised it, last Thursday. Peanut in a rage. Told Ho his *tz'u changs* [departmental chiefs] were no good and said he was risking the loss of the Burma campaign. Also got after him about the ration. Wonderful. Maybe now the fire is hot enough to fry Ho Ying-ch'in!!!!

Chapter 8

AT THE END OF NOVEMBER the masters of the Allied world gathered for two sessions in the Middle East, the first at Cairo, the second at Teheran.

At Cairo, Roosevelt and Churchill summoned Chiang K'ai-shek to their presence to discuss the war against Japan. At Teheran, Roosevelt and Churchill met Stalin to discuss the war against Germany.

The two conferences, linked by a global war, were interdependent. At Cairo, despite much friction between Chinese, British, and Americans, the Allies agreed to a major offensive in Burma to be set in motion immediately; it was to be a fully mounted offensive with a heavy British landing in south Burma, the participation of American troops, the Ramgarh-trained Chinese of the X force to attack north Burma from India, the Chinese Yoke force to make an all-out drive on east Burma from Yünnan.

Such technical details as these were worked out by the combined staffs of the Chinese, British, and American armies meeting on the functional level. At these conferences, the duty of representing China fell on Stilwell. When

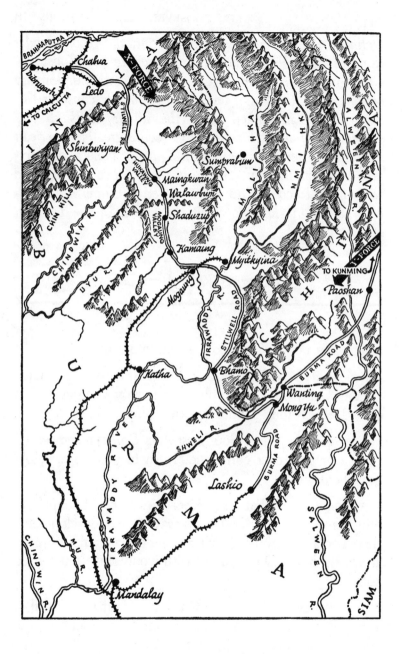

technical details had been worked out, the recommendations of the military men were passed to the Roosevelt-Churchill-Chiang level. After much unrecorded diplomatic bargaining at the senior level, Chiang finally consented to the general plan worked out by the military staffs. He was still unhappy about his failure to secure greater American aid within China for the bolstering of his general military-political structure; but on the basis of Allied promises he was willing to co-operate. He returned to China while Stilwell tarried in Cairo to await the results of the Teheran conference.

NOVEMBER 15　Off at 2:00 p.m. Kunming at 4:30.

NOVEMBER 16　Off at 3:40 in C-87. Smooth trip. In [at Chabua] at 7:00. Three hours and twenty minutes. Off at 8:00. Delhi at four. To headquarters on papers.

NOVEMBER 18　10:30 Southeast Asia Command meeting. Long squabble over command. Rush to get off. 2:35. At Karachi at 7:05.

NOVEMBER 19　Off at 7:50. Basra at 4:30. Eight hours forty minutes. Flew over Abadan on way in. Big developments there and along river at Basra. Masses of date palms. Stayed at airfield hotel. Duck dinner with wonderful French-fried potatoes.

NOVEMBER 20　Off at 8:00. Gassed at Habbaniyeh. Off at 10:35. Passed Jerusalem at 1:00. Cairo. Payne Field at 3:40. Seven hours and forty minutes. Barbed wire all over the

place. Limeys protecting Dicky [Mountbatten]. To Shep-
heards [Hotel] for haircut. Down to camp PX—astounding
stock.

NOVEMBER 21, CAIRO   Breakfast at 8:00. Scribbled on plans
[for] Canton [offensive which was planned for following
spring].

P.m. Saw Shang Chen and Company. Took a walk and
got lost. Routed out at dinner by Shang Chen and Lin Wei.
Madame after me. Went out and saw Generalissimo.
Madame gone to bed. Barbed wire everywhere. Then to
No. 4 [House]: George [Marshall], Pat [Hurley] and
Somervell. Talked till 11:30—F.D.R. doesn't like me to call
Chiang K'ai-shek Peanut.

NOVEMBER 23   Meeting on [of Combined Chiefs of Staff].
Sounded off on the plan [for Burma]. 11:00 [Admiral]
King [1] to plenary session. Mountbatten gave a spiel on the
plan. Lunch at Mena House. 2:30 to preliminary meeting.
G-mo phoned "Do not present proposals." Message the
G-mo would come. Then he wouldn't. That he would.
Christ. Brooke [2] got nasty and King got good and sore. King
almost climbed over the table at Brooke. God, he was mad.
I wish he had socked him.

3:30 Chinese came. Terrible performance. They couldn't
ask a question. Brooke was insulting. I helped them out.
They were asked about Yoke and I had to reply. Brooke fired
questions and I batted them back. At 6:00 went to G-mo's
and helped Chinese get questions ready. Tired.

NOVEMBER 24   Dead beat till 10:00. Wrote notes for
Madame—reasons for United States troops [to participate in

[1] Admiral Ernest King, chief of naval operations, U.S. Navy.
[2] Field Marshal Sir Alan Brooke, chief of the British Imperial General
Staff.

Burma campaign]. Went out at noon and gave them to her. She was in bed. Told her she would have to get up for lunch with George Marshall. He talked a streak during lunch, and afterward G-mo held forth on the plans. Not much hope for United States troops. Peanut first said he'd go to meeting and then reneged, telling me to tell them his views.

3:30 meeting, and the Chinese asked their questions which I had written. The one about the number of British troops [to participate in the Burma campaign] got under their skin. We worked through it, with George [Marshall] laying it on the line about U.S. planes, U.S. pilots, U.S. dough, etc. A grand speech for the G-mo [to hear] and incidentally for the Limeys. Louis [Mountbatten] told to go fix it up with the G-mo. Welcome change from telling *me* to fix it up.

NOVEMBER 25   4:30 with George to see F.D.R., who said Peanut had agreed [to the Burma plan].

His [F.D.R.'s] plan for French Indo-China—three commissioners—Chinese, British, American. Not to go back to France. Got after him for troops. His plan was a brigade of Marines in Chungking! George Marshall's plan is small combat teams. O.K. with us—just give us men.

Hopkins sent for me at 9:30. Car lost. Got there at 10:30 band playing—whoopee—talked to Churchill. Hopkins says G-mo as of 6:00 p.m. does not like the plan [for Burma]. My God. He's off again.

NOVEMBER 26   Louis [Mountbatten] in at 11:00 to spill the dope. He is fed up on Peanut. As who is not?

11:30, to see Peanut, with Hap [Arnold], Somervell, Wheeler, Stratemeyer, and Chennault. John Liu green with fright because we were three minutes late. Shang Chen peering out the door with ashen face and trembling knees. What a life for those boys. Scared witless all the time. I told him not to worry but he was very anxious about it.

Peanut went into his song and dance. We talked him down. He wants Louis to keep his hands off the ATC [Air Transport Command—the Hump line]. Must have his 10,000 [tons a month over the Hump]. Finally said O.K. Sat around till 3:00. Napped.

NOVEMBER 27   Everybody beat it for Teheran. We wait till they come back and act. No minutes for us [CBI command]. Wedemeyer has them and his stooge Lincoln. I'm getting tired of that important young man. "War by Committee" is a bust. The executors are left out on a limb.

NOVEMBER 30, EGYPT: LETTER TO MRS. STILWELL   The censor let me name the country, but not the city. So you'll have to guess. Maybe you know about the walla-walla here; it's been going on for a week and isn't over yet. I brought Frank [Merrill] and —— and we've been fighting for dear old Rutgers. I have had to represent the Peanut in all this business since his own people are completely at sea, and strangely enough I believe he is beginning to appreciate my efforts. Our principal trouble is where it has always been, right at the top.

On Sunday we played hooky and flew up to Jerusalem. Went first to Bethlehem, five miles south, and then rushed through the sights of the city. I learned some astonishing things. (1) Jerusalem has been destroyed by fire and earthquake and battle—32 times. (2) Each time the city was built up again on the debris, so the original streets at the time of Christ are now thirty or forty feet below the present levels. (3) The present walls were built only in the sixteenth century but are probably accurately located on the original trace. (4) There is a terrific controversy where Christ was crucified and buried. (5) Every one of the so-called "holy places" has been grabbed by some religious sect—who claim to own them and who have built churches right on top of them. The old surroundings have disappeared entirely and all that is needed to make you believe you are at Coney Island is a hot-dog stand. Christ's birthplace, which was in a big cave used in part as a stable, is now just a hole filled with junk lamps and horrible marble bathroom decorations which you approach through a church and enter by going down into the cellar behind the altar. It made me sick. When you think how the place might and should have been treated it makes you mad. (6) You probably know that Jerusalem is a holy city to three religions, Christian, Mohammedan, and Jewish. The Jews started in there with Abraham, the Christians with Christ, and Mohammed took off from there for heaven. So, since it was holy to all three, they have been fighting over it for two thousand years and taking turns at killing one another and tearing the place to pieces. Jerusalem, outside the walls, is new within the past twenty-five years and looks like the outskirts of Philadelphia. The most pretentious building in town is the Y.M.C.A., built with American money for some nondescript local yokels to disport themselves in. Well, there were some high spots—like the citadel, the native city, the old crooked streets, the mixed population, the probably authentic tomb of Christ outside the walls, the view of the Dead Sea, the country scenes. But the pious and reverent who go there with solemn ideas are due for a shock.

How different here in Egypt. The pyramids are untouched. The restorations are all dignified and authentic. Everything is left just as it was, with enough clearing so you can get to it. The Sphinx and the Gizeh pyramids are right here at our door, of course. (The Cheops pyramid was 480 feet high.) We went up to Sakkara, about ten miles out, to see the "step" pyramid—5000 B.C. and the oldest masonry structure in the world. Near-by is the tomb of the Sacred Bull, an amazing cave hollowed out of the rock, where successive bulls were buried, each in its massive granite coffin in its own side chapel. This was about 3000 B.C. Then nearby again is the tomb of Thi, prime minister and high priest, with the most delicate stone carving you can imagine. The walls are covered with scenes from the life of his time, and the drawing and carving would be high class today. We thoroughly enjoyed it. Of course there are a lot of antiquities that we haven't time for, but these two tombs were so satisfying that we can pass up the rest without regret.

DECEMBER 1, LETTER TO MRS. STILWELL Played hooky again, and flew up to Luxor, the site of ancient Thebes. Two-hour flight up the Nile. What a day! Went through the tombs of Seti I, Rameses III, and Tutankhamen. Astounding things, all at the end of long rock tunnels, with the walls covered with decorations in color. Hidden away in the hills west of the Nile and now well taken care of. Saw the Colossi of Memnon and Rameses' temple. Then back on the east bank, the temples of Luxor and Karnak. This was the center of Egyptian culture for over a thousand years and it must have been simply magnificent. The temples of Karnak covered 1,000 acres. (Our place is less than one acre!) We had a guide named Abhoudi. He knew his history and his archaeology, too. Runs a souvenir store on the side and picks up loot in the tombs.

I am all smoked up over Egypt. I am a sucker for antiquities and this is where they are. I could spend months wandering around here, and I hope to come back and do it sometime. If it hadn't been for this conference I probably

never would have seen these things. We shove off in a
couple of days back to the manure pile. I wanted you to
know what a grand interlude this has been.

The Teheran conference forced a drastic alteration in the
Cairo plans. At Teheran Stalin, with American military
agreement, insisted on a massive cross-Channel invasion in
1944. The decision to make this invasion forced the Amer-
ican-British planners to curtail sharply the quantity of landing craft they had allotted to the south Burma landing and
consequently altered the entire strategy of the plan for the
Burma offensive.

Roosevelt and Churchill returned to Cairo and there they
reopened study of all the decisions that had been made the
week before. Without a strong south Burma landing, the
British refused to go through with the over-all Burma operation to which they had previously committed themselves.
Chiang was absent from this second session—he had flown
back to Chungking confident that all was arranged. It was
now Stilwell's task to go back and tell him that the Allies had
reneged on their commitment.

It was essential for Stilwell to know how to deal with
Chiang in this situation and he sought and received an interview with Roosevelt. His purpose was single-minded—what
American policy should he announce to Chiang? His notes
on this conversation he recorded in question and answer
form.

Roosevelt followed the conversation with a personal cable
to Chiang requesting his opinion. Chiang replied with an
equivocal answer; and Stilwell returned to Chungking to
the same weary task of urging Chiang to attack in Burma
using no compulsion greater than the force of his personality.

CONFERENCE ON POLICY IN CHINA

December 6, 1943, at Alexander Kirk's home, Cairo. After Teheran.

Present: Roosevelt, H.H. [Harry Hopkins], J.W.S. [Joseph W. Stilwell], and ——[3]

F.D.R. Well, Joe, what do you think of the bad news?

J.W.S. I haven't heard yet how bad it is.

F.D.R. We're in an impasse. I've been stubborn as a mule for four days but we can't get anywhere, and it won't do for a conference to end that way. The British just won't do the operation, and I can't get them to agree to it.

J.W.S. I am interested to know how this affects our policy in China.

F.D.R. Well, now, we've been friends with China for a gr-e-e-at many years. I ascribe a large part of this feeling to the missionaries. You know *I* have a China history. My grandfather went out there, to Swatow and Canton, in 1829, and even went up to Hankow. He did what was every American's ambition in those days—he made a million dollars, and when he came back he put it into western railroads. And in eight years he lost every dollar. Ha! Ha! Ha! Then in 1856 he went out again and *stayed there all through the Civil War*, and made another million. This time he put it into coal mines, and they didn't pay a dividend until two years after he died. Ha! Ha! Ha!

J.W.S. I take it that it is our policy to build China up.

F.D.R. Yes. Yes. Build her up. After this war there will be a great need of our help. They will want loans. Madame Chiang and the G-mo wanted to get a loan

[3] Name of the fourth American deleted.

now of a billion dollars, but I told them it would be difficult to get Congress to agree to it. Now, I'm not a financial expert (!!) but I have a plan to take fifty or a hundred million dollars and buy up Chinese paper dollars on the black market. It wouldn't take much. (!!) When the Chinese found out that these notes were being bought up, they would tend to hold them and the rate would come down. We might beat the inflation that way. And I'd share the profit with the Chinese government—I'd put the notes in escrow and when they were needed I'd sell them to the Chinese for what I paid for them.

—— The effect on the Chinese of failing to reopen communications—

F.D.R. Yes. Yes. How long do you think Chiang can last?

J.W.S. The situation is serious and a repetition of last May's attack might overturn him.

F.D.R. Well, then we should look for some other man or group of men, to carry on.

J.W.S. They would probably be looking for us.

F.D.R. Yes, they would come to us. They really like us and just between ourselves, they don't like the British. Now, we haven't the same aims as the British out there. For instance, Hongkong. Now, I have a plan to make Hongkong a free port: free to the commerce of all nations—of the whole world! But let's raise the Chinese flag there first, and then Chiang can the next day make a grand gesture and make it a free port. That's the way to handle that! Same way in Dairen! I'm sure that Chiang would be willing to make that a free port, and goods could come through Siberia—in bond—without customs examinations.

—— What in your opinion caused the noble attitude of the Russians in allowing China to have Manchuria?

F.D.R. Well, I think they consider they've got enough as it is. You can put a hundred million more people into Siberia. Stalin doesn't want any more ground. He's got enough. He agreed with me about Korea and Indo-China. We should set up commissions to take charge of those countries for twenty-five years or so, till we get them on their feet. Just like the Philippines. I asked Chiang point-blank if he wanted Indo-China, and he said, "Under no circumstances!" Just like that—"Under no circumstances."

J.W.S. Chiang will have trouble explaining to his people the Allied failure to open Burma.

F.D.R. Yes. Yes. But if we don't put on this operation, we can put more tonnage over the Hump. Yes, we can get more freight into China that way.

H.H. Is this CNAC a Pan American subsidiary?

J.W.S. Forty-nine per cent is American, fifty-one per cent is Chinese.

F.D.R. Well, that's all right. The Chinese can run their airline *inside of China*. I have no objection to that. Now, I would agree to the British, after the war, running passenger planes for Australia from England to New York, letting off passengers for New York, taking on passengers for *Australia*, and then flying to San Francisco, letting off passengers from England, and taking on passengers for Australia. But not to take passengers on at New York and letting them off at San Francisco. Oh, no. No, sir.

J.W.S. We need guidance on political policy on China.

F.D.R. Yes. As I was saying, the Chinese will want a lot of help from us—a *lot* of it. Why, K'ung one time asked me for a loan of fifty million dollars for developing transportation and I said to him, "Mr. K'ung, that's a *lot* of money!" Then I said to him, "What are you going to use this money for?" and he said, "Construction materials," and he said, to try and influence me, "If we get this loan, we'll buy those materials right here in the United States." And I came right back at him and said, "Mr. K'ung, in your country you have construction materials already. You have cement, you have sand, you have rock—you have all those materials." Then he said, "Yes, but we need technical help—engineers and other technicians. We would pay a good engineer $100,000 a year, and give him a house and twenty servants." And I said, "Mr. K'ung, when I was governor of New York State, I had a superintendent of highway construction named Green—(ever know Green?)—and he was paid $15,000. And he was the best road engineer I ever saw. But he's dead. But don't pay $100,000— pay $15,000—no house, no servants. You don't want to pay $100,000. Why, there are any number of good engineers in the Army—not the regular service, men from civil life—and you can get them for $8,000. They can do that kind of work. But no exploitation."

STOOGE The Prime Minister is here.

F.D.R.   Well, now, there you are and remember, YOU'RE AMBASSADORS! Ha! Ha! Ha! Yes, sir, you're my Ambassadors.

End of Conference
Draw your own conclusions.

H.H.   What do you think would be a good religion in Japan?

[The Following Are Some Undated Passing Notes on Cairo Found Among the Papers.]

George C. Marshall says a good chance for Germany to crack by February, 1944.

In September George Marshall was going to let me out and give me the Fourth Army, if I wanted it. He asked me what my decision would have been.

Kirk says the Army should mutiny and take control. It makes him wild to watch the antics of the politicos. "Here I've been a —— for thirty years and my muscles ought to be all relaxed," etc.

Antics by Peanut. The boys got a faint idea of what it means to work with him. Demanded change in plans, and 600 more planes to make it work. F.D.R. made everything worse by telling him we were going to haul 12,000 [tons monthly over Hump].

George C. Marshall's outburst: "Now let me get this straight. You are talking about your 'rights' in this matter. I thought these were *American* planes, and *American* personnel, and *American* material. I don't understand what you mean by saying that we can or can't do thus and so." Chu Shih-ming had overreached himself a bit.

DECEMBER 7   Found out F.D.R. had wired Chiang K'ai-shek about the bust. No answer.

[The following are undated notes in General Stilwell's Papers.]

After Teheran, plan changed. F.D.R. to Chiang K'ai-shek. "Will you accept altered plan?" or "Will you postpone till November?" Chiang K'ai-shek came back with a squeeze play. "O.K. if you give me a billion dollars and double the air force and ferry route."

Stalin dominated at Teheran. He laid it down and they took it. Overlord and Anvil [4] are on. Stalin jumps in at same time. So Louis [Mountbatten] loses a lot of landing craft and can't do Buccaneer [5] (he had 58,000 men allotted to it) .

Stalin kidded Churchill. "Let's execute 50,000 German officers." "Oh, but we can't subscribe to any such plan as that." So Stalin kept at him. It was like a blood transfusion to see Stalin put backbone in our gasbags.

DECK-HAND DIPLOMAT A brief experience with international politics confirms me in my preference for driving a garbage truck. This is admittedly not the proper approach to the matter of international politics. It is a very serious business. A lot of Big Figures indulge in it, and a host of little ones trail along. Those who make the grade are of course interested to dignify and even glorify the profession, which can be done in a wink of the eye by using the term "diplomacy"—a word we usually utter on a hushed and respectful note. The term "diplomat" to the average American evokes a vision of an immaculately dressed being—pinstripe pants, spats, cutaway, and topper—and a coldly severe and superior manner which masks the lightning-like play of the intellect that guides the Ship of State, moves the pieces on the board with unerring precision, and invariably turns up in Washington without his shirt. Or rather our shirt. There was a curious misprint once in a Peking-English language newspaper. The word "diplomat" came out "doplomat" and I am still wondering about that typesetter.

It is very confusing to a deck-hand to be pitchforked in among this class of people, especially if he is a military deck-hand. It is common knowledge that an Army officer has a one-track mind, that he is personally interested in stirring up wars so that he can get promoted and be decorated and that he has an extremely limited education, with no appreciation of the finer things of life. He has two strikes on him as soon as he appears, and everybody waits with keen anticipation for the third one to come over and send him back where he belongs. Even in time of war, when presumably the military aspect of the situation should be of primary importance, the fact that he may attempt to infringe on the prerogatives of the Sacred Cow of Diplomacy makes a warm welcome somewhat problematical. People lose sight of the fact that he is there because he is ordered, not because he wants to be.

I was lucky to find old friends in the Chungking Embassy who were disposed to help me in a job that their experience had proved to them held little hope of accomplishment, whatever their opinion as to the choice of an instrument. We have a lot of good boys in our Foreign Service: if they could only make themselves heard and get to positions of responsibility a little more quickly, we'd be all right, but as long as we go on paying off political debts with the top posts, we handicap ourselves out of the race.

Our fundamental conception of this game is wrong. We are idealists; we have the sporting instinct; we want to meet people halfway and shake hands. We forget that as the richest nation in the world we are a standing temptation for chiselers. We readily forget the experiences of the past and naïvely hope that the next time it will come out better. Under the actual setup, it can't be anything but a tough game for us, unless we are prepared to share our wealth with

[4] Code names for the invasion of France.
[5] Probably code for the south Burma landing.

all comers. A little more realism is the medicine we need, and we have a good example in the case of Russia. Have you noticed how they do it? There you have the direct approach. When they want to get an idea across, instead of saying, "Accept, dear Mr. Ambassador, my sincere hopes that the present harmonious relations between our two great nations will long endure," etc., etc., they simply say, "If you don't throw those troops out of Shinegazabo right now, we will have to throw them out." Regrettably crude, perhaps: remarkably effective, however. Remember that gem of diplomacy that settled a knotty little problem of Japanese encroachment in Siberia? The message read: "If you Japs don't keep your pigs' snouts out of our garden, it will be too bad." The Japs needed no interpretation by the protocol boys to tell them just where they stood.

I am not proposing that we assume a truculent or belligerent attitude; I am merely proposing a readjustment of mental attitude on a basis of realism, because, after all, life is real, life is earnest. For instance, a matter comes out that makes a military effort by an ally desirable in a certain place. (As you see, I am diplomatic and I don't come right out and say Great Britain and Burma.) So the ally proposes a different move in a different place, one that would have no earthly bearing on the outcome of the war, and after a spirited struggle agrees very handsomely to give in. That puts us under the necessity of meeting them halfway, in the interests of harmony, so we agree to forego our contention, too, and make it 50-50. Then we make a date for another conference and go home and buy another shirt.

I once took my family out for dinner at the San Diego Club, and told them to order whatever they wanted. The youngest boy, Ben, six years old, at once said, "Roast duck." That seemed a little heavy for his age, so I suggested cream

of wheat. He leaned back and said, "Duck." Then the family
pitched in and suggested some nice spinach, or some vegeta-
ble soup and mashed potatoes. He said, "Duck," once more
without budging. I made one more attempt, to which he
answered "Duck," so I then wiped the perspiration off my
brow and ordered duck. He had never heard of Joe Stalin,
but he knew the technique. He'd make an excellent secretary of state but for the fact that he's going to be a doctor.

Playing international politics is much like playing poker.
To make it remunerative, all you need in a fairly large group
of contestants is one sucker, especially if he has plenty of
dough and is sensitive to insinuations about his sporting
blood. It is best to make him feel that it is a favor to be
allowed to sit in—once get that idea firmly in his mind, and
all the other players are assured of a merry evening. He can
be easily induced to play table stakes, with real money in
front of him, while those among the other contestants who
have forgotten to bring their pocketbooks can write I.O.U.'s
on little pieces of paper and pass them over in full confidence that they will end up in the fireplace. You can even
go so far as to express, very politely of course, a supercilious
disapproval and a well-bred sense of injury when the sucker
decides to go home and get some sleep.

My introduction to the game of international politics was
in the Orient. The first shock of immersion is severe, but
rapidly passes over, due to the numbing effect of repeated
dunkings. I had batted around China, Japan, the Philippines, the Dutch Indies, Indo-China, Siam and Malaya
somewhat, but had always watched the show from a back
seat in the balcony. This was my first opportunity to go behind the scenes and observe some of the headliners without
their grease paint and other trappings, and I ran into many

things back there that are not visible from the front. [This paper was never finished.]

DECEMBER 8   Off at 6:30, Basra at 3:30. Hotel full. Rode around: "Beware of Pimps"—the romantic East as per Basra restricted area.

DECEMBER 9   Off at 6:30, rough over Persian Gulf. No stop at Sharja. Karachi at 6:00 p.m. Took off at 7:30, Delhi at midnight.

DECEMBER 11   Off at 11:30, Chabua at 7:00. Kunming at 6:30.

DECEMBER 12   Saw Glenn. Talked with Dorn. Off at 11:30, in Chungking at 2:00. Slept all the way. Mail.

DECEMBER 13   A.m. papers, office. Phoned Snow White [Madame Chiang]. Ho Ying-ch'in for conference. All the usual crap on roads, replacements, rations, etc., etc. He made the usual notes. Period.

DECEMBER 14, LETTER TO MRS. STILWELL   Christmas cards from you and Garry. Don't open till Christmas. Like hell. Where will I be by Christmas? What a marvelous idea. I came nearer to crying than at any time since I saw you. This mail came at just the right time. Things were pretty gloomy. Got back from Cairo day before yesterday, we got the usual answers down there, and after Bloody Joe [Stalin] got through laying down the law up there at Teheran, we were lucky to get away with our shirts.

Our Big Boy doesn't seem too interested in us. What am I kicking about? Didn't he give me a shoestring when I came out and haven't I still got it? Human nature being what it is, I am still playing a lone hand. The day of the giants is gone and most of the biggest statues have clay feet. I don't care for a guy who greets me as "Joe" and reaches for a knife when I turn around. Well, that's past now, etc. Now I've got to pop back and lend the boys a hand in Burma. Our lads have been in contact for over a month, and in spite of considerable casualties have stuck to it. Certain parties are making capital out of the fact that they haven't made more progress— (Ain't that generous?) —but nobody else in Burma has so far held on to their ground. We have to go through a rathole as we go. A lot of guys deserve a lot of credit. So do the boys that keep the [Hump] ferry line going—and that's no picnic either. We haven't any presidential candidates here, but we do have a lot of people with guts, working without any publicity and also without any squawks. Take it from me that Americans are all right. Smiths, Cohens, Slavinskis, Theissens, Giambatistas, Jonsons, and what have you. White, black, and yellow—they are all playing the game. I feel like a dog—I've sent no presents home for Christmas. Every day will be Christmas at Carmel. I found out what Carmel means. In a guidebook at Palestine! It means the "Vineyard of the Lord." And ain't that the truth.

Stilwell's stay in Chungking lasted a week. The Generalissimo flatly refused to commit the Chinese Yoke force to action against Burma so long as the Allies were unwilling to make a major landing in south Burma. Nothing that Stilwell could say could shake him; but to prove his good faith, he yielded to Stilwell for the first time complete command of the Ramgarh-trained X forces in India to use as he saw fit.

For a year and a half Stilwell had been training the X forces in India. Two divisions were already concentrated in northern Assam on the Burma border protecting the advancing Ledo Road. They were trained, equipped, ready for action. Stilwell decided that further negotiations in Delhi or Chungking would be fruitless. On December 20 he left

Chungking, flying toward the Burma border where combat troops awaited his command. With these he planned to drive into Burma as deeply as possible, striking for the Chinese border.

[UNDATED]   Return from Cairo. Graduation exercises at [Chinese] Military Academy. As Peanut mounted rostrum band leader counted 1-2-3, but unfortunately band sounded off at 2. Peanut was furious, stopped band, bawled out leader: "Either start playing [on 1] or start on 3. Don't start on 2!" Then a speaker pulled his notes out of his pants pocket. This infuriated Peanut. He bawled him out, and told him that *tsai wai kuo* [in foreign countries] you could put a handkerchief in your pants pockets but not papers. Papers go in lower coat pockets, and, if secret, in upper coat pockets. Then someone stumbled on procedure and Peanut went wild, screaming that he ought to be shot . . . *Ch'iang pi* [shoot him] and repeating it at the top of his voice.

DECEMBER 15   The Reds are no longer afraid [of Chiang K'ai-shek]. The Central Government men desert to them. One whole company deserted and the Reds sent the rifles back. "We can't force the men to return, but here are the rifles." More troops moved up to contain the Reds, but their propaganda is working. They feel that Chiang K'ai-shek's position is weak.

CONFERENCE WITH PEANUT   Put it to him as to possible results of reneging on Burma operation. He has a trick solution: accept *both* of the plans offered by President:[6] i.e., get ready [for Burma offensive] and be in position and then "when spring comes" decide if "conditions are favorable." If so, fight. If not, wait till November [1944]. Told him it was necessary to decide *now*, so troop moves could start. Asked him who would decide the case and he said he would!

In other words, no fight. The little bastard never intended to.

[He] keeps coming back to the amphibious operation,[7] promised by President. Told him present plan better than old one, except for size of amphibious operation. No soap. This amphibious operation is just "no good." We ought to attack Moulmein and "cut off the rear." Says we mustn't risk being defeated in Burma. The effect on the Chinese people would be too serious. The little hypocrite. Even at expense of remaining cut off—still he won't risk defeat. Of course, next November the same argument will be just as weighty.

May did her best. She realizes the implications and it drives her nuts. Wants a meeting with K'ung tomorrow to dope out something, but I can see she is pretty low and hasn't much hope of changing the little bastard over.

DECEMBER 16 Saw May and Ella. They're close to nervous prostration. Can't sleep. May said she prayed with him [Chiang] last night. Told me she'd done "everything except murder him." Ella says when he's tired he takes refuge in being "noble." We doped out what to do and decided on asking F.D.R. to send him a radio. "Expect you to lend same wholehearted co-op that the British gave Eisenhower."

Session with ———, in which I gave him some dope to feed the Peanut. Asked him how come they had 300 divisions and couldn't fill up 10 [full strength divisions]. He said they were "useless." Imagine that.

Session with Ho Ying-ch'in.[8] His usual line of crap. "U.S.

[6] Offered by Roosevelt at Cairo, see page 255.
[7] For attack on Japanese in southern Burma.
[8] At this time, Stilwell was trying to place U.S. Army officers with front-line divisions of the Chinese Armies to observe their use of American equipment and instruct them. The Chinese were for a long while reluctant to let Americans live with their troops.

instructors can't live with Chinese troops—they wouldn't be comfortable. We can't *chao tai* [accommodate them] properly," etc., etc. Told him I had done so [9] often and my people would, too. [He said] the Russians [previous Russian observers] had complained; it was very unpleasant. Told him we wouldn't and that we'd relieve the kickers. He pulled some stuff about training programs and time limits and crap, and I told him the G-mo said we were welcome in all units, for indefinite stay. He said of course if I did not trust the Chinese officers we could send checkers to watch the motor movement. I told him that wasn't the reason: U.S. [money] was being spent and I was responsible for it and had to report. We got him on every count, and had him running so much that McCammon couldn't look at him toward the end.

(4:00 p.m.) Conference with the Peanut. More history made. When he says anything, it's so: i.e., "There are eight Jap divisions in Burma." He just says it, so it must be so. If I say everybody agrees that there are five divisions, he just says "No, there are eight." Again flatly—"We have only one chance in a hundred of winning." Again—"We have even less chance of winning now than we had in 1942!" Good God. And if I mention air, artillery, tanks, 200,000 Chinese, and 180,000 British he still sticks to it.

He "reasons" that "we have a better chance to win if we take the defensive and let the Japs attack." I asked him where we would be if the U.S. had adopted that attitude two years ago. No answer. He has an idea that the British won't fight, and that he will sit on his ass till the Americans come and save him. "We'll get ready and tell Mountbatten to go ahead with his plans—and then, if everything is favorable, we'll fight. We must wait for the opportune time."

Good God. He's so ignorant of military matters that he thinks he can get an offensive started at the word "Go." Very nice guarantee of co-operation for the British to lean on.

"Let the British go ahead and attack Akyab." [10] I told him *they* would naturally expect *him* to do something to take pressure off of them, just as *he* is insisting in treble notes that *they* attack and take pressure off him. Oh, no, that's different. "We must have three to one to beat the Japs." I tell him we have more than three to one—in Yünnan we have fourteen divisions against one and a third. "Oh, no, they have several divisions there." Nothing is possible without a big amphibious operation. He doesn't know what a big amphibious operation is, but unfortunately Mountbatten was honest about it. So now that it is on a reduced scale, he screams. It is fatal to promise anything.

Another unfortunate thing was the President's message, giving him a choice of jumping off [in Burma] in March, or waiting till November, and promising "heavy amphibious operations" then. *That* will be insisted on now. F.D.R. should have insisted on his co-operating as planned, under pain of cutting off all supplies. Now he believes he can go just as far as he likes and the U.S. will cringe and take it. He's not going to fight at any time, regardless of what he says.

The pay-off is that I can go ahead and fight with the Ledo force. He is afraid that even concerted attack by all available forces has only one chance in a hundred and yet he'll sit back and let a small force take on the Japs alone. Madame is discouraged, disgusted, and a little dismayed. She can't do a thing with him.

[9] Lived with Chinese troops in the field.
[10] A port in southwestern Burma.

DECEMBER 19   First time in history. G-mo gave me full command of the Ledo [X force] troops.[11] Without strings—said there would be no interference and that it was "my army." Gave me full power to fire any and all officers. Cautioned me not to sacrifice it to British interests. Otherwise, use it as I saw fit. Madame promised to get this in writing so I could show it to all concerned.

It took a long time, but apparently confidence has been established. A month or so ago I was to be fired and now he gives me a blank check. If the bastards will only fight, we can make a dent in the Japs. There is a chance for us to work down to Myitkyina, block off below Mogaung and actually make the junction, even with Yoke sitting on its tukas. This may be wishful thinking in a big way, but it *could* be.

LETTER TO MRS. STILWELL   Every time I say to myself, "That's the last gasp—we can't possibly chew that over any more," Peanut has to see me again, with a further drain on my small stock of patience.

Put down December 18, 1943, as the day, when for the first time in history, a foreigner was given command of Chinese troops with full control over all officers and no strings attached. Can you believe it? May was a witness and I have a letter to the army and division commanders to take orders from me as though I were the Peanut himself. This has been a long uphill fight and when I think of some of our commanders who are handed a ready-made, fully equipped, well-trained army of *Americans* to work with, it makes me wonder if I'm not working out some of my past sins. They gave me a shoestring and now we've run it up to considerable proportions: the question is, will it snap when we put the weight on it? I've had word from Peanut that I can get away from this dump tomorrow. That means I'll spend Christmas with the Confucianists in the jungle. "Jungle Bells, Jungle Bells, jungle all the way. O what fun it is to ride in a jeep on Christmas Day." Until this mess is cleaned up I wouldn't want to be doing anything but working at it, and you wouldn't want me to either, thank God. So, it's all as it should be and we are a lucky crowd.

DECEMBER 20 Off for Burma again. Under better auspices than last time. CAN WE PUT IT OVER?

[11] The two Chinese divisions that had been trained at Ramgarh.

Chapter 9

IN DECEMBER, 1943, it could be truthfully said that never in history had Chinese troops launched a successful strategic offensive against a modern enemy. In the second Burma campaign, Stilwell proposed to rewrite history, staking his reputation on the unproven thesis that, given proper equipment and training, Chinese soldiers were, man for man, as good as any in the world. In his belief in Chinese valor, Stilwell stood alone. Not only did the British and the overwhelming portion of the U.S. Army staff in Asia believe it was impossible for the Chinese to attack and destroy battle-proved Japanese divisions of roughly equal strength in northern Burma, but the Chinese general staff in Chungking held the same low opinion of its soldiery.

What Stilwell proposed to do was this: to take raw troops, divorce them from the possibility of retreat, abandon fixed supply lines as completely as did Sherman in Georgia, make them dependent on air drops alone, drive them two hundred miles through jungle, swamp, and mountain to conquer a skillful, entrenched, and desperate enemy.

The bare outlines of the campaign were simple enough. The great objective was the open lowland of north-central

Burma, where the meter-gauge railway wound its way through the linked towns of Mogaung and Myitkyina. If these two towns could be seized, a road might be built through the jungle from India to reach them, and then pushed on toward the Chinese border of Yünnan, to end the great blockade. (See map, page 43.)

No one spoke seriously of Myitkyina when the campaign was steaming up at Stilwell's headquarters on the Indian border in December, 1943. Myitkyina was a word, a phrase, a label on a dream that existed in Stilwell's mind alone. From the Allied position on the tangled mountain-jungle border of India, the road to Myitkyina seemed incredibly distant. Ultimately—perhaps in 1945—it would be taken, but before then the campaign would have to proceed chunk by chunk in slow, plodding steps. First, there was the Tanai River to be cleared to make the Shingbwiyan clearing safe.

Beyond the Tanai valley lay the Hukawng valley, studded with Japanese garrisons.

Beyond the Hukawng lay the Jambu Bum hills and more Japs.

Beyond the hills lay the Mogaung valley.

And beyond that, over a 6,000-foot mountain range carpeted with jungle, was Myitkyina and its garrison.

Stilwell had at his command two Chinese divisions—the 38th and 22nd—which had ben moved from Ramgarh to the India-Burma border in 1943. In reserve, in Central India, another Chinese division was finishing training. All three divisions totaled about 50,000 men. Opposing them were between forty and sixty thousand battle-tested Japs, dug in deep.

The main burden of combat rested directly on the Chinese divisions, commanded by their own officers, but tightly subordinate to Stilwell's personal urge. The Chinese, however, were only one strain in an association of races and nations that made the north Burma campaign of 1944 one of the war's great galleries of curiosities. In central Burma, far to the south of the main drive, British Commando forces under Wingate and Lentaigne operated. Kachin scouts under American direction raided Japanese outposts far and wide. An American Commando force—Merrill's Marauders—wheeled about the flanks of the main advance, unpinning each position the Japanese established against the Chinese by cutting around the jungle to their rear. The entire combat movement was fed by parachute drops executed by the U.S. Tenth Air Force, performing superbly its strategic functions in an infantry war. Behind the Chinese troops crawled the Ledo Road, struggling toward China—American engineers (Negro and white), Chinese, Indians, Nagas built the road through the jungle and over the hills under the treads of the tanks and the wheels of the trucks that were carrying combat troops forward to clear the trace.

On the map, the campaign for north Burma was a line that wriggled tortuously from unpronounceable name to unpronounceable name. On the ground, it was rain, heat, mud, and sickness. It was snakes in camp at night; K rations and dried rice; snipers and ambush; darkness during the day and the rustling jungle at night. It was hike, kill, and die, or, as Stilwell noted in his diary after one of his everyday marches through the muck: "Up the river, over the hogback—slip, struggle, curse, and tumble."

Stilwell was in the jungle from January to July of 1944, and for his personal participation in the campaign he was later severely criticized. He was, at the time, a three-star general of the United States Army and commander of a war theater, but he had abandoned his headquarters to command troops in the jungle. In the mouths of his critics, his personal command became a frolic, a Rover Boy's holiday in the woods. But in Stilwell's mind his course had been determined by the history of the previous two years. It was impossible to persuade either Delhi or Chungking by words or logic that Chinese troops could defeat entrenched Japanese; it could be done only by demonstration in the field. It was more important in Stilwell's mind to dispose Chinese battalions, companies and platoons in combat and prod them to victory than to argue their worth in conference elsewhere.

Stilwell realized that for ultimate success in breaking the blockade he would need a co-ordinated drive by the Yoke force sallying out of Yünnan in the east under the direction of Brigadier General Dorn. He had been refused this co-operation in Chungking immediately after the Cairo conference. He hoped to wring it out of Chiang's pride by the example of personal action and success in field operations in north Burma. By wire and courier, he kept up constant pressure on Chungking to commit its troops to action.

During the period of the second Burma campaign Stilwell's diaries consist almost exclusively of technical military notations, the movement of regiments, battalions, divisions. Only enough of them are included in this chapter as is necessary to give the bare bones of action and the movement of events. His references to divisional and regimental numbers always refer to Chinese troops; his American Marauders are usually recorded simply as "Galahad"—the code word for the Marauders' project.

Here are some of the names of the commanders with whom Stilwell dealt:

Major General Daniel Sultan, U.S.A.—deputy commander of the China-Burma-India theater, whose office was in Delhi.

Major General Frank Merrill—commander in chief of the Marauders.

Brigadier General Lewis Pick—General Pick was the engineering officer in command of the construction of the Ledo Road.

Brigadier General Donald Old—commander of the air support operations that supplied the campaign with food, munitions, and airborne troops.

Colonel Frank Hunter—executive officer of the Marauders, who exercised field command on the march to Myitkyina when Merrill was invalided.

Colonel Rothwell Brown—American commander of the Chinese-American tank unit used in the north Burma campaign. This outfit consisted of approximately ninety light and medium tanks.

Lieutenant General William Joseph Slim—British Army. Slim was Mountbatten's appointee in command of the entire Burma front, both British and Chinese. Stilwell's operations in north Burma were technically subordinate to Slim, though in the hierarchy of command Stilwell outranked Slim.

Major General Sun Li-jen, Chinese Army—Sun was commander of the Chinese 38th Division, and Stilwell was fonder of Sun, a Virginia Military Institute graduate, than of any other Chinese leader in his command. Sun was later promoted to command the Chinese New First Army.

Major General Liao, Chinese Army—commander of the Chinese 22nd Division, later commander of the New Sixth Army.

These were the men and forces with whom Stilwell had to deal.

When, in the last week of December, 1943, Stilwell flew across the Hump armed with Chiang's vermilion seal of command, the Chinese 22nd Division on the Burma-India border had been skirmishing fitfully with Japanese outposts for months without success. Stilwell's first purpose was to force this division to take aggressive action, to blood it in battle by clearing the matted valley of the Tanai River. His first limited objectives were Taipha Ga and Yupbang Ga (see map, page 271). By clearing these he would clear the area about the village of Shingbwiyan which he planned to make the base for his Hukawng valley drive.

A cold trip across the Hump brought him to Assam from China, and from the airbase next morning he drove by jeep over the rough new road trace reaching out of Ledo toward the jungle and Chinese combat headquarters.

DECEMBER 21   Up at 1:30. [Arrived] Chabua [in Assam] at 6:30. Cold trip to Ledo. Saw Sun [Li-jen]. Went over plan.

DECEMBER 22   Up at 7:00 for breakfast. Oatmeal, hot cakes, bacon, coffee, jam, and butter. Off [over the Ledo Road] at 8:00. 14 miles to Ningam. Arrived 2:00 p.m.

No action for past ten days. Insisted on serious attack on Yupbang. Apparently only two platoons, "surrounding" Chinese in front of Yupbang. Japs dug in at river; changed plan to put weight against them there with artillery and air support. Chances look good. Five hundred casualties so far. Q. How long would they have sat on their asses here?

DECEMBER 23   Good sleep in dugout. Breakfast: chicken soup, coffee, sausage. Jap assurance that Chinese will not react may have gotten them in a hole. If we take out Yup-bang, those up north will be bagged. 9:00 a.m. conference [with Chinese]. Made a speech and told them this is important and must go. Bummed around all day. Much objection to my going forward. Ambush, etc. Compromise on tomorrow early. Pigs dropped [by parachute] for [Dr.] Seagrave [commanding hospital for Chinese Army] for Christmas party.

DECEMBER 24   Breakfast at 6:00. Off at 6:30 [on foot] for the party. Arrived at 3rd Battalion command post at 8:40. Artillery put in 370 rounds [from] nine to ten. Infantry off at 10:05, closing in from both flanks and gradually cleaning up. One pocket left at 5:00, surrounded. Pulled out at 5:00, back at 7:00. Tired.

Li and Han [Chinese battalion commanders] did good day's work, Japs tough. All things considered, Chinese did a good job. The men are fearless and the junior commanders did O.K. Very tough going to get Japs out of this jungle.

DECEMBER 25   *Christmas.* Report at 9:00, pocket all cleaned. Japs in pocket killed themselves with hand grenades. One Jap officer captured—wounded in arm.

DECEMBER 26   Got Sun [commander of Chinese 38th Division] in and gave him a heart-to-heart talk. He seems sincere. Swears they are trying to do a good job for the *lao hsien sheng* ["old gentleman"—meaning Stilwell], that the troops are all bucked up to have me with them, but commanders are uneasy for fear I get hit and they be held responsible. Insistent that I stay back and let them do it.

DECEMBER 29   Delayed start till 7:20. Sun reports entire [Jap] position overrun. At dark, Li got going and went into main position, where they had little trouble. Two islands were left along river, and a few wandering bands were being worked on. One major, three captains, three [Jap] lieutenants bagged. Good work by Chinese: aggressive attack, good fire control, quick action. They are full of beans and tickled to death at beating the Japs. Went to command post and saw the gang. Firing all around as the roundup proceeded. Considerable loot. All very nervous about me. Stayed an hour and then came back. Two and a half hour hike, stopped once for suspected ambush.

Annoying news from Chungking and Delhi. Louis [Mountbatten] trying sly tricks. G-mo may commit Yoke force [to Burma campaign].

DECEMBER 30 *Turkey* for supper. No fooling, with cranberry sauce and sweet potatoes.

DECEMBER 31 Cold and damp, cleared by 9:00. Last day of 1943, R.I.P.

A lot of messages from Chungking and Delhi. Screaming for me to come to both places and decide on this and that. Got them all answered by noon. Decided to jump to Delhi and get it over and jump back.

DC-3 came in at 1:00, and we took off at 1:55. In at Delhi at 1:00 a.m. New Year's—shooting fireworks.

JANUARY 1, 1944, DELHI   Office 8:30. Saw Sultan, Covell, Merrill, Ferris. Saw Louis [Mountbatten] at 2:00. Wallawalla. He won't take command; doesn't know where he is. Saw Wedemeyer, Wheeler, Sultan, Ferris at 3:30. Got a haircut. To field at 12:00.

JANUARY 2   Chabua at 7:15. Decided to try for Shingbwiyan [1]—good landing. Sun [Li-jen] not moving; preposterous demands for ammunition, air support and artillery.

[1] The main Allied headquarters of the Stilwell campaign, in northern Hukawng valley.

Word from Chungking, G-mo still bucking [the commitment of Yoke force to offensive]. F.D.R. perhaps implied threat to divert supply.

JANUARY 4   Off for Yupbang at 8:20. Li's command post for lunch and then down to river. Quiet. Big banyan tree strong point, regular hotel and fort combined. Tarzan vine to slide down from machine-gun nest. Extensive Jap trenches. Under observation at river positions—went to forward observation point through tunnel on riverbank and had view of river and Japanese side up and down. Back at 5:00—17 miles [on foot].

JANUARY 8   Radio from Sultan—Louis [Mountbatten] welches on entire program [for Burma offensive]. G-mo's fault of course. Limey program: (1) Stop road at Ledo. (2) Do not attack Burma. (3) Go to Sumatra. (4) Include Hongkong in SEAC!

JANUARY 9   The Long Range Penetration Group [Merrill's Marauders] is arriving at Ledo January 20, and expects to jump off February 15. My God what speed. Snorted at him and he allowed they might better the time. Expect to ride in trucks to the river! Went to bed at 6:30.

JANUARY 10, LETTER TO MRS. STILWELL   Just a line to let you know I am pecking away with the help of my Chinese friends on a tough assignment. Since the Limeys control the communiques, you will hear very little about our endeavors, but so far the boys have performed very creditably and chewed up quite a few Japs. I get numerous howls to come up to Chungking or come down to Delhi but so far have managed to fight them off and remain with the troops. I'd like a vacation after the weary mental struggle I've been having with our allies.

JANUARY 12   Cleveland back with bad news. Generalissimo now demands [before committing Yoke force] amphibious operations on Andaman Islands plus . . . plus . . . plus cutting of communications between Bhamo and Lashio. No replacements in sight. We are out on a limb.

LETTER TO MRS. STILWELL   We eat straight rations or Chinese chow and we live where we have to and the trails are tough, and we get wet and muddy, but we sleep soundly and the food tastes good because we are usually hungry. The principal hazard is being hit on the head by a bag of rice dumped out of a plane. Once in a while the Japs' patrols get ambitious but they have pulled in their horns lately and the trails to the rear are quite safe. Progress is slow; the jungle is everywhere and very nearly impenetrable. Yesterday, on a cut trail I took 3½ hours to do 3 miles, tripping and cursing at every step. It takes a long time to even locate the Japs, and a lot more to dig them out. We are in tiger and elephant country although I haven't seen any yet. Some of the men have and I've seen droppings and tracks. When an elephant leaves his card in the trail, it takes a pole vaulter to climb over it. I expect to see Tarzan any day now. The jungle is full of his long swinging vines. This experience is different from the last time. Now we have aviation and ammunition and artillery and a certain amount of training, so we don't have to take it on the nose as we used to, with no chance of answering. The Chinese soldier is doing his stuff, as I knew he would if he had half a chance. It's only the higher-ups who are weak and they are still pretty terrible. The Americans are all doing a good job and they all enjoy the life. If I could just have a couple of U.S. divisions. But the Brain Trust won't turn them over, so I've got to go on struggling with my shoestring. The Glamour Boy [Mountbatten] is just about that. He doesn't wear well and I begin to wonder if he knows his stuff. Enormous staff, endless walla-walla, but damn little fighting. And of course the Peanut is unchanged. The jungle is a refuge from them both and I am leaving the shoveling of manure to a couple of my boys.

JANUARY 13   Long talk with Sun. Again impressed on him extreme importance of this operation and serious consequences of failure. He protests he means business and will take Taipha.

JANUARY 21   To Ningam, arrived at 11:00. Saw Brown [Colonel Rothwell Brown, tank commander] at Shingbwiyan. 87 tanks in, remainder in [from Ledo] today. One lost. Fine job [over road] under terrible conditions, Brown says worse than anything he can imagine. Everybody performed. One Chinese killed—tried to jump out of tank. Gave them three days to rest and refit. P.m. doped out plan of advance to south.

JANUARY 28   Off [at] 7:00 down the river, 9:00 at boathead. 9:30 to 12:00 getting to [front]. Went over Jap position; it was too small and the mortars gave them hell. Not well dug in, in spite of occupation from January 19 to January 24. Thompson claims probably 325 dead Japs. They were all over the place with heads and feet sticking out, rather hurried burial; plenty in the river. They ran their guns in the river.

JANUARY 30   [Reached] Delhi at 7:30. Long talk with Sultan and Ferris on the situation here. The Limeys are welching.

JANUARY 31, DELHI   Office. 10:00 a.m. to the big wallawalla [conference]. The Limeys take me more seriously now. But *they* won't fight if they can help it. Blew off my head about "the plan" that "we global strategy" experts have evolved. Fancy charts, false figures, and dirty intentions. Got nowhere, of course. Told them "To hell with logistics." And mentioned Clive and his 123 soldiers.[2] Dead silence.

FEBRUARY 1   At 11:00 started for Shing. At Shingbwiyan got message that Taipha Ga was taken today.

The Chinese had tasted their first jungle victory. They were now ready to set out on the conquest of the Hukawng valley. Stilwell's diaries record the rains, the long waiting for the road to dry, the gradual formulation of plans for the next phase as the Chinese gnawed their way through the jungle in February.

Maingkwan, about fifteen miles south of Taipha Ga, was his next objective. Maingkwan was the main Japanese supply and communication base in the Hukawng valley, and its loss would speed them on their way south. By late February, Stilwell was ready to use Merrill's Marauders on their first mission. The Chinese would advance through the jungle, taking Maingkwan frontally, while the Marauders would sweep around wide to the east and fall on the Japanese at Walawbum, cutting them off eight miles to the south. The tank column, also employed for the first time, would cut through jungle trails and drive in on the Japanese communications between Walawbum and Maingkwan.

FEBRUARY 8, LETTER TO MRS. STILWELL   Don't believe any slop you hear about my being in any danger. Hell, I don't want to be knocked off in this morass, and I assure you that I will take good care of myself. I have gotten together a few tough eggs to keep an eye out—front, back and sides, and

[2] Robert Clive had established British imperial dominion over India with 123 men almost two hundred years before.

they would all enjoy a little bout of assassination. Things are going slowly but satisfactorily. We are chewing them up in bunches, but the aggregate is getting to be fairly respectable. And the boys opposite are tough eggs.

FEBRUARY 15   Pontoon bridge in at Yupbang. Brown's reconnaissance outfit going up.

FEBRUARY 17, LETTER TO MRS. STILWELL   Just a line during a lull while waiting for dope on whether or not we have taken a step in the right direction. We are getting a break on weather. The chow is arriving regularly. I am getting plenty of sleep and am generally enjoying myself.

FEBRUARY 21   It rained last night from 11:00 to 1:00, and I lay there cursing till long after it finally stopped. About one more day of that and I'll be a raving maniac. Went to Ningbyen and saw Merrill's gang. Tough-looking lot of babies. Told Merrill what his job would be. Had to wade river to see 1st Battalion. With Merrill ready and Brown ready, we can go now.

FEBRUARY 24   Merrill starts.

FEBRUARY 25   Last night, first word of appreciation from Peanut. Merrill's patrols at Tawang Hka.

FEBRUARY 26   Rain. Christ again.

MARCH 3   The big day. Ominous quiet. No Jap artillery. Up at 5:30 and over to see tanks move out. Not well done. Jam on road. Truck stuck. Start one hour late. Message from Merrill—will reach Walawbum at noon. 8:00 p.m., message from Merrill—hit Japs at Wesu and Lagang. No U.S. casualties. Jubilation. Chinese all pepped up.

MARCH 4   Sequence of messages: 8:00 p.m. last night, Merrill arrives, jubilation; 10:00 p.m. Brown's first message—

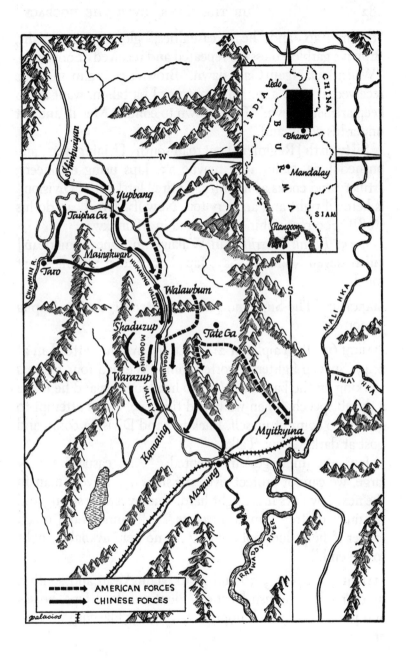

AMERICAN FORCES

CHINESE FORCES

"enemy trap" and "heavy casualties," gloom; at midnight, Brown's garbled message repeated and received at 9:00 a.m. "Will attack Ngam Ga at dawn." Brown's 5:00 a.m. message received at 7:00 a.m.: "Do not need battalion, want air to keep artillery down." Told Brown to contact Merrill and get under his command.

Sixty-sixth [Regiment] cut road south of Maingkwan, ambushed Japs, claim 100, maybe 25. Japs using engineers, artillery and cooks as infantry. Entire [Jap] 56th [Division] is here all right and artillery too. Now if Merrill can do his stuff!! 3:00 p.m. Chinese reported in Maingkwan.

5:45: *Frank Merrill is in Walawbum.* One [American] killed, seven wounded. Says Japs lost at least 25 times that much.

MARCH 5   The Supremo [Mountbatten] is due at Taipha tomorrow.

MARCH 6   To Taipha at 2:15. Louis [Mountbatten] in at 2:45. Sixteen fighters escorted him. (We had four fighters working on the battle.) Went to headquarters and he made a dumb speech. Then we talked till 4:45. Usual attempt to get me to commit myself. Back to 22nd Division command post at dark. Chow. Talk.

Japanese messages intercepted: ". . . casualties very large, we cannot protect river crossings . . . every man in the next few days must fight hard. Enemy is very strong and we must destroy him at all costs . . . cannot hold much longer if help does not come . . . no help available, fight to the end."

MARCH 7   Up at 5:30 and in to Maingkwan and south a mile or so to ambush location. Plenty of dead Japs, horses and junk. Louis much impressed. Doesn't like corpses. Left at 9:00.

MARCH 9   Liao [commander 22nd Division] feeling his oats. ("22nd Division beat the best division of Jap Army at Kun Lun Kuan. Now it has beaten the second best division of the Jap Army." The 1942 interlude [Burma retreat] is forgotten.)

LETTER TO MRS. STILWELL   Still in the bushes but pushing along. Louis has been up but didn't like the smell of the corpses. Now it has been proved that I was right about Chinese troops and the opposition is entirely tongue-tied. It's grand. Louis and I get along famously even if he does have curly eyelashes. Dorn is frothing at the mouth because for certain reasons his gang[3] are still on leash. Health, excellent. Disposition, nasty. Sleep, plenty. Food, too much. Patience, still some left.

MARCH 12   Flew to Ledo at 1:00 p.m. Went to 20th General [Hospital], saw Chinese wounded. Flew along Ledo Road on way back. "Radio" from G-mo to halt advance till British advance in the Arakan. Oh, Jesus. Now *that* starts. Message from Joe Stalin in answer to my congratulations on 26th birthday of Red Army. Fly eggs in my blanket. Like cheesy candle grease. Boiled them out.

MARCH 13   Begins to look like Shaduzup for the rainy season anchorage.

Stilwell's plans were suddenly affected by the offensive the Japanese launched in late March against the British Indian border, two hundred miles to the south. Three Japanese divisions, in a surprise drive, struck across the border with their apparent target Imphal and their purpose the penetration of India deep enough to cut off Assam province. Japanese success in cutting off Assam would not only break off Stilwell's rear supply but also put an end to all supplies for

[3] The Yoke force.

China which depended on the Hump airbases located in Assam.

The larger problems of the campaign, too, began to press on Stilwell. Chiang kept urging Stilwell to halt his advance south, lest he overextend himself and lose what had been won. But Stilwell, determined as ever, was now framing plans for the push that was to carry him in the next few weeks out of the Hukawng valley to the hills around Jambu Bum and Shaduzup, which separate the Hukawng from the Mogaung valley. His tactical problem was simple: Should he halt for the season, before the torrents of the monsoon began, on the hills at Shaduzup, or should he plan to push ahead?

Stilwell decided not to break off his campaign in the jungle to brace the British, whose resources exceeded his manyfold. Instead, he joined the British in urging Chiang K'ai-shek again to thrust across the Burma border with the Yoke force from the east. Brigadier General Dorn was the senior American officer with the Yoke force on the Salween at the time, and while Dorn pressed for action at the front, Stilwell flew to Chungking to press action on Chiang directly. Chiang had been impressed enough by Chinese success under Stilwell to yield to this urging: he released a Chinese division (the 50th) to be flown across the Hump for direct action under Stilwell and finally promised to set the Yoke force in action.

Stilwell returned to Burma hoping that the British would turn the Japanese back at Imphal, that Chiang would this time move, that when the hills at Jambu Bum and Shaduzup were reached he might have a fighting chance to strike at Myitkyina.

MARCH 15 More rain in night, thunderstorms. Wired Dorn to needle Wei.[4]

Sixty-sixth [Regiment] now attacking at Jambu Bum. Item: *It pays to go up and push.* At least, it's coincidence that every time I do, they spurt a bit.

MARCH 16   After lunch *bad news from Imphal.* Limeys have wind up. Flying in 5th Division from Arakan and looking for more troops. This about ruins everything. Shoved off for 38th Division, caught in thunderstorm, backed and filled, and then went on and made it.

MARCH 18   Japs crossed [Indian border] on 16th at Homalin, Tonhe, and Tanngut. Imphal threatened. This ties a can to us and finishes up the glorious 1944 spring campaign.

MARCH 19   Sixty-one today. Well, we got Jambu Bum on my birthday anyway.

MARCH 20, LETTER TO MRS. STILWELL   The 61st birthday, cake with "Uncle Joe" on it. It was a cheerful day anyway. The Japs found it too hot on Jambu Bum and pulled out. That's the divide, so now we are out of the Hukawng at last, starting downhill in the Mogaung valley. (This war is just one damn valley after another.) And today we get the news that yesterday, also, the Japs pulled out of Sumprabum—bum really means hill or mountain—and started south. That is a great relief to me for it was a strong position on our flank and I had just decided we must go get it. Double birthday present. There is a Nsopzup and Yudam Bum.

T. V. is out of the bank now and is he humble. Sent word by Dorn that he hopes I understand that certain things he did were by order of the Peanut. I understand all right. Well, anyway I think we have proved that the Chinese can fight, and you may remember how many people agreed with me on this point.

⁴ Wei Li-huang was commander in chief of the Yoke force.

MARCH 23 Japs [on Imphal front] in Ukruhl![5] My God. Slim getting two divisions from south and hopes to smack them. Wired me to get Yoke in.

MARCH 24, LETTER TO MRS. STILWELL We have had a hard scrap in this bitched-up jungle. I'm getting tired of it but the damn Japs won't let me come out in the open without an argument. I have been on a strain, but now it has eased off and I can see the way a little better. So there won't be quite so much cursing around the command post.

MARCH 27 Off for Kunming, in at 7:00.

MARCH 28 Chungking at 9:30. To house and slept till 2:00. Date with G-mo at 5:00. Got a division to fly in [to Burma]. *Nobody* particularly interested in [Burma] campaign.

MARCH 29 Fiftieth [Chinese] division can go, filled up. Other division, no decision. Merrill has had heart attack.

MARCH 30 Off at 9:00. Lin Wei at field. Told me to get more and more [Chinese troops] to India, only way to make them fight.

Hell of a trip, terrible weather. Pitched around like a leaf. Made Maingkwan about 7:00. Four hours to get back to command post. Rain for five days out of last six. Saw Merrill at Maingkwan. Medicos say he is out of the picture. Bad news from Imphal, *bad*. Got to bed at 1:00.

MARCH 31 We are below Shaduzup. Sixty-fifth [Regiment] attacking Laban against light opposition. Radio to Louis [Mountbatten] for date. Situation at Imphal worse than ever.

Sixty-fifth got into Laban at 6:00.

APRIL 1   Rain. Has the monsoon started? Dubby day. Radios back and forth to Louis [Mountbatten] and Sultan. Arranged to see Louis at Jorhat April 3. Japs astride Imphal road in two places. Very serious now. Slim wants help.

LETTER TO MRS. STILWELL   Just a line before hopping off to see Louis who, to put it mildly, has his hind leg over his neck. If they don't buck up on their side, we also will have our tit in the wringer. What a mess the Limeys can produce in short order. Ben, take care of that flag. It is the first Jap flag captured by the Chinese in the first action in the first sustained offensive they have ever made.

APRIL 3   Jorhat at 10:00. Big gang gathering. Supreme Commander [Mountbatten], Slim, Lentaigne, Old, etc., etc. Talked to Slim, after chow Louis came. "Conference" —usual slop. Reviewed the situation. Much to my surprise, no question of help from us. On contrary, Slim and Supreme Commander said to go ahead.

Left at 5:00 for Maingkwan. Back at Tingkawk at 10:30.

At the beginning of April, Stilwell decided to risk all on a strike for Myitkyina. The monsoons, he knew, could not be long delayed, and thereafter the rains would halt further advance. But capture of Myitkyina would seal his winter-long campaign with a victory that could not be belittled anywhere in the world, would place him halfway across Burma to China, and make the ending of the China blockade a matter of routine.

Stilwell had, by mid-April, Chiang's promise to unloose the Yoke force for a co-ordinating drive into north Burma from the Salween. The situation on the British front at Imphal had passed the critical stage and the Japanese were

5 Town twenty miles within the Indian border.

being pressed back. Stilwell therefore decided to move his frontal Chinese troops across the ridge into the Mogaung valley for an assault on Kamaing, and at the same time secretly dispatch Merrill's Marauders through the jungle to Myitkyina, a march of almost one hundred miles over a 6,000-foot mountain range. He hoped that the main Chinese assault on Kamaing in the Mogaung valley would so focus Japanese attention that Myitkyina would fall to a surprise attack before reinforcements could be sent up. The Japanese considered it secure from any penetration and garrisoned it lightly with less than a thousand men.

At the end of April the Marauders set off in three columns, one Chinese regiment following them in close contact. Their combat leader was Colonel Frank Hunter, for Merrill was too sick to march. The plans were carefully laid. As soon as word of Hunter's arrival and seizure of the airstrip should be received, Stilwell planned to fly in two or three regiments of Chinese troops to reinforce him, and ferry in enough supplies to secure the position.

The date for the attack on Myitkyina was set at May 12—ominously close to the seasonal beginning of the monsoon rains.

APRIL 4 Sweated out and decided to bring 114th [Regiment] up, keep 65th [Regiment] in, and go on. Put rest of 112th [Regiment] in at Janpan—and if, as, and when go for Myitkyina. Meanwhile push south and hope for best at Dinapur [in Imphal area].

APRIL 5 Another fine day. Waited for Brown to come down. We must organize a push and break into Kamaing in a hurry.

APRIL 6 Cloudy day. Kachins [6] predict early monsoons. At noon, moved up to Shaduzup, camp not ready. Walked down to river and back to command post—full of Jap dugouts and bashas and crap. At 6:00 went to 22nd Division command post for conference. Back and forth, pro and con. Told them this [the Myitkyina-Kamaing drive] was our chance—our *only* chance. And we would all have to make a big effort. Division commanders push columns and break through this crust. "Speed to Kamaing." Let Sun [Li-jen] have 112th [Regiment]. Brown lent thirty trucks. 114th [Regiment] to march. We concentrate on Kamaing and Sun promises to go to Myitkyina, rain or no rain. Called on us to witness. (Now to keep pressure on.)

APRIL 10 Radio from Hearn on F.D.R.'s latest [message to Chiang]. "Inconceivable that the Yoke force should not attack after all our efforts to equip and train it."

APRIL 11 Took Sun [Li-jen] down to see Fu [a subordinate regimental commander]. [Fu] still not in Wakawng. About half the [Jap] position taken. Jap orders say to hold to the last. Jap wounded found killed by cuts in neck and belly. Some Japs hung themselves in the dugouts. Seventy corpses *claimed* counted. Back through heavy traffic. Met tank company going to Wakawng. They went in 1,000 yards ahead [of the] 1st Battalion of the 66th [Regiment] and had two tanks knocked out.

APRIL 13 Better feeling at Imphal today.

LETTER TO MRS. STILWELL We are still plugging our way down the rathole, the Japs objecting quite strenuously to the process. This last scrap at Wakawng has been tough. It has now broken up, however, and perhaps we can get going again. If and when this war gets finished, I am going to

---

[6] North Burma is inhabited by a people called the Kachins who co-operated with the Allies wholeheartedly during the campaign.

economize on clothes and go strong on fancy eats. Corned beef and salmon are out the window forever, and the fancy grocery and butcher shops are going to get my money. You must think my mind is all on my belly, but it really isn't. I have other things to worry about and dreams of breakfast in our kitchen help to keep me from going crazy. Nearly four months steady of this party now and I'm beginning to be nasty to people without any reason.

APRIL 15   We [U.S. bombers] smack Kamaing and Mogaung tomorrow and for four days more.

APRIL 17   Talked to Merrill about Mitch [Myitkyina] plan. Hit Mitch, May 12. God grant it doesn't rain.

Lunch, then the avalanche. Fenn in . . . Godfrey, Davis in . . . Asensio in. Sent for Pick. He came in and we went to it. Limeys wanted Pick to pay for trees cut down in making Ledo Road. Tie that. Session with Liao [commander of 22nd Division]. He says G-mo has not interfered with operations, but frequently writes to him. Has told him to obey me, even if I'm wrong. Pick here for supper. Kept him overnight, so he could sleep.

APRIL 19, LETTER TO MRS. STILWELL   The villages are just a few charred poles, in a clearing. Everything in Burma was burned down when the Japs ran us out. We had tough going the first ten days this month, but a lot of Japs assumed horizontal positions and we are on the move again. A great deal depends on God—if He will hold up the rains for a month, it might be very useful to me. The Glamour Boy [Mountbatten] was over addressing our troops the other day. His own back yard was on fire and that was the time he chose to make a pep talk to us. Impressing his personality on his troops.

A Limey forestry official came to our headquarters and made the proposition that the United States pay the British for the trees we are cutting down in Burma to make a road to China.

APRIL 23   Merrill left for Dinjan and Tate Ga. Will jump [for Myitkyina] on 27th. Our last effort.

APRIL 26   Joe [7] has news that Japs are building up on us at Myitkyina. Uh.

APRIL 27   Merrill all set to go on 28th. We will keep in touch by plane. (Chinese wounded man calling for water. Finally got it. "Give it to him," pointing to patient beside him.)

MAY 1   Rain. (Depression days, commander's worries: I start them off for Myitkyina, it rains. The resistance grows here. Why didn't I use them on our front? Is the gap too big? Will they meet a reinforced garrison [at Myitkyina]? Does it mean we'll fail on both sides, instead of only one? Can I get them out? Are the Japs being sucked towards Mogaung or is the new [Jap] unit staying in Mitch? Etc., etc., and nothing can be done about it. The die is cast, and it's sink or swim. But the nervous wear and tear is terrible. Pity the poor commanding officer.)

[UNDATED] PSYCHOLOGY OF COMMAND A good commander is a man of high character (this is the most important attribute), with power of decision next most important attribute. He must have moral backbone, and this stems from high character; and he must be physically courageous, or successfully conceal the fact that he is not. He must know the tools of his trade, tactics and logistics. He must be im-

[7] Colonel Joseph W. Stilwell, Jr.—who had been ordered to his father's staff in the north Burma campaign as G-2, intelligence officer.

partial. He must be calm under stress. He must reward promptly and punish justly. He must be accessible, human, humble, patient, forbearing. He should listen to advice, make his own decision, and carry it out with energy.

Unless a commander is human, he cannot understand the reactions of his men. If he is human, the pressure on him intensifies tremendously. The callous man has no mental struggle over jeopardizing the lives of 10,000 men; the human commander cannot avoid this struggle. It is constant and wearing, and yet necessary, for the men can sense the commander's difficulty. There are many ways in which he can show his interest in them and they respond, once they believe it is real. Then you get mutual confidence, the basis of real discipline.

Generals get sharply criticized. They are the birds who shelter themselves in dugouts and send the soldiers out to get killed. They cover themselves with medals, won at the expense of the lives of their men, who are thrown in regardless, to compensate for faulty or poorly thought-out plans.

There are really not many [generals] like that. The average general envies the buck private; when things go wrong, the private can blame the general, but the general can blame only himself. The private carries the woes of one man; the general carries the woes of all. He is conscious always of the responsibility on his shoulders, of the relatives of the men entrusted to him, and of their feelings. He must act so that he can face those fathers and mothers without shame or remorse. How can he do this? By constant care, by meticulous thought and preparation, by worry, by insistence on high standards in everything, by reward and punishment, by impartiality, by an example of calm and confidence. It all adds up to character.

Q: If a man has enough character to be a good commander, does he ever doubt himself? He should not. In my case, I doubt myself. Therefore, I am in all probability not a good commander.

FORMULA:

Character	80%
Power of decision	10%
Technical knowledge	5%
Everything else	5%

MAY 1, LETTER TO MRS. STILWELL   This is the month when the heavens open and the floods descend and the fields become lakes and the roads disappear and there is hell to pay generally. I hope the Japs are as tired of it as we are. If the little bastards insist on fighting during the rains, I don't know what I'll do, but there are indications that they have been chewed up here and there, so maybe they won't be so ambitious this time. The "dry season" in this country is a joke, anyway. We have had rain in December, 12 days in January, 18 in February, 10 in March, 10 in April, and now it's *really* going to rain. From now till fall we'll be in the Navy. Did I tell you this one? I was crossing a river in a pontoon and the colored soldier running the boat looked me over and shook his head sadly. Said he: "It sure is tough to make an old man like you come up and work in this country!" I occasionally overhear similar remarks by the Chinese soldiers. They think I am about ninety years old and comment on their own senior officers.

MAY 2   Another cloudy day. We sat and gloomed. The 22nd Division has had 57 company officers killed. Can't push the 22nd Division under the circumstances and can't help them. It's hell. Joe up for supper and checkers. Christ but I feel helpless.

MAY 4   Louis's latest is proposal to withdraw [our] force so as to save planes, presumably to use in Imphal. Back at 3:00. Liao is now making all the known excuses for not moving. He and Sun have been hobnobbing for three days. He's going to lie down and dig in.

MAY 5   Liao in at 1:30. Long talk. He is affected by losses, particularly company officers.

MAY 6, LETTER TO MRS. STILWELL   Your letters are grand and help me to remember that *everything* is not double-crossing, obstruction, and stupidity. Probably we are getting a bit jumpy: the boys have been plugging for four and a half months and it hasn't been easy. I've just heard we have been sent some "war dogs." They won't give me any doughboys but they send me some dogs. It will be difficult to get them educated on the different smells of Americans—black and white—Chinese, Kachins, Nagas, Indians, Garos, Darjeelings, Burmese and Japs. The British of course don't smell —they tub regularly. By God, the longer I live the more I appreciate George Washington and the boys of the Revolution. Raining again. We have this constant threat of the monsoon hanging over us.

MAY 8   Shoved off at 11:30. Picked up Sun [Li-jen] at 38th [Division] command post and went up to 113th [Regiment]. Hot. 1:30 to 3:30 hike up to 114th Command Post near Nawngmi Kawng. Hill, 2,000 [feet high]. Damned near killed me. All out of shape. No wind, no legs. Swore off smoking then and there. Felt like an old man when I staggered in. Li [regimental commander] there. Went over the dope and there was the usual bustle and stir by Sun. Overnight at 114th [Regiment]. Sun went back—too much for him.

MAY 9 Li went up to battalion command post. I let him go to give him [a] chance to push the boys after I had orated at length on his slowness and need for haste. Told him to get going. Period. We left at 1:00 down 1,500 feet to river, then up 1,000 feet to command post. The goddam shoes were killing my feet. Skin off toes. No others with me. Pretty dumb. Fell up the hill and into command post exhausted. Again told them what I wanted. Japs fired artillery all night long, all over the lot.

MAY 1C Lay around all morning waiting for news of attack on Hkatang Kawng. Third company going to Samlan around left flank. First company straight in. (They did and lost a platoon commander and six casualties from fire from flank.) About 1:30 Li [regimental commander] went to see P'eng [battalion commander] horrified that I should go too. Too much loss of face. Told them to fight or I would go and stand in the trail up front. This makes them move and is the only thing that does. Down the hill to regimental command post and spent the night there. Chinese troops staggering uphill as we came down. All cheerful, they deserve better company officers.

MAY 12 *Yoke jumped off yesterday*—maybe.

MAY 14 Hunter expected to give us the 48-hour signal [8] tonight. I told Merrill to roll on in and swing on 'em. 48 HOUR NOTICE.

MAY 15 (2:00 p.m.) 24 HOUR NOTICE!!
Old here. All set for moves to Mitch. Took a walk. Hunter

---

[8] The Marauders' column was to preserve radio silence all the way through the jungle till they judged themselves within forty-eight hours' march of Myitkyina itself. Then they were to radio in by prearranged code, so that the air force could alert its units for the troop carrier movement to the airstrip when it should have been seized.

[at Myitkyina] set by night of 16th. Hiding out till 17th or 18th.

MAY 17 Clear. By God a break. Got commanding officer of 149th [Regiment] up and told him about the job, except destination [Myitkyina].

At 10:50 message "in the ring" came in. That meant— "at the field."

Old flew over [Myitkyina] at 12:00 and saw nothing. Hunter getting in place probably. We'll just have to sweat it out.

Merrill in at 2:50. Had been over field which was clear [of Japs]. He saw trench mortar fire well to northeast. About 3:30 we got "Merchant of Venice"—i.e., transports can land. WHOOPS! Enormous relief to get Merrill's report. At once ordered machinery and reinforcements started. About 3:30 two transports landed. At 4:00 we saw transports and gliders going over. Thereafter, a stream of planes both ways. Told them to keep going all night. We may have 89th [Regiment] in by morning—WILL THIS BURN UP THE LIMEYS.

Monsoon coming in on south Burma now. Myitkyina due [for monsoon] June 1.

MAY 18 Not much sleep. Ants and worry. 9:30 Theissen took us into Myitkyina. About twelve correspondents. Heavy clouds. We let down and got in O.K., about 10:00. 89th [Regiment] coming in, 150th had not started attack. First Battalion [of] Galahad [Marauders] had gone to the Zigon ferry. No Jap reaction, Japs not yet located. Planes bombing the town. Shoved off at noon and came back around the Mogaung corner. Got an L-1 and flew back to Shaduzup.

MAY 19 Flock of visitors continues. Merrill in—he has had another [heart] attack. Peterson gave him morphine and put him to bed. Progress terribly slow at Mitch. I am worried about the Jap reaction. 150th [Regiment] moved this a.m. and overran two Jap positions. A Jap group up by north field has not moved. Counterattack last night at Zigon ferry.

MAY 20 Last night Sun [Li-jen] in with plan to take Kamaing. O.K. by me. I kidded him along and then agreed. Anything to get the 38th [Division] moving. If we get to Kamaing, we tell the Limeys to go to hell.

Merrill passed by medicos. I let him go back—they [the Marauders] are to finish the job [at Myitkyina].

One hundred fiftieth [Regiment] has command post in [Myitkyina] railroad station. Japs backed into bazaar section. Resistance now localized and we are reasonably sure of the place. Japs apparently all in confusion and trying to pull out, Chinese casualties heavy.

Within a week, the success at Myitkyina had transformed itself from a brilliant coup to a squalid, heartbreaking campaign.

The 150th Chinese Regiment, which was the first flown in to consolidate, had but lately arrived from China and was unblooded in war. In their first action, several of its battalions mistook each other for Japanese and succeeded in inflicting disastrous casualties on themselves before recognition was achieved. Panic spread. Before the troops at Myitkyina could be pulled together the Japanese had had time to bring in all their outpost garrisons from the field, to rush supplies and reinforcements from the south and dig in for desperate resistance.

The Japanese force, variously estimated at from five to seven thousand men, decided to make a suicide stand of it, and each individual pocket had to be dug out in intensive fighting. Two full months dragged by while their stronghold *was being reduced. Two American commanders were re-lieved. The Marauders, exhausted from their previous four months of fighting, were decimated with disease. The rains poured down, the battle area became a quagmire, it was impossible to withdraw from the struggle through the jungle without disaster.*

Although this was a period not unmarked with success—for the Chinese had captured Kamaing and gone on to Mogaung beyond—it was a period of bitterness and worry for Stilwell.

Not till the end of July was the decision sure; and by then Stilwell was more than willing to leave the jungle and fly to Ceylon. Lord Louis Mountbatten of the Southeast Asia Command was called to London. Stilwell as deputy of the command was ordered to SEAC headquarters at Kandy in Ceylon to watch affairs from the commander's chair.

MAY 21   Six p.m. Cannon in from Mitch. BAD NEWS. Panic in 150th [Regiment]; they ran away and had to be taken out. What goes on at Mitch. A bad day mentally. Good deal of strain and worry—if the troops are undependable, where are we? I'm looking forward to a full stop to this business. Wish it would pour right now.

MAY 22   BLACK MONDAY. Bad news from Mitch. Now they saw 800 Japs go into Charpati [9] last night. And 200 crossed the river from the east. McCammon says "situation is critical." Not a thing I can do. It has rained heavily all morning. We can't get troops in, also the field is in bad shape at Mitch. Radioed McCammon to take out Charpati if information was true. Later message said Japanese both in front and behind of 3rd Battalion of Galahad. General air of discouragement down there, and of course corresponding worry here. We've got to sweat it out, but it's no fun. Q:

Get Pick's engineers [as reinforcement]? Yes. At least alert them, and use as replacements for Galahad. Meanwhile push 42nd [Regiment] in, and follow with 41st [Regiment] if necessary.

If the goddam rain will only let us use the field for a few days. If we can't land planes, can't land troops.

This is one of those terrible worry days, when you wish you were dead. 10:00 p.m., still raining heavily.

[UNDATED]   I'm a worrier. I am always imagining dangers, and experiencing them mentally. Many never occur, but those that do I'm mentally prepared for, so maybe it pays. They say the coward dies a thousand deaths, the valiant dies but once. But possibly the valiant dies a thousand deaths too, if he is cursed with imagination. The valiant who dies but once must be an unimaginative clod, or else he has something I can't understand. Enough will power to dismiss from his mind all the possibilities of trouble and disaster that may occur. That would take balance that I know I could never attain. I have to drive myself through the mental stress of anticipation. Q: Am I by nature a coward? And if so, can it not be proved that it is harder to be a coward . . . and not quit . . . than a hero?

To be able to live with the family . . . with a free mind . . . I have to risk never living with them. Probably this thought would never occur to a guy of strong character.

Imagination again. I often dream of going down into holes to pull the kids out, or looking for them frantically underwater. I think of situations . . . quite needlessly . . . that turn my guts to water. Is it the same thing that makes me worry about covering the flanks, about checking on location of units, delivery of orders, execution of move-

⁹ Village near Myitkyina.

ments, arrival of supplies, etc., etc.? Wouldn't a stable mind dismiss the needless worry and concentrate on the important things? Or must I pay for one by suffering the other as well?

Strangely enough I do not worry about my own lot. It never occurs to me that my plane will crash or that the next bomb has my name on it. The possibility occurs to me, but it does not weigh on my mind at all. I wonder what that indicates.

In connection with the above, many things have happened close to me in time or space, without making any impression of danger on me. The plane ahead of mine has crashed, the plane behind has been shot down, a place has been bombed just before my arrival or just after my departure . . . Someone else, doing just what I was doing, has been a casualty. And still no apprehension is created in my mind . . . I know how Win would explain it, but if so, why isn't *everyone* taken care of?

MAY 23   Cleared up at 11:00. Myitkyina field closed to C-47 [troop carrier planes]. Sent [Brigadier General Hayden] Boatner in [to Myitkyina] with Hu and P'an. Boatner back at 7:00, matters fairly satisfactory. Attack on 25th, tomorrow to get lined up.

MAY 25   Disturbing news from Mitch. McCammon gloomy. Decided to go down. Rain, in at Mitch, O.K., runway very wet. Got the dope on the attack. All night firing all along the line, very little sleep. Rain.

MAY 27   Rain again, discouraging. No air support. Worry-worry-worry. Off at 9:30 [back to Shaduzup].

MAY 29   CLEAR! Thank God, got the engineers in yesterday and the air will start on Galahad replacements today. One more day and we are set—Christ again, will God give

First Burma campaign. Stilwell (wearing campaign hat, far left) tells his tired men they must abandon their vehicles. Behind them was the enemy and defeat, before them the roadless jungle.

The Stilwell party is shown here resting during one of their brief pauses on the long hike out. Stilwell supervised every detail of the march, counting cadence, setting rations, inspecting rifles and packs.

"Holcombe out, Merrill out; heat exhaustion. Lee out. Sliney pooped. Nowakowski same. Christ, but we are a poor lot. Hard going in the river all the way. All packs reduced to ten pounds."

"Sun came out. Nurses put the roofs on the rafts. Long scramble getting rafts ready. Mat sheds by Seagrave's group. Always willing. Four piece rafts and an advance guard of one piece. Ten polers."

Stilwell eating from mess kit. The rations were rice and tinned food.

Hiking on to the Chindwin at one hundred five paces to the minute.

LIFE *photograph* Stilwell leading last lap over mountains. "Pinky" Dorn follows.

This Thibetan mule pack train, bringing up the rear in the march, was found wandering leaderless by Stilwell during the retreat. He attached it to his group, loaded it with baggage, and led it to India.

Stilwell emerged from the first campaign (left of center) smarting
with defeat but determined to return to Burma and smash the
blockade as soon as possible. For a counteroffensive he needed the
co-operation of British Field Marshal Sir Archibald Percival Wavell.
Wavell, shown above in conference at right of Stilwell, had been
Allied Commander in the disastrous battle for the South Seas in
1942. Wavell felt that an offensive against the Japanese could be
undertaken only after long and massive preparation. In conference
after conference, month after month, Wavell and Stilwell differed
on the conduct of the war in Asia. Against the paper-and-map calculations of Wavell's impressive staff, seen here at their Delhi headquarters, Stilwell opposed his single-minded passion for action. On
the other side of the Hump, in Chungking, his energies were
drained by similar conferences with Chiang K'ai-shek's staff.

Stilwell is here inspecting a few of his Chinese infantrymen at an American training camp. Camps like these in India and China introduced American weapons and procedures to Chinese soldiers.

The General found Madame Sun Yat-sen to be "sympatica."

Stilwell visits Chennault. They rarely smiled when they met. *International News*
Stilwell and the Chiangs in 1942. They smiled in the beginning.

Chinese troops of the Yoke force perched on the eastern heights of the Salween gorge. Five thousand feet below ran the river. Facing them were the Japanese, holding the western line of blockade.

Stilwell flew the Hump as if it were a commuters' run, cat-napping as he went. His plane was a beaten-up transport that held a few chairs, several parachutes, a case of rations, and a cot.

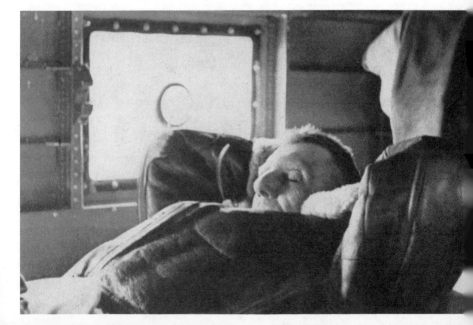

Conference on Policy in China.

Present — FDR, H. Hopkins, JrS

Q FDR "Well Joe, what do you think of the bad news?"

A JoS I haven't heard yet how bad it is.

FDR We're in an impasse. I've been stubborn as a mule for four days, but we can't get any — where, and it won't do for a conference to end up that way. The British just won't do the opera- tion, and I can't get them to agree to it.

JoS I'm interested in how this affects our policy in China.

FDR Well now, we've been friends with China for a gre-e-e-at many years. I ascribe a large part of this good feeling to the missionaries. You know, I have a China history. My grandfather went out there, to Swatow and Canton, in 1829, and even went up to Hankow. He did what was every American's ambition in those days, — he made a million dollars; and when he came back, he put it into western railroads. And in 6 years he lost every dollar. (Ha! Ha! Ha!) Then in 1856 he went out again, + stayed there all through the Civil War, and made another million. This time he put it into coal mines, and they didn't pay a dividend till 2 years after he died. Ha! Ha! Ha!

Associated Press Stilwell looks out over the Tanai River at the jungle in January, 1943. The clearing of the Tanai was the first step in Burma's reconquest. It was eight months to final victory at Myitkyina.

Debonair Lord Louis Mountbatten is shown here visiting the jungle front. Mountbatten, who commanded from his Ceylon headquarters, often amused, often irritated Stilwell.

International News Service

The war in Burma was a walking war, and Stilwell, seen here with carbine across his back, grew as tired of foot-war as any infantryman. The Chinese feared Japanese would ambush him on such trips.

Chinese troops such as these bore the main burden of reconquest. Eighteen months of American training at Ramgarh had prepared them for the campaign and China's first successful offensive.

Stilwell (hands on hips, back to camera) stares back over the muddy road trace. Widened, paved, cleared of the enemy, it finally stretched hundreds of miles to pierce China's three-year-old blockade.

Sun Li-jen (right) commanded China's New First Army. Stilwell thought him the ablest of his Chinese field commanders.

Streams like this became, in the rainy season, torrents of angry water. Scores of such bridges marked the Ledo Road.

LIFE Magazine

An American of Merrill's Marauders gazes at a dead enemy. Most of the Marauders were hardened fighters who had learned to handle the Japanese in the Pacific and had volunteered for Burma duty.

LIFE Magazine

Some of the American combat troops that Stilwell commanded are seen resting beside their glider. These men fought as spearhead battalions, operating frequently deep behind the Japanese lines.

Stilwell at Myitkyina airfield, during Japanese counterattack. "The private carries the woes of one man; the general carries the woes of all. He is conscious always of the responsibility on his shoulders, of the relatives of the men entrusted to him."

Stilwell's field headquarters were a bamboo shack, his rations GI. He preferred this to the pomp and luxury of Chungking or Delhi.

We can't expect to be told about the
future. If we want to find out, we
must march toward it. Let's go –

I'm a worrier. I am always imagining
dangers, & experiencing them mentally.
Many never occur, but those that do
I'm mentally prepared for, so maybe
it pays. – They say the coward dies
a thousand deaths, the valiant dies but
once. But possibly the valiant dies
a thousand deaths, too, if he is cursed
with imagination. The valiant who
dies but once must be an unimaginative clod, or else he has something
I can't understand, – enough will power
to dismiss from his mind all the
possibilities of trouble and disaster that
may occur. That would take balance
that I know I could never attain.
I have to drive myself through the mental stress of anticipation. Question: Am
I by nature a coward? And if so, can
it not be proved that it is harder to be
a coward – and not quit – than a hero?

Burning plane at Myitkyina. As the troops fought to extend the perimeter of the airfield, enemy artillery potted at the planes as they stood exposed. For the first two weeks, defeat seemed very close.

A staff officer, Stilwell, General Wei Li-huang confer at Yoke force headquarters. Wei was a sturdy soldier and eager to fight — but he could not move until Chungking permitted him to act.

Stilwell and Patrick J. Hurley, shown during Hurley's first visit to China in 1943. Stilwell enjoyed this visit and looked forward eagerly to the Hurley-Nelson mission sent to aid him late in 1944.

Chungking was a narrow spit of rock that lay at the confluence of the Yangtze and Chialing rivers. This view looks down at Chungking's airport, awash during the Yangtze's seasonal high water.

General and Mrs. Stilwell in their garden at Carmel in 1944. However far he traveled, it was to Carmel that his thoughts always returned. It was here he planned to spend his years of retirement.

General Stilwell, playing on the beach at Carmel with Garry, his dog, after relief from command. He wrote: "If a man can say he did not let his country down, and if he can live with himself, there is nothing more he can reasonably ask for."

LIFE Magazine

me one more day of clear weather? Took a swim with Joe, in the Shadu. Clouding up.

MAY 30 CLEAR! Another break. God is good (sometimes). Today we move 42nd [Regiment into Myitkyina by air] and begin on fillers (Galahad) from Ramgarh. Decided to take Boatner to Mitch, [in] at 5:15.

Just as I left it only not so good: [only] 12 men left in 2nd Battalion of Galahad. Galahad is just shot.

Made general plan for tomorrow, put Boatner in command, he took hold at once.

JUNE 2, LETTER TO MRS. STILWELL The pressure has been on me for a month: worry over the weather, worry over the Myitkyina business, etc. Some of our troubles have ironed out, the break in the weather I had been praying for came at just the right time (Great is God—*Allah il Allah—Wo mi t'o fu*) and now we have a fighting chance. Certain of our allies don't care for the *fighting* chance. The situation in China looks pretty bad.[10] I believe the Peanut is going to pay dearly for being stupid and stubborn. The jackass had salvation offered him free, and wouldn't take it. Now it's too late and he's screaming. This is just what I told them a year ago but they knew better. The rains have held off miraculously, but we are about to run into them now.

JUNE 3 Evening, word from Boatner. Got bumped yesterday hard—42nd [Regiment] had 240 [casualties]; 150th [Regiment] had 80 casualties. Attack *stopped.*

JUNE 4 Kuo, [of] 38th [Division], in to announce capture of Tumboughka. That's grand. And Liao has told Fu to get into Kamaing tomorrow.

10 In East China, the Japanese had just launched the great summer offensive of 1944 that was to carry them from Changsha to Kweilin in the next five months.

Chiang K'ai-shek says: "Come up for Christ's sake," so shoved off at 4:00. Kunming at 7:00.

JUNE 5 Up at 5:15, off at 6:30, Chungking at 9:00. Date with Peanut at 3:30. As expected, chiseling gasoline for the Fourteenth Air Force. All he wants is the world and nothing in return.

Peanut much surprised over north Burma success.

JUNE 6 Off at 11:00, Kunming at 2:00, saw Chennault and his staff and told them what would be done. Off again at 3:00—Tingkawk [Shaduzup] at 7:15 Indian time, hot and humid. Joe up and played accordion till midnight.

JUNE 9 1,867 Chinese casualties evacuated from Mitch.

JUNE 11 Wheeler back—Supreme Allied Commander [Mountbatten] going to United Kingdom and deputy [11] to take over. Louis wants to know what about it. Well, what about it?

The wear and tear on the nerves continues. Are we attempting too much? Can they hold us? Is there a surprise ready? Counterattack? Will our people stick it out? Casualties too heavy? I can tell that I've had nearly enough of this. It looks easy for an outsider to command, but it's rough as hell on a worrier.

Beat Joe at checkers.

[UNDATED] COMMANDER Principal load is standing disappointment and upsetting of plans. Everything conspires against him—dumb execution, weather, breakdowns, misunderstandings, deliberate obstruction, jealousies, etc. Must be prepared to accept fifty per cent results in twice the time calculated. One small block delays the entire move—not just the unit affected. Tendency of Chinese commanders to change the plan if easier for them. Constant check. Constant prodding. Constant smoothing. As Foch said, "To accomplish even a little on the battlefield, much effort is needed." All he can hope is to keep going. A brilliant success is an accident, because accidents are certain to occur; it is only a happy one, that fits into a mistake, in time or place or disposition by the enemy, that brings a result quickly. A dumb mistake by the enemy may put a unit in an unexpected place and wreck a perfect plan. War is a gamble. All we can do is try and keep a small percentage on our side.

JUNE 12   114th [Regiment] *is* moving—they are already beyond Padawnyang. We are too ready to crab and criticize. Kamaing being pounded.

JUNE 13   Just bellyaches from Boatner [at Myitkyina]. "He's pushing—but—" etc., etc.

JUNE 14   Gloomy report from Boatner. Everybody running away and hell to pay generally, and Japs about to take the offensive. Hard rain early a.m.

LETTER TO MRS. STILWELL   Underhanded bastardy. Ben graduated from High School. I always visualized being around some of the time he was in school and here we are in a goddam war for 2½ years and we haven't started yet. He'll be an old married man before I get home. On the other hand, if some of the people who are trying to stick a knife in me have some luck, I may be home any day.

Our Chinese soldier cooks continue to turn in good performances. The other day one of them had been out foraging and on the way in, heard a noise in the bushes which turned out to be a Jap major. The cook pulled out the pin of his grenade—laid it down in the grass and stepped out

11 Stilwell was the deputy.

and lay down in the bushes until it went off, making another minor Shinto god out of the major. Then he picked up the souvenirs and came on in.

Five stray Japs charged the regimental command post, 113th Infantry. The pings [Chinese soldiers] shot them all except one, a great big Jap whose ammunition ran out. He kept coming, with a surprised look on his mug and the pings began to shoot at his feet to make him dance. Then the colonel stopped them and told them to grab him. About fifty pings sailed into him like ants on a caterpillar and there was a hell of a fight to see who would get the Jap tied up. He was very dilapidated when they unpiled and produced him, all laughing like hell. Queerly enough they harbor no rancor against the Japs. We've been making a killing lately. Got the Japs cut up into several separate hunks and they are paying for it at the rate of ten to one. We're close to a couple of places we want, badly. We've had some torrential downpours and some sunny interludes. But we can expect only rain, mud, leeches, mosquitoes and more, etc. It is better than being in Delhi or Chungking or in Kandy [12] with Louis.

JUNE 15   Rain all night, still raining all morning. Struggled with papers. Terrible letter from Boatner, bad news from Myitkyina. *U.S. troops are shaky.* Hard to believe. Either our officers are all rotten, or else Boatner is getting hysterical. I'll have to go down.

Article in *The Saturday Evening Post.* The one man of genius in Asia is Chennault. "Walking Joe and the Platoon War in Burma," "World War I foot-soldier." In other words, just a dumb bastard. What we should do is give Chennault 500 planes and watch him "go to town." And at the end of the article, this fool says we are getting ready for the great battle on the mainland of Asia, against the Japanese ARMY. (Fight with planes and be up to date.) Such jackass stuff gets under my skin. There is a deliberate plan in the Fourteenth Air Force to belittle everything I do and to invent catchy phrases to make me look like an old-fashioned stooge.

JUNE 16 Good news at last. 22nd in Kamaing and having a hell of a time. Before noon. That should have been a killing.

JUNE 17 P.m. at [Myitkyina] airstrip.

JUNE 18 With Captain Johnson and two squads of intelligence and reconnaissance platoon to south Charpati, Sitapur and Mankrim. About six miles of hard going, in mud and rain, in two hours and ten minutes. No Japs. Saw Hunter and talked it over, not so bad as painted, the men looked good.

JUNE 20 Rain. Off at ten and in at Warazup [field headquarters].

JUNE 21 [Chinese and British] attack on Mogaung tomorrow. In general, situation [at Mogaung] seems pretty good, Japs chopped up and starving, easy killings in large numbers, with no casualties on our side.

JUNE 22 Remnants of [Jap] 18th Division cooped up southwest of Kamaing. The end for them.

Radio from Merrill, Louis wants me relieved as deputy supreme Allied commander and has approached Marshall. Substitute to be Wedemeyer or Sultan. Good God—to be ousted in favor of Wedemeyer—that would be a disgrace. Just a feeling of relief if it's done.

12 Headquarters of SEAC were located at Kandy in Ceylon.

JUNE 25   Boatner has malaria.

JUNE 26   Chased Boatner to showers. He cried and protested, told him no argument.

JUNE 27   Good news from Mogaung. *We have it.*

JULY 2   Rain. No further news from Mitch. Message from George Marshall: "How about going to China and fixing things up!"

LETTER TO MRS. STILWELL   The rain is pouring down, day after day, and night after night and the mud is getting deeper, and we still go on fighting these bastards. A tough and persistent race, but in the Kamaing-Mogaung area we have broken their backs and had numerous cleanup parties. Over in Myitkyina, they are dug in deep, etc. It's a great pleasure to have a hand in this but it's a hell of a drain on nervous energy. I'll be glad of a rest myself. Mountbatten has been up again. He had the nerve to make a speech at our headquarters but he doesn't fool our GIs much. They are getting a look at the British Empah with its pants down and the aspect is not so pretty. You can imagine how popular I am with the Limeys. I have been thinking of Mountbatten as a sophomore but I have demoted him to freshman. How lucky we all are that your grandparents and one of mine had the good sense to come to the United States. How much we owe George Washington and the few helpers he had that put over the Revolutionary War.

Over in China things look very black. It would be a pleasure to go to Washington and scream, "I told you so," but I think they get the point. This was my thesis in May last year, but I was all alone and the air boys were so sure they could run the Japs out of China with planes that I was put in the garbage pail. They have had their way and now the beans are spilled, but what can anyone do about it? It's just one of those sad might-have-beens. The people who are principally to blame will duck all criticism and responsibility. If this crisis were just sufficient to get rid of the Peanut, without entirely wrecking the ship, it would be worth it. But that's too much to hope.

JULY 3 Got radio off to George Marshall on China crisis. Nothing new at Myitkyina. Rain.

JULY 5, LETTER TO MRS. STILWELL We have pretty well cleaned up the Japs around Mogaung. It has been a satisfactory party. We still have our troubles elsewhere and you can readily believe that all is not love and kisses among the various ill-assorted fragments I have to work with. However, I can only do my best. And to hell with it.

JULY 8 Radio from F.D.R. to Chiang K'ai-shek and from George Marshall to me. They have been pouring it into him about me. F.D.R. told Chiang K'ai-shek to give me full authority to run the show, promotion to full general.

JULY 11 Ben's birthday—17. Sore throat—papers all day.

JULY 13 Yesterday small gains [at Myitkyina] but everywhere.

JULY 19 Japs at Mitch, shoving off on rafts. Three groups yesterday, [we] picked up or killed 47.

JULY 21 SAC [Supreme Allied Commander—Mountbatten] leaving August 2. He is working to abolish the China-Burma-India [theater].

LETTER TO MRS. STILWELL Still whanging away at Mitch but indications are now that we have the noose good and tight and that very few will get away. We should finish the job in reasonable time and then Ole Pappy is going to take a day off. I have had a hard two months what with one thing and another and you know what I mean when I say that undercover maneuvering continues in all camps and I have to watch my step and keep my throat protected. The Japs continue to be the least of my troubles. When I see what gets into the papers it nauseates me. The Chinese troops have been grand—and they will do what I say now. Their tails are up and they tear into the Japs with full confidence that they can beat the hell out of them. It is what you might call very satisfying to say the least. Also that our score of dead Japs counted is now over 20,000. (Confidential.) Rain, rain, rain, mud, mud, mud, typhus, malaria, dysentery, exhaustion, rotting feet, body sores. If we are badly off, what about the Japs with little medical help and their supplies shut off? This has been a knockdown and drag-out affair. The physical conditions I speak of are worse with the British and Japs. Not nearly so bad with the Americans, and the Chinese are in excellent shape after seven months of it. We have taken good care of them, but even at that it is remarkable. I feel guilty about Mitch [Myitkyina] but we'll get it in due time.

With my experience, I should do well in the rackets in peacetime.

The damn snakes are beginning to appear. One got into the office and one tried to get into my tent. Now I look around before I put my bare feet on the floor and shake my shoes before I put them on.

JULY 22   Big news from Germany. Riots and what not, opposition to Nazis has broken out. Russkies are pouring on to Warsaw, and they must be in East Prussia.

JULY 26   Prisoner of war [from Myitkyina] says conditions [of Japs] very bad. Morale low, wounded kept in line, short rations—one quarter bowl of rice daily. About 400 left.

JULY 29 (3:00 to 4:00 p.m.) Flew with Randall all over Mitch and up and down river. Watched fire bombs, which were not very effective. Looks from air as if we should finish it off soon. Took off with Joe for Shaduzup at 5:45. Worked till I nearly fell asleep. Cleaned up papers and packed [to go to Ceylon].

Stilwell's three-week stay in Ceylon was a pleasant interlude in a year of struggle.

Stilwell was enormously amused by the pomp and ceremony of the great headquarters at Kandy. His first official act was to cancel the sequence of endless meetings that occupied the attention of the higher brass of headquarters. Thereafter he proceeded to relax, napping, reading, driving about the island.

Myitkyina had fallen by the time he had settled comfortably into his chair at Kandy and the campaign in north Burma had halted for the monsoon season. In Ceylon he received news of his promotion to the rank of four-star general of the United States Army, a dignity he shared at the time only with Generals Marshall, MacArthur, Eisenhower and Arnold. The Chinese situation disturbed him greatly— but Roosevelt had demanded that Chiang make Stilwell commander in chief of the Chinese Armies, and Patrick Hurley, the wealthy oilman from Oklahoma, was coming to China to conduct the delicate negotiations. Someone quipped that Vinegar Joe and Oilman Hurley might not mix any better than oil and vinegar—but Stilwell at the time was delighted with the news.

On Mountbatten's return, Stilwell flew to Delhi to greet Hurley, and together the party flew on to China.

AUGUST 1, [CEYLON] Saw Louis [Mountbatten] at 10:45. Eleven to 1:30 a cockeyed conference. They came to the conclusion that they had better get a directive somehow. They are just fumbling trying to guess what the Prime Minister [Churchill] wants. A dead giveaway on the function of Southeast Asia Command. Three p.m. a very sad G-2 meeting. Goodbye to the Supremo [Mountbatten].

AUGUST 2 British Broadcasting Company broadcast promotion [to full general]. Wires from Sultan and MacArthur, just the same as before, no thrill.

Saw Pownall [Lieutenant General] and told him to run the show. Went through the crap and beat it. P.m. to the Temple of the Tooth—no tooth.[13] And nothing to see. "Shopping" sad. Silver, and ebony elephants, saw the museum. Now I've done all the sights. Read, had a nap.

AUGUST 3 Office at 9:00, radios and stuff. Read, had a nap. 6:45 to Swiss hotel for cocktail party. Merrill was introducing me to Kandy society, mob of about 300. Good news from Myitkyina, big gains.

LETTER TO MRS. STILWELL "What though the tropic breezes blow soft o'er Ceylon's isle—

Where every prospect pleases, and only man is vile." Correct in every detail. Kandy is 2,000 feet up. Climate like Hawaii. Plenty of fruit. The views are beautiful. In contrast with north Burma, this is a paradise. Why am I talking about Ceylon? Mountbatten has left temporarily, and as heir to the throne, Little Willie, the Country Boy, had to come down and take over. This is a laugh. A goddam American in the driver's seat, etc., etc. I'm going to read and rest and get a lot of sleep. Read *Life in a Putty Knife Factory*. It's screwball but it's lovely. He comes right out with a lot of things I have always wanted to see in print. Also read *A Tree Grows in Brooklyn*.

AUGUST 4 Radio about Myitkyina—over at last. Thank God. Not a worry in the world this morning. For five minutes anyway.

AUGUST 5 Office, press conference. P.m. read. George Marshall radio on Hurley (oil and vinegar). O.K.'d it.

AUGUST 6 7:30 by car to Newara Eliya. This island is a park all the way; 48 miles up there. Tea and rubber all the way, one estate after the other. Everything trim and clean, waterfalls everywhere, deep and distant views. The air took me back to 1906 in Yellowstone, clean and bracing. Big cypress trees—a lake. What a place to bum in—crowd of Limeys though. We walked around and breathed it in, left at 1:00 after lunch along the road, and came back the long way. Easter lilies grow wild. Ceylon exceeds the advertising.

AUGUST 8, LETTER TO MRS. STILWELL Went up to Newara Eliya on Sunday. Limey resort, 7,000 feet up. This is some war. Eating papaya and avocados, sleeping, reading and sitting. I have abolished the "conferences" and have the chief of staff handle the rest. Everything is lovely and the Limeys just can't make it out.

AUGUST 13 MacArthur in a sweat over Chennault trying to bomb Manila.

AUGUST 15 Last night, BBC broadcast. "Headlines of the news." To wit: "A British patrol moving down the Tiddim Road has crossed the frontier of Burma," and right after it— "The Russians have isolated the German armies in the Baltic States." Colossal, Watson, colossal!

---

[18] One of Ceylon's much-advertised tourist spots is the temple where supposedly one of Buddha's teeth is enshrined.

AUGUST 22, LETTER TO MRS. STILWELL   The enclosed letter from the 12th Engineer Regiment is to my mind a gem of prose. "At the communique stating you have been promoted to be one of the very few four-star generals of the U.S. Army. Here the whole of this regiment renders you its warm congratulations and does believe there is nothing competent for expressing your consummate achievement in this theater which was taken for granted impossible except in Iliad." (Back up, Homer, and give me room. Move over, Hector—*I'll* dance with Helen.)

There is undisguised apprehension on the part of Louis's staff here on account of his impending return. I have let them do their work and canceled most of their bellyache meetings. Now they realize they must again face the daily blast of wind and paper, and they don't relish the idea. We almost had it on a common-sense basis.

AUGUST 23   Louis [Mountbatten] here tomorrow. Message from George Marshall: Chiang K'ai-shek through K'ung has AGREED to do it [i.e., appoint an American commander in chief] for Chinese Armies. Nelson [14] and Pat [Hurley] are leaving today. Copy of F.D.R. [message] to Peanut came in later. Sunbath, dead beat.

AUGUST 24   Got started at 8:30 for Colombo [to await Mountbatten's arrival]. In there at 11:00. Ordered crabs and went to the field. Estimated Time of Arrival now 1:30. Went to Mount Lavinia beach, and to White House for lunch. Back to Ratmalana [airport]. Estimated Time of Arrival now 3:30. Christ—went and got ice, picked up the crabs and went to zoo. Good selection of monkeys—one with a big red ass. One gibbon. Highly colored macaws. Back to the field. Finally came at 3:30. Fooled around and then I shoved. He was not at ease with me. Admirals Fraser and

Layton there. Back home at 6:30. Dumb day, but now I am all through with Colombo.

LETTER TO MRS. STILWELL   The situation in Europe looks good. I began to believe the crackup can come almost any time. Then with one war on our hands, maybe Mr. Churchill will allow Mr. Roosevelt to give me some help. (The presidential backbone seems to be stiffening with Hurley and Nelson coming over.) Help on the shoveling!

I went down to Colombo to welcome Mountbatten on his return. I went to the zoo first to look at the monkeys just to get in the mood. He was not at ease with me which is not surprising, because his trip had to do with an operation on his deputy's throat. Maybe the fourth star threw a monkey wrench into the machinery. At one time or another all the Best People have attempted to get the can attached, but have somehow slipped up on it—up to now—anyway. We finally got Mitch [Myitkyina]. It was a bitch of a fight and with the raw troops we had, full of anxiety, but we are sitting pretty now. What a bitter dose that was for the Limeys. They had said it was impossible so often and so vehemently that they just couldn't believe it was true. Satisfaction. The Chinese generally are all pepped up over the fight their soldiers have put up down here. The FIRST SUSTAINED OFFENSIVE IN CHINESE HISTORY AGAINST A FIRST-CLASS ENEMY.

AUGUST 25   Blah blah meeting with SAC [Mountbatten] telling how he put it over [in London]. 3:00 p.m., "G-2 meeting." Terrible. 3:45, commander in chief meeting till 5:00. One day—three meetings; net result—zero.

AUGUST 26   Office, no meetings! Just papers. P.m. partial sun bath and read A Bell for Adano.

14 Donald Nelson—wartime chief of the U.S. WPB.

Chiang K'ai-shek wants me to go up for "important conference."

AUGUST 28 Office—this and that. 11:45 meeting. Just crap. 3:00 p.m., G-2 meeting. Terrible. 3:30 SAC [supreme Allied commanders] meeting, more crap. On and on till 5:30 or later.

AUGUST 29 Last day in Ceylon. Papers all morning. 3:30 SAC meeting. Sad. Packed till midnight.

AUGUST 30 Up at 3:30, off at 7:40, Delhi at 6:00.

SEPTEMBER 4 Office, to airfield at 10:00 and met Hurley, Nelson, etc. Talked with Pat [Hurley] and Nelson till lunch and afterward till 4:30. [At] dinner more talk on Russia. (Mountbatten tried to ditch me at Cairo. F.D.R. said no. Pat says George [Marshall] is for me and realizes difficulties.)

SEPTEMBER 5 Up early and off at 9:00. Pat, Sultan, etc. Nelson to Agra in other plane. Chabua at 4:00.

SEPTEMBER 6 Off at 9:20 [across Hump] in C-54 with Hurley and Nelson. Over Kunming at noon, Pei Shih Yi [Chungking] at 2:00 and at the house at 3:00. All as usual, big mail. Hurley and Nelson in. Worked till 11:15.

Chapter 10

THESE NOTES, written over a period of months and found among General Stilwell's undated papers, help set the background for the developing conflict of 1944 that culminated in the Stilwell crisis.

CHIANG K'AI-SHEK I never heard Chiang K'ai-shek say a single thing that indicated gratitude to the President or to our country for the help we were extending to him. Invariably, when anything was promised, he would want more. Invariably, he would complain about the small amount of material that was being furnished. He would make comparisons between the huge amounts of Lend-Lease supplies going to Great Britain and Russia with the meager trickle going to China. He would complain that the Chinese had been fighting for six or seven years and yet we gave them practically nothing. It would of course have been undiplomatic to go into the nature of the military effort Chiang K'ai-shek had made since 1938. It was practically zero.

Whether or not he was grateful was a small matter. The regrettable part of it was that there was no quid pro quo. We did what we could, furnished what was available, without being allowed to first ask what he would do, etc. The result was that we were continuously on the defensive and he could obstruct and delay any of our plans without being penalized.

* * *

[I have] faith in Chinese soldiers and Chinese people: fundamentally great, democratic, misgoverned. No bars of caste or religion. . . . Honest, frugal, industrious, cheerful, independent, tolerant, friendly, courteous.

I judge Kuomintang and Kungchantang [Communist party] by what I saw:

[KMT] Corruption, neglect, chaos, economy, taxes, words and deeds. Hoarding, black market, trading with enemy.

Communist program . . . reduce taxes, rents, interest. Raise production, and standard of living. Participate in government. Practice what they preach.

* * *

CHINESE ARMY   In 1944, on paper, the Chinese Army consisted of 324 divisions, 60-odd brigades and 89 so-called guerrilla units of about 2,000 men each. This looks formidable on paper, till you go into it closely. Then you find:

1. That the average strength per division instead of 10,000 is not more than 5,000.
2. That the troops are unpaid, unfed, shot with sickness and malnutrition.

3. That equipment is old, inadequate, and unserviceable.
4. That training is nonexistent.
5. That the officers are jobholders.
6. That there is no artillery, transport, medical service, etc., etc.
7. That conscription is so-and-so.
8. That business is the principal occupation. How else live?

How would you start to make such an army effective?

* * *

RADIOS I DID NOT WRITE:

You don't have to join in singing "God Save the King," but you will at least stand up when the rest of them sing it.

I don't mind standing up. All I object to is (1) standing on my knees and (2) having my feet kicked out from under me when I do stand up.

* * *

Chiang K'ai-shek is confronted with an idea, and that defeats him. He is bewildered by the spread of Communist influence. He can't see that the mass of Chinese people welcome the Reds as being the only visible hope of relief from crushing taxation, the abuses of the Army and [the terror of] Tai Li's Gestapo. Under Chiang K'ai-shek they now begin to see what they may expect. Greed, corruption, favoritism, more taxes, a ruined currency, terrible waste of life, callous disregard of all the rights of men.

* * *

[An Undated Paper, on the dominant military doctrine of the Chinese Army.]

It wasn't just a question of recruiting, organizing and training an army. The big job was to change the fundamentally defensive attitude of the Chinese to an offensive attitude. They were fixed and set by long years of custom—Chiang K'ai-shek had made the defense his policy in the present war. He was going to trade "space for time," a very catchy way of saying he would never attack.

My own theory is that this predilection for the defensive wherever possible is based, not only on the long succession of Chinese failures when in contact with modern methods and weapons, but also to the fact that most Chinese are Taoists at heart. Taoism teaches nonresistance to outside forces; it is foolish to struggle against a general trend. Float with the stream and avoid trouble. If you struggle, you will only bruise yourself on the rocks or be stilled along the shore and you will get nowhere. I have seen the subconscious effects of this feeling in action. The Chinese commander hesitates to challenge fate. If he makes a decision to take positive action and it results badly, it is his fault for having tried to influence events. If he lets nature take its course, everything may come out all right, but if it does not, he cannot be blamed for what has occurred, since he did nothing to bring it about. A scapegoat is always being sought for, under conditions where repeated failures must be explained and the inevitable tendency is to avoid any chance of being picked. This attitude is general in the Chinese Army. There is an added reason—a Chinese command is the property of the commanding general: if he risks it, he risks an investment. A division reduced to the strength of a regiment by an attack cannot expect to be filled up at once to its former strength. The division commander thus becomes in effect a regimental commander, and such reduction is to be avoided at all hazards.

The Chinese were dominated by the idea that the Japs were so superior in training, armament, and equipment that it was not practicable to attack them. Chiang K'ai-shek has said on many occasions that a Chinese division did not have the fire-power of a Jap regiment, and that three Chinese divisions were not a match for one Jap division. Naturally, his commanders eagerly accepted this statement as full excuse for running away. A new spirit had to be built up. It was vitally necessary that the fresh contacts should be successful. If they were, we could gradually build up confidence —if not, it would be almost impossible to keep them on the offensive.

The Chinese had no confidence in themselves. We started out to give them some.

PHILOSOPHY AS APPLIED TO SUPPLY

Conversation with the second in command of the Xth war zone:

Q. "General Wang, now that the Japs have taken the salt mines in south Shansi doesn't that seriously affect your supply?"

A. "Oh, we've still got the salt in Yünnan to draw on."

Q. "Yes, but you have now lost the Tangku field, the Kiangsu field, and the Shansi field. Is there enough salt in Yünnan to supply the whole country?"

A. "Well, we won't have as much as we had before."

Q. "Then there's the matter of gasoline. What are you going to do about that?"

A. "Oh, we'll get along all right."

Q. "But you can't import any, and you don't produce any. As time goes on, you'll be in a bad fix. This matter of salt and gasoline supply is serious. Aren't you worried about it?"

A. "Oh, no, there's really nothing to worry about. Of course, without resupply, our stocks will get smaller and

smaller, but you don't seem to understand that as the
Japs occupy more and more of the country, the part left
to us will get smaller and smaller, and we won't need
so much salt and gasoline."

In time of war you have to take your allies as you find
them. We were fighting Germany to tear down the Nazi
system—one-party government, supported by the Gestapo
and headed by an unbalanced man with little education.
We had plenty to say against such a system. China, our ally,
was being run by a one-party government (the Kuomintang), supported by a Gestapo (Tai Li's organization) and
headed by an unbalanced man with little education. This
government, however, had the prestige of the possession of
power—it was opposing Japan, and its titular head had been
built up by propaganda in America out of all proportion to
his deserts and accomplishments. We had to back the existing regime in order to have any chance of getting China to
pull her weight. To change the structure during the emergency would have been next to impossible. All through the
Chinese machinery of government there are interlocking
ties of interest . . . family, financial, political, etc. No
man, no matter how efficient, can hope for a position of
authority on account of being the man best qualified for the
job: he simply must have other backing. To reform such a
system, it must be torn to pieces. You build a framework to
grow grapevines on: in the course of time, the vines grow all
over it, twisting in and out and around and pretty soon the
frame is so tightly held by the vines that if you start pulling
them out, you will tear the frames to pieces. We could not
risk it, we had to take the instrument as we found it and do
the best we could. But because it was expedient to back this
government to get action against Japan, it was not neces-

sarily advisable to endorse its methods and policies. We could have required some return for our help.

Chiang K'ai-shek made a great point of how badly the U.S.A. had neglected China, who had been fighting desperately for so long, while Lend-Lease materials had been poured into Great Britain and Russia by the billion. His case was that we owed him a great debt and that it was a crying shame that we didn't do more to discharge it. This attitude met with sympathy in the U.S. It was true that large quantities of Lend-Lease materials were going to Russia and Great Britain. It was also true that Russia and Great Britain, particularly Russia, were making good use of this material against Germany. It was also true that there was no possible way of delivering the goods to Chiang K'ai-shek unless he made an effort on his part to help break the blockade. It seemed reasonable to expect Great Britain to use the huge Indian Army for the purpose. The U.S. was fighting Germany in Europe, and Japan in the Pacific. She was supplying enormous quantities of munitions and food to all the Allies. Under the circumstances it seemed reasonable for somebody else to display a little energy in Burma.

To keep the show going, I had to overlook some of these incongruities and pretend, like the other players. If not, the critics would say it was a bum show, and we are very much afraid of the critics in our show.

[This paper was never finished.]

SOLUTION IN CHINA [Probably July, 1944]

The cure for China's trouble is the elimination of Chiang K'ai-shek. The only thing that keeps the country split is his fear of losing control. He hates the Reds and will not take any chances on giving them a toehold in the government. The result is that each side watches the other and neither gives a damn about the war [against Japan]. If this condition persists, China will have civil war immediately after Japan is out. If Russia enters the war before a united front is formed in China, the Reds, being immediately accessible, will naturally gravitate to Russia's influence and control. The condition will directly affect the relations between Russia and China, and therefore indirectly those between Russia and U.S.

If we do not take action, our prestige in China will suffer seriously. China will contribute nothing to our effort against Japan, and the seeds will be planted for chaos in China after the war.

Chapter 11

THE SUMMER OF 1944 fed China the final portion of the long war's bitterness. Chungking, the capital, reeked of corruption, and Chungking's officials were drenched in cynicism.

In the rear, hunger ravaged the countless villages of the nation, while the peasants twisted to evade the grain tax and conscription. The ancient hostilities of the Kuomintang and Communist party split the nation in two to prevent the mobilization of fresh energy or effort.

At the front, the armies starved and the soldiers sickened and died. The Japanese, alarmed by the depredations of American sea-raiding planes, had launched a massive campaign—their last great offensive in history—to destroy the East China bases that launched the American planes. As the offensive unfolded through the hot summer months it cut across all of East China, severing Chiang K'ai-shek's China almost in two, threatening to bring about the total collapse of the Chungking government. By September, the Japanese were approaching Kweilin, the greatest American military center in East China. This background of disaster

323

in the field hung as a dark backdrop on the stage of September's negotiations.

American policy, so closely twined with China in Asia, could not help sharing a sense of emergency. Nor, considering our own vast interests in the continuing disaster in East China, could America refrain from insisting on immediate corrective steps. The only bright spot in the pattern of war in Asia at the moment was the campaign General Stilwell had conducted personally in North Burma. There, Chinese troops, supplied and led by Americans, divorced from the conspiracy and corruption of their General Staff at Chungking, had written a spectacular scroll of success. The United States, viewing the situation in China, contrasting it with the situation in Burma, decided that Stilwell's nominal role as Chiang's chief of staff in China was an ineffective one. It demanded that Stilwell be given direct field command over Chinese troops on the China front, similar to those he had possessed in Burma and used so effectively.

Chiang had consented to this in principle during the summer; and the diplomatic negotiations to work out details were confided to Donald Nelson and Patrick J. Hurley. Nelson was to offer the Chinese vastly increased quantities of Lend-Lease materials and discuss huge postwar aid in reconstruction. Hurley was charged with binding the Chinese government to certain hard-and-fast commitments: the granting to Stilwell of direct command functions; an agreement that American Lend-Lease war materials be distributed as Stilwell directed for war uses; an agreement that Stilwell be permitted to bring the Communists under his joint command for use against the Japanese.

It was impossible at this point to evade the issue of civil war in China. The Communists were fighting valiantly against the Japanese in North China. But, at the same time, an undeclared civil war continued between the Communists and Chiang K'ai-shek. The blockade line between Communists and government troops in North China absorbed the energies of about 200,000 of the best government troops and perhaps 50,000 Communist troops—a tremendous waste of manpower. Stilwell insisted that all Chinese troops everywhere be moved to the front, that political disputes be settled by political means. The Communists declared that they were willing to submerge their differences and place their troops at Stilwell's personal command, if Chiang would do the same for all Nationalist troops in China. To Stilwell, charged with defeating the Japanese on the mainland, preparing for an eventual American landing in North China where Communist help might be vital, the unity of all Chinese parties seemed to be essential. Such a unity, moreover, sealed by common war against a common enemy, would bring China through to peace as a mighty unified nation, able to face and repel all foreign enemies with her own resources.

Early in September Stilwell accompanied Nelson and Hurley from Delhi to Chungking to assist in the negotiations that were to determine his fate.

[UNDATED NOTES] Hurley and Nelson arrive full of P. and V. They are going to pound the table and demand:
1. Real unification in China. 2. Unification of command. Then and only then will they talk about what the U.S. will do for China economically.

It is one thing to make a brief call on Chiang K'ai-shek, when he is on his good behavior, receive his assurances that he is liberal minded, admires the U.S., and is going to give full participation to the people in a democratic government. It is another to make him take *action* along these lines. (After concessions that give him a blank check and tie me up.)

SEPTEMBER 7   The G-mo calls. Date at 9:30, Hurley and Nelson at 11:00. Why me, ahead of them? Love feast. Peanut went right into it, and told me that up to now my work had been 100 per cent military—now, AS COMMANDER OF THE CHINESE ARMY, it would be 60 per cent military and 40 per cent political.

[He] said that if I used the Reds, they would have to acknowledge the authority of the National Military Council. He would advise me from time to time. He wanted no *k'o ch'i* [politenesses] between us. He had full confidence in me. Kidded about my saying Chinese commanders were no good—asked about commanders and divisions in Burma.

Hurley and Nelson saw him at 11:00.

LETTER TO MRS. STILWELL   I brought Bill Bergin along to help fight the gloom. I oscillate from Glamour Boy [Mountbatten] to Wonder Man [Chiang K'ai-shek] and I don't know which is worse. My arrival here has reduced my temperature so far that I expect to have fallen arches by morning.

SEPTEMBER 8   G-mo wants us to go to Bhamo and relieve Lungling.[1]

The Burma campaign has sure changed the attitude of these dodos. No patronizing airs any more.

Pat [Hurley] saw T. V. at 5:00; T. V. is climbing back.

He tried to get a lot of conditions agreed to. And then let the cat out of the bag: The G-mo *must* control Lend-Lease. Pat told him to write down "Disagreed" in capital letters. We can't even control the stuff we make ourselves. What a nerve. That's what the G-mo is after—just a blank check. Now we come to the showdown.

SEPTEMBER 9 Disaster approaching at Kweilin, nothing to stop the Japs—about 50,000 demoralized Chinese in the area against nine Jap divisions. Chinese have had no replacements. Jap units are filled up. It's a mess and of course all they think of is what we can give them. Sun Fo wants us to fly in American troops. Another wants weapons. What they ought to do is shoot the G-mo and Ho and the rest of the gang.

Newsboys in for an hour. G-mo's party at 8:00. These gloomy gatherings are more funereal than festive and endured rather than enjoyed.

Pat [Hurley] much impressed with the antics of the Peanut, T. V., etc., and Nelson discussing dams on the Yangtze, area that might be irrigated, cost of plant, cost per kilowatt, time to amortize cost, etc. Hour after hour, with no thought of the war. Crisis in Kwangsi, several hundreds of thousands of men lost. Crisis at Lungling. (Never mind: let's talk about money. That's more fun.)

SEPTEMBER 10 Covell in. He and I and Pat and Sultan crashed in on Ho [Ying-ch'in] at 11:00. He was expecting me alone. I attacked at once and got him on the spot. He

---

[1] The X force in north Burma, tired from the long summer fight, were consolidating at Myitkyina. Stilwell wanted them to rest and recuperate before going on. The Generalissimo, on the other hand, was insisting that they set forth immediately to attack Bhamo, ninety miles farther through the jungle, to divert the Japanese from Lungling, which the Yoke force were attacking. Stilwell refused.

was at a decided disadvantage all through the session. Stalled and floundered. He promised 10,000 [replacements] to Dorn and I gave him some Canadian Bren [guns].

Pat says all Allies are as bad or worse than Chinese. The "Beggar Nations"—Russia gave Persia tanks and rifles, while we were busting ourselves to give them to Russia! All on Lend-Lease. Christ again. The Limey reverse Lend-Lease is a racket. They refuse cost figures, and are purposely gumming up the accounts so the snarl can never be untangled.

LETTER TO MRS. STILWELL   Hope the tea gown was successful and you're not being just polite. To hell with being polite: I am so fed up with smiling at rattlesnakes that I can be decent to friends. I put the bug on the war minister and had him floundering and hanging on the rope. We are "conferring" and dickering and it's slow work.

SEPTEMBER 12   Chiang K'ai-shek agrees to appoint Joseph W. Stilwell [as commander in chief of all Chinese ground forces] and give him his "full confidence." Dickering proceeds.

T. V. is back in the game.[2] Hurley has agenda [for negotiations] ready, so maybe we can get down to cases now. Papers again.

Pat in in p.m. Rather discouraged—G-mo very difficult, says he must control Lend-Lease and that I have more real control in China than he has. Wants to dicker about powers for me. "Thinking" about a diagram to show my authority.

Bad news from Timberman [in East China]. Collapse. Decided to go to Kweilin and see about it.

Urgent crises were making themselves felt both in East China and in the Salween campaign of the Yoke force.

In East China, the Japanese had broken through the Chuanhsien pass, the last great natural defense barrier above the lowlands of Kwangsi. Their breakthrough left the American air net about Kweilin in Kwangsi almost defenseless, for the Chinese armies in the East were now disorganized units. It fell to Stilwell to order the preventive demolition of these installations while at the same time drawing up plans for their last-ditch defense.

On the Salween, the crisis was a crisis of opportunity. The Yoke force, commanded by Dorn, had crossed the Salween River in bitter fighting, struggling over 11,000-foot mountain ranges toward a junction with the X force in North Burma. They were embattled on the outskirts of Lungling, the lynchpin of the Japanese defenses. Dorn needed reinforcements desperately for the last drive.

All the military problems of China seemed to come to a confluence. The Generalissimo wished to cancel the Yoke campaign at once without pressing the Lungling advantage, and use its men and materials to shore up the East China front. He would continue, he said, only if Stilwell immediately urged an all-out advance by the Chinese forces in Burma to relieve the Yoke men. Stilwell felt that the twenty divisions of Chiang's troops held useless in a blockade of the Communist rear areas should be the main source of strength for bolstering the East China front.

SEPTEMBER 14, KWEILIN   [Arrived] noon. Sent for Chang Fa-kwei [Chinese commander of Kwangsi defenses]. He came out; he says plan [is] to fight in Kweilin due to orders of G-mo, against his judgment. Three divisions in town, two of Thirty-sixth Army, one of Forty-sixth Army. Only two

² T. V. had been in disfavor with Chiang K'ai-shek ever since the late fall of 1943. He had been stripped of most of his powers, and only with the arrival of Nelson and Hurley was he called back to Chiang's council.

regiments left at Liuchow, and one a student regiment; nothing else available except Ninety-third Army of two divisions now retiring [from north]. G-mo said [Chinese could hold] three months at Chuanhsien,[3] actually three days.

Chang [Fa-kwei] says he can hold Kweilin for two months, cannot protect airfield except with Ninety-third Army, which is not reliable. Remnants of Thirty-seventh Army presumably moving toward Kweilin. Chang cannot estimate strength or time of arrival; no Jap tanks yet. Chang does not know location of Ninety-seventh Army.

Junk [American base equipment] all out of Kweilin today. Demolition on fields tonight; all our forward groups coming out.

Shoved off at 1:30, Kunming at 4:30.

Middleton says 200th Division [on Salween front] had a battalion of nine French 75s hidden away, with 4,000 rounds of ammunition. Five of these guns went to the Salween— the damned fools had concealed the existence of these guns. Middleton also says no fillers [replacements] have reached any unit west of the Salween. Grabbed off by Fifth Army and nondescript bureau organizations along the road. Bed at nine.

SEPTEMBER 15   Off at 8:10 a.m. Chennault reports Chou Chih-jou [chief of Chinese Air Force] as not co-operating, refused gas to United States planes from common stock. Maybe they are learning at last in the Fourteenth Air Force.

Chungking. G-mo calling for me. Took Hurley down at 12:00; one and a half hours of crap and nonsense. Wants to withdraw from Lungling, the crazy little bastard. So either X [4] attacks in one week or he pulls out. Usual cockeyed reasons and idiotic tactical and strategic conceptions. He is impossible.

SEPTEMBER 16 The G-mo insists on control of Lend-Lease.[5] Our stuff, that we are giving him. T. V. says we must remember the "dignity" of a great nation, which would be "affronted" if I controlled the distribution. Pat [Hurley] told him "Horsefeathers." "Remember, Dr. Soong, that is *our* property. We made it and we own it, and we can give it to whom we please." (We must not look, while the customer puts his hand in our cash register, for fear we will offend his "dignity.") Pat said there were 130 million Americans whose dignity also entered the case, as well as the "dignity" of their children and their children's children, who would have to pay the bill. Hooray for Pat! (If the G-mo controls distribution, I am sunk. The Reds will get nothing. Only the G-mo's henchmen will be supplied, and my troops [the Yoke force] will suck the hind tit.)

(4:00 p.m.) Plain talk with T.V. Soong, all about the situation. He is appalled at gap between our conception of field commander and the G-mo's. I proposed Ch'en Ch'eng for minister of war. Pai Chung-hsi as chief of staff. Gave T. V. the works in plain words. I do not want the God-awful job, but if I take it I must have full authority. Two-hour bellyache.

SEPTEMBER 17, THE MANURE PILE: LETTER TO MRS. STILWELL We are in the midst of a battle with the Peanut, and it is wearing us out. Crises are arising in quick succession here and there; there is disaster in Hunan and Kwangsi: Dorn [in command on the Salween] is screaming for help:

[3] Chuanhsien was the major Chinese defense line, seventy miles north of Kweilin.
[4] The X force—the Chinese Army in north Burma.
[5] Control here meant the Generalissimo's right to use Lend-Lease supplies at his own discretion within China; as versus the Stilwell concept that Lend-Lease be used for strategic units and tasks commonly agreed on.

and hell to pay generally. Hell has been to pay before so I guess we can take it again. You may be interested to know that everything is turning out exactly as I told them it would in May, 1943, when I was the Voice of One Howling in the Wilderness and when I was voted the Horse's-Neck-Most-Likely-to-Succeed-in-that-Role. I don't know if the Knowit-alls have learned their lesson or not, but even if they have it has been an expensive experiment for me. A year and a half lost. In the so-called campaign for Changsha, Hengyang and Kweilin, the Peanut insisted on conducting operations by remote control and by intuition as usual, with catastrophic results. The enormity of his stupidity is shown by the fact that he thinks it was a pretty good show, considering. Considering what? I don't know. They throw away 300,000 men in Hunan [East China] without batting an eye and I break my back trying to get 10,000 to replace battle casualties [in the Burma campaign]. Co-operation in capital letters. Why can't sudden death for once strike in the proper place. It would really be funny if it weren't so tragic. The picture of this little rattlesnake being backed up by a great democracy, and showing his backside in everything he says and does, would convulse you if you could get rid of your gall bladder. But to have to sit there and be dignified, instead of bursting into guffaws, is too much to ask for the pay I get. What will the American people say when they finally learn the truth?

I see that the Limeys are going to rush to our rescue in the Pacific. Like hell. They are going to continue this fight with their mouths. Four or five old battleships will appear and about ten RAF planes will go to Australia but in twenty years the schoolbooks will be talking about "shoulder to shoulder" and "the Empire struck with all its might against the common enemy" and all that crap. The idea, of course, is to horn in at Hongkong again, and our Booby is sucked in.

SEPTEMBER 18 Long talk with ———.[6] He knows about [American] command proposal. He came clean on G-mo and his cockeyed handling of [East China] situation; with phone [from the front] to Chungking, [he says] command is impossible. I clamped down on handouts, told him, in view of rotten performance, all stuff had been wasted. Artillery improperly used, proposed defense plan stupid. He agreed. Suggested I get after Peanut. Cat came out of the bag. G-mo's plan: "Hold for two months at Kweilin till the Americans can get a decision in the Pacific." There you are —coast, boys.

SEPTEMBER 19 Mark this day in red on the calendar of life. At long, at very long last, F.D.R. has finally spoken plain words, and plenty of them, with a firecracker in every sentence.[7] "Get busy or else." A hot firecracker. I handed this bundle of paprika to the Peanut and then sank back with a sigh. The harpoon hit the little bugger right in the solar plexus, and went right through him. It was a clean hit, but beyond turning green and losing the power of speech, he did not bat an eye. He just said to me, "I understand." And sat in silence, jiggling one foot. We are now a long way from the "tribal chieftain" bawling out. *Two long years lost*, but at least F.D.R.'s eyes have been opened and he has thrown a good hefty punch.

I came home. Pretty sight crossing the river: lights all on in Chungking.

SEPTEMBER 21, LETTER TO MRS. STILWELL A lot of mail in but nothing but junk. I throw it at Carl. The only mail I

[6] A Chinese general.
[7] On this day a telegram arrived at U.S. Army Headquarters, from Franklin D. Roosevelt for Chiang K'ai-shek; General Stilwell was instructed to deliver it personally. Its precise text has never been revealed. But it was the sharpest worded American demand for reform and action on the part of the Chinese government that the war had evoked.

want to see has the Carmel postmark. It has taken two and
a half years for the Big Boys to see the light, but it dawned
finally and I played the avenging angel.

> I've waited long for vengeance—
> At last I've had my chance.
> I've looked the Peanut in the eye
> And kicked him in the pants.
>
> The old harpoon was ready
> With aim and timing true,
> I sank it to the handle,
> And stung him through and through.
>
> The little bastard shivered,
> And lost the power of speech.
> His face turned green and quivered
> As he struggled not to screech.
>
> For all my weary battles,
> For all my hours of woe,
> At last I've had my innings
> And laid the Peanut low.
>
> I know I've still to suffer,
> And run a weary race,
> But oh! the blessed pleasure!
> I've wrecked the Peanut's face.

"Rejoice with me and be exceeding glad, for lo! we have
prevailed over the Philistine and bowed his head in the dust,
and his heart is heavy."

The dope is that after I left the screaming [Chiang's]
began and lasted into the night.

SEPTEMBER 22 Bad news from Salween. Further attacks [by Chinese on Lungling] stopped by Chungking till X [in India] and British move. The Peanut again. Japs on move toward Kweilin again.

SEPTEMBER 23 Ho took me inside for very private talk; Peanut has told him nothing [about progress of negotiations]. He was hot for dope, I gave him general terms. Then he said that in his opinion it was the Lend-Lease angle that was holding things up. I believe Ho is right, the Peanut's face aches; Russia and Great Britain have no strings on them [in using Lend-Lease]. He has and it hurts him.

Decided to try and break the deadlock, showed Pat my agenda and he leaped at it: "This will knock the persimmons off the tree."

SEPTEMBER 24 Madame Sun [Yat-sen] wants me to represent China at the Peace Conference. Says I would do more for China than the Chinese. That I have a reputation among the Chinese people for standing up for them. The Burma campaign made them feel respectable again.

LETTER TO MRS. STILWELL Just after I squawked, two letters came from you and one from Ben. Nance is right—if you have time to think it's bad. The mills of the gods grind slowly. It takes the snappy chief executive of this unhappy land an average of one month to come to a decision which any child could make in five minutes. The fact that his house is on fire doesn't seem to worry him at all, and he goes merrily on slapping his best—and only—friends in the face and expecting them to like it. Well, our score is no longer zero. He has at last had one resounding kick in the pants that nearly brought on apoplexy. Even the dumb stooges around him are worried about his antics, and their changed attitude toward me is interesting. Now they get me out in the back room and get down to cases. We could go to town but for the blight at the top. I am sitting around waiting for the Peanut to pronounce the Oracle.

Oh, Oh, the Oracle has spoken and of all the cockeyed performances. Got to go to work now and write radios.

SEPTEMBER 25 Pat in with bad news. The Peanut reversed the field yesterday. Pat put in hours talking but you might just as well talk to a blank wall. The Peanut lied about me and made astounding statements to effect that I was bucking him. I "peremptorily refused" to make a feint from Mitch [Myitkyina] on Bhamo. No other claim; said he wouldn't specify further. His face is gone over the President's message and he is afraid of my influence in the Army. Had the nerve to say he would have a mutiny on his hands!

Pat saw him again at 4:00 p.m. More walla-walla. At 9:30 the "aide memoire" came in. "Throw out General Stilwell. He's a nonco-operative s.o.b. He has broken his promises. General Stilwell has more power in China than I have." Etc., etc.

N.B. The decision was made after I handed him the President's message. That, according to the Peanut, made him my subordinate. It was then impossible for him to direct me. T. V. undoubtedly wrote the thing, which was just a personal attack on me.

SEPTEMBER 26 Two years, eight months of struggle and then a slap in the puss as reward. Jap broadcast said I was plotting to oust Chiang K'ai-shek and make myself czar of China. Clever. Just what would make Chiang K'ai-shek suspicious. (Or was it manufactured in Chungking to make his action plausible?)

Saw Pat at 3:00. Nothing new there. Got radio off to George [Marshall] giving him the lowdown. [Congressman] Judd, Hurley and McNally for dinner. —— here. Kept him for dinner and movie. He blames war minister [Ho Ying-ch'in] for twenty million deaths. Judd kept the floor against Pat and that's going some. I went to sleep.

SEPTEMBER 27 Dubbed all day. Hot. Played records.

SEPTEMBER 28 —— saw Lin Wei. He does not know [about Chiang's demand for Stilwell's relief]. Thinks the trouble is on account of the Reds. Thinks that Peanut believes I insist on arming them and that if I drop it, he will agree on other points: the Peanut has not told them about the aide memoire. No word from Washington yet. Pat says G-mo indicated conciliatory attitude toward Reds. K. C. Wu's in. Movie.

SEPTEMBER 28 Ho Ying-ch'in has [been given] Chinese and English versions [of the following]:

1. The suggestion for using the Communist troops was raised because it seemed advisable to make use of any and all military assets in this crisis. I was not insisting on the use of the Communists as a condition for agreement.

2. The matter of using the Communists can be dropped, and we can proceed advantageously with our other plans:

Build up the Ledo force. Train and equip the Yoke divisions not now in action. Withdraw the Yoke force as soon as possible, build it up, train and equip it. Meanwhile start in on the Kweiyang area, to organize a nucleus of the Z force from the units that can be salvaged from South China.

This plan can be started at once. It will give us the security we want. It will also give us the nucleus of a force sufficient to take the offensive within six months.

SEPTEMBER 29 Saw Pat [Hurley]. T. V. had been there, close to nervous prostration. T. V. asked if I had gotten the

President to send the ultimatum. Pat refused to ask me. A-ha! Maybe this is the lowdown. It fits in. The G-mo thinks I had it done and then tore his face off with it. So he has to tear me down. I wired George about this. The delay in answering the G-mo's blast has them worried sick. But the G-mo has not informed anybody, so perhaps he is holding on to an out for himself.

SEPTEMBER 30   Nothing new. Told Pat to throw the hooks into T. V. about the squawk I may make over this. They are frothing over Churchill's speech, boosting Louis [Mountbatten] and putting the hard word on us. T. V. is getting out an answer. Office in a.m. Isaacs [8] in to get dope.

Pat says in November, '43, Louis asked him why he didn't get me out of here.

LETTER TO MRS. STILWELL   Tomorrow is October. 1944 is three-quarters gone and we are still floundering around with a gang of morons who can't see beyond their noses. You can see by the papers what is happening in South China. The pity of that is that it could all have been avoided if certain men of genius and amateur strategists had kept their hands off. Right now we don't know where we are, and the whole structure is tottering in the breeze. There may possibly [be] a loud bang out here before you get this and if you look carefully in the debris which will be flying through the air you may see yours truly with his pants blown entirely off.

Did you see Churchill's speech about Louis's Great Campaign in Burma? They apparently feel it necessary to pump a little prestige into him. Today's news is that Eden announced that the "beloved" commander of the South East Asia Command was in London. He didn't tell me he was going so I suppose there is more skulduggery afoot. One more sniper makes little difference: sooner or later they'll slip it over on me and have it their way. I'm getting damn tired of it, however, and someday I'm liable to open my big mouth and let out a resounding squawk. I asked Hurley about Franklin D. Roosevelt and he said that he had undoubtedly been sick, but he didn't know how seriously.

At this point, a wry twist was given the negotiations. H. H. K'ung, the Generalissimo's brother-in-law, was then in Washington and had been invited to a dinner party at which he met Harry Hopkins. According to K'ung, Hopkins had informed him that if the Generalissimo insisted on Stilwell's recall Roosevelt would yield to the request and send another American to command the Chinese Armies. The conversation has been in dispute, but whatever its actual import, K'ung cabled this tidbit to Chungking. The effect of this message on the charged political atmosphere of the Chinese capital was electric.

OCTOBER 1   Pat in with news of K'ung to G-mo. F.D.R. "delighted" that U.S. commander will be appointed, and other point [Stilwell's appointment] is a matter of sovereignty. F.D.R. proceeds to cut my throat and throw me out. Pat feels very low about it. I don't. They just can't hurt me. I've done my best and stood up for American interests. To hell with them.

LETTER TO MRS. STILWELL   It looks very much as though they had gotten me at last. The Peanut has gone off his rocker and Roosevelt has apparently let me down completely. If old softy gives in on this, as he apparently has, the Peanut will be out of control from now on. A proper fizzle. My conscience is clear. I have carried out my orders. I have no regrets. Except to see the U.S.A. sold down the river.

⁶ Harold Isaacs, *Newsweek* correspondent.

So be ready, in case the news isn't out sooner, to have me thrown out on the garbage pile. At least, I'll probably get home and tell you all about it. God help the next man. It hasn't happened yet, but it is a thousand to one that it will soon.

OCTOBER 2   Caught up on correspondence at last. Read and wrote.

OCTOBER 3   Told Bergin yesterday to stop uneasiness about preparations. He wants to go along. Bummed. Wrote adiós radios. All caught up on correspondence.

Gauss told Hurley that at meeting of the [Kuomintang] Central Executive Committee G-mo said he would refuse demands of U.S.; that I must go, that he would not appoint an American commander; that Nelson had promised him control of Lend-Lease. G-mo said I had refused to obey his orders to move on Bhamo after Myitkyina and I had to go.

[UNDATED]   Chiang K'ai-shek is the head of a one-party government supported by a Gestapo and a party secret service. He is now organizing an S.S. of 100,000 members.

[He] hates the so-called Communists. He intends to crush them by keeping any munitions furnished him and by occupying their territory as the Japs retire.

[He] will not make an effort to fight seriously. He wants to finish the war coasting, with a big supply of material, so as to perpetuate his regime. He has blocked us for three years and will continue to do so. He has failed to keep his agreements.

[He] has spoken contemptuously of American efforts and has never said one word to express gratitude for our help, except in one message to the President, in which he attacked me.

[He] is responsible for major disasters of the war. Nan-

king, Lan Fang. Changsha and Hengyang. Kweilin and
Liuchow. Red blockade.

But [he] is the titular head of China and has marked me
as *persona non grata*.

Therefore I cannot operate in the China theater while he
is in power—unless it is made clear to him that I was not
responsible for the September 19 note, and that the U.S.
will pull out unless he will play ball.

Ignored, insulted, double-crossed, delayed, obstructed for
three years. Orders to [my] subordinates during operations. False charges of disobedience and nonco-operation.
Constant attempts to put the screw on U.S. Use our air
force. Borrow our money. Refuse us men for the equipment we hauled. Attempts to get the munitions at Ichang
and Sian, and let Y [force] and Z [force] starve.

OCTOBER 4 Merrill in last night [from Washington].
Brought candy and cakes. Photos from home.

War Department is with me apparently, but this theater
is written off and nothing expected from us. No [Amer-
ican] troops will be sent. Stiffening attitude toward the
Peanut, including President. No decision on splitting theater. One day yes, next day no. In general, nothing new.
Japan [to go] down eighteen months after Germany.

OCTOBER 6 Friday. Shoved off for Mitch [Myitkyina] to
see 475th battalion. And of course Sultan had the message as I landed. "Important communication from Washington." It's always that way. So I had to work all night
and start back at 3:30 a.m. Saturday.

OCTOBER 7 Kunming at 7:30. Off at once. In at 10:15.
Bergin there with "important" message. The message was
rather encouraging. Not at all like the crap H. H. K'ung

has been sending. F.D.R. "surprised" and "regretful" at G-mo's "reversal" on command. Drops a hint about Fourteenth Air Force and Hurley. Says situation on ground has deteriorated so badly that now it wouldn't do to put an American in over-all command. Then insists that Japs will interrupt ferry [the Hump airline] unless I retain command of X force and in addition get Yünnan province. With supply and fillers from Chungking. Then puts a stiff one on the end. "Consequences of pulling Stilwell out of Burma battle might be far more serious than Generalissimo apparently realizes." (Agrees to put me out as chief of staff. Sultan to control Hump tonnage. Lend-Lease to be divorced from my control.) It might have been a soft capitulation.

OCTOBER 8, LETTER TO MRS. STILWELL   After waiting for weeks for a certain message, [Frank] Merrill and I hopped off on Friday for Mitch [Myitkyina]. As I got off the plane at 4:00 p.m. I was handed a radio. "Important message from Washington." It always happens that way. Talked to the troops, etc., including Sultan until 2:00 a.m. Back to Mitch in a deluge, went over plans with Sultan, met the plane at 4:00 a.m. and back in Chungking at 10:15 a.m. Message important but needn't have broken our backs over it. It was much stronger than I expected and maybe Ole Pap won't get tossed out on the pile, with the other garbage. We are not yet completely sold down the river. Routed out of bed by the boy at 1:30 a.m.—an air alert—half asleep I leaped out and made a crash landing. One leg was sound asleep and I fell down twice before I woke up enough to realize what I was doing. Stood around awhile and went back to bed. Japs went on to Chengtu and we all felt silly.

OCTOBER 9   Pat [Hurley] coming at noon, but T. V. went there and they both went to see the G-mo. Now what's up?

Answer: Nothin'. Pat came and acknowledged that all he'd done was to keep Chiang K'ai-shek from sending a bum answer. He got them to finally send a message that can't be handled well. Some diplomat. So we're sunk.

I tell George Marshall that the case is hopeless and give him the real issue. "Is China to make an effort?" Suggestion of a local combined staff as a solution.

Meanwhile Nelson goes home after promising the Chinese God knows what, and convinced that Chiang K'ai-shek is a great man who should under no circumstances be spoken to sharply.

OCTOBER 10   Office. P.m. McNally in with Hurley's come-down message to F.D.R., cutting my throat with a dull knife. Got off our proposal for joint policy board. Pat in— I gave him my slant and he pulled a few of the barbs out of his message.

OCTOBER 12   No word from Washington.

OCTOBER 13   Sitting. Waiting. Twiddling our thumbs. Peanut still on a High Horse. Some indications F.D.R. will get tough but I don't trust politicians. Valuable time is lost and nothing done. Today is Friday the 13th. I was about to shove off for down south and the weather stopped me.

OCTOBER 14   Off for Liuchow at 9:30.[9] Went over plan of concentration and attack. All fairly optimistic. Shoved off for Chengtu at 5:00.

OCTOBER 15   Cold and sore throat. Poor sleeping. Back to Chungking.

[9] The Chinese were gathering forces for a last defensive stand in east China at Liuchow and Kweilin. The U.S. Air Force was flying supplies to the last airfield open at Kweilin, and Stilwell hoped that he might persuade the Chinese to a last counterattack.

Hurley convinced that he has failed and accepts defeat on the command question. Then he gets excited about the Communists, seeing a chance to make a noise by "unifying" the Chinese war effort.

OCTOBER 16 Saw Teddy White and Atkinson [10] and told them some home truths.

OCTOBER 17, LETTER TO MRS. STILWELL We are in the doldrums for fair, just sitting and waiting for the Big Boys to make a decision. If a military commander took two months to make a decision, he would be drawn and quartered, skinned, hung, burned at the stake and otherwise suitably disciplined. But any goddam politician can horn in and keep the war dangling indefinitely. I am in the dark about the attitude our people are taking. But whatever the reason we are the stepchildren of World War II. (Election coming up.) I am getting sour enough about this pusillanimous proceeding to warrant being called Vinegar Joe. Japs announcing they have sunk half our Navy so evidently they have been hurt. The Peanut sits on his hands and watches with great glee the fool Americans who actually get out and fight. This is not a letter, I am just scribbling to keep from biting the radiator.

OCTOBER 17 To date only one radio from George Marshall giving gist of F.D.R. reply (October 5) to G-mo's first blast. (Serious consequences.) No word of any kind covering policy. President probably will not act without George Marshall's advice and George Marshall may be in France. Also election is coming and the whole thing may be held over.

[LATER] Hurley gets radio from F.D.R. telling him to ask Chiang K'ai-shek for his three names.[11] ("Remember I have not yet come to a decision—I want to see how his mind works.")

[LATER]   G-mo suggests Eisenhower, Handy and Patch. I suspect F.D.R. of delaying till after elections. Believe his mind is made up. Last radio to Hurley went via Navy. First time Hurley has failed to show it to me. The thing begins to stink badly. John Davies arrived. I enlightened him. Hurley in for dinner and movies.

OCTOBER 18   Thirty-fourth [Wedding] Anniversary. Bergin had radio from Win [Mrs. Stilwell] for me at breakfast. Decorated the air boys at office. T. V. says G-mo will be adamant in getting rid of me. A hell of an anniversary. Raining.

OCTOBER 19   THE AX FALLS. Radio from George Marshall. I am "recalled." Sultan in temporary command. Wedemeyer to command U.S. troops in China. CBI to split.

So F.D.R. has quit. Everybody is horrified about Washington.

Told White and Atkinson. They also were horrified and disgusted. Atkinson going home to blow the works. Did some packing. Hurley feels very badly. Told me he had lost me the command. Sees his mistakes now—too late. Says Peanut accepts Wedemeyer. Everything will now be lovely.

LETTER TO MRS. STILWELL   (The day after our Anniversary.) The ax has fallen and I'll be on my way to see you within a few days. The politicians are in full command, so this kind of monkey business is to be expected. Some of the

---

[10] Brooks Atkinson of *New York Times.*

[11] Roosevelt asked Chiang to suggest the names of three American generals whom he, Chiang, would be willing to accept as a replacement for Stilwell.

boys here were confident that F.D.R. would stand up to the
Peanut. I felt from the start that he would sell out. "The
war is more important than the individual," etc.

So now I am hanging up my shovel and bidding farewell
to as merry a nest of gangsters as you'll meet in a long day's
march. I have to go to Washington, of course, but I think
George will turn me loose promptly.

OCTOBER 20 Rush and hurry. Adiós radios. Brooks [Atkin-
son] and White in. Teddy White has written a last article.
Hurley in with "roses." The Peanut offers me *China's highest decoration*. Told him to stick it up his ——[12] Saw Madame Sun Yat-sen. She cried and was generally broken up.

5:00 p.m. date with Generalissimo. Lin Wei came, also
Hurley. T. V. interpreted.

Peanut said he regretted all this very much; I had done
a great deal for China training troops—leading them—etc.,
etc. *It was only because of the difference in our make-ups
that he was asking for my relief*. Hoped I would correspond
with him and continue to be China's friend. Asked about
personnel—who were most trusty of the Americans, and
what good Chinese prospects there were. Asked for criticisms and suggestions about organization, particularly in
higher echelons. Asked about situation in Liuchow. Surprised I had gone down. He said I was to continue in command in Burma till President made decision. I told him
whatever he thought of me, to remember my motive was
only China's good. Gave him the old *"Tsui Ho Sheng Li"* [13]
and beat it. The G-mo even came to the door.

Back to No. 3 at 5:45. Staff all there. Met them all and
they beat it. A dinner for several Chinese.

OCTOBER 21 Called on Gauss (he is going to resign).
Said goodbye to Hurley. Twenty minutes of blah. Called

on Ho Ying-ch'in—also blah. Said adiós to the staff at 2:00 and shoved off at 2:30. Rough trip to Kunming. 5:00. After dinner, Pat O'Brien's show—excellent.

OCTOBER 22   Off at 7:15. Paoshan [14] at 9:00. Out to Dorn's command post and talked. Met officers. Back to field. Decorated seven liaison pilots, and off. Myitkyina at 5:00—played Joe cribbage.

OCTOBER 23   Finished up with Sultan [at Myitkyina]. Rode around and saw the sights. Morale good here. [Ledo] Road coming fine. Shortage of trucks.

OCTOBER 24   Off at 8:00. Beautiful weather. Letter from Dorn. The boys are shocked. Ranchi at 1:00 p.m. Delhi at 6:00. Radio in during night for Wedemeyer to go to Chungking and take over.

OCTOBER 25, DELHI   Office. Reports, etc. Al Wedemeyer is calling "important conferences." He must have some dope.

[These Undated Papers were probably written immediately after Stilwell's relief from command.]

I. Competent authority, for good and sufficient reasons, ordered my relief from duty in the CBI theater. Since I am

[12] Chiang K'ai-shek's offer of a decoration was transmitted to Stilwell's staff via a minor functionary of the Chinese military council; Stilwell rejected the offer through an American officer of similar rank, giving as his formal reason the excuse that a U. S. Army officer of his rank felt it unwise to accept any foreign decoration. The diary notation here is probably a recording of the remark he made to his aide when news of the offer was first brought to him. He did not see Chiang K'ai-shek till later that afternoon for a farewell call.

[13] For the Final Victory. This was the war slogan of China—"Carry On to Final Victory."

[14] Headquarters on the Salween front where Brigadier General Dorn was in command of the American Liaison and Advisory Group attached to the Yoke force.

persona non grata with the existing Chinese government, it
was the only thing to do.

The trouble was largely one of posture. I tried to stand on
my feet instead of my knees. I did not think the knee position was a suitable one for Americans. Since promotion was
intended to give me appropriate rank for a position that did
not materialize, I am requesting reduction to my permanent
grade and assignment to a combat division.

II. It has been announced by competent authority that
I was relieved of command in the CBI theater because of
friction that developed between Chiang K'ai-shek and myself. At all times my relations with Chiang K'ai-shek were
on an impersonal and official basis, and although we differed
often on questions of tactics and strategy, once the decision
was made, I did my best to carry it out. My mission in China
was to increase the combat effectiveness of the Chinese
Army, and an agreement was in effect that China would
supply the manpower and that we would train and equip it.

Burma was in the hands of the Japs, and the only way to
get supplies in quantity into China was by reopening the
communications by ground. The demands of other theaters
made it impossible to assign combat divisions to the CBI
theater, and the solution accepted was to develop the air
ferry, and confine the war in China to an effort in the air.
This resulted in using almost the entire air lift in supplying
the Fourteenth Air Force. It was expected that command of
the air could be maintained in China and bases built from
which the mainland of Japan could be bombed. In May,
1943, the decision was reached in Washington to give the
bulk of the tonnage to the Fourteenth Air Force and depend on the Chinese ground forces to protect our bases.
I argued that as soon as the Japs felt the effect of an attack

from bases in China, they would stage an attack to take the bases from us, and that the Chinese troops available were not competent to prevent it. This opinion was not accepted by the Combined Chiefs of Staff. We have now lost all our bases east of Kunming and have nothing to show for all the effort and expense involved.

OCTOBER 26   Thirty-two months of this. Last day in CBI. Radio about split of theater arrived. Shoved off at 1:00 p.m. Bergin, Arnold, Young and I. Felt like hell. Karachi at 5:00.

OCTOBER 27   Left the field at daylight. 8:00 a.m. last of the CBI.

[AMONG STILWELL'S UNDATED PAPERS]   The personal experience of an individual fades into insignificance in the enormous scope and ramifications of war, especially if there is a grievance connected with it. And when the general result is success, who cares about the squawks of the disgruntled? If a man can say he did not let his country down, and if he can live with himself, there is nothing more he can reasonably ask for.

AFTERWORD

[*The story of General Stilwell's return to the United States is told in Mrs. Stilwell's words in the following narrative.*]

General Marshall's office informed me of General Stilwell's impending return to the United States. Knowing from letters that my husband did not expect to remain in China much longer, I realized that this news meant that his service in the China-Burma-India theater was at an end. Arrangements were made for me to travel east in order to meet General Stilwell on his arrival in Washington.

I reached Washington on November first in General Bonesteel's plane and stayed at the Officers' Club at Fort Myer. The next day I was taken to the field in great secrecy, and at the expected hour—3:00 p.m.—"Uncle Joe's Chariot" arrived. General Stilwell jumped off at once and came over to me, hugged me, and then we entered the car. We looked back and were surprised to see the entire crew lined up by the plane, and later we learned that they were being given instructions on how to conduct themselves. There were to be "no discussions whatever of the China situation."

351

We went to the Officers' Club by car, and I had a few moments in which to look Joe over. The expression in his eyes was easy to read and he was thin and weary. We got out of the car and were amazed to find another car also stopping behind ours; as we went on to our apartment, had we taken a step backward we would have walked on both General Handy and General Surles. They followed us very closely, right into our living room. General Stilwell looked at me and said, "I believe someone wants to have a few words with me." I took the hint and walked into the hallway, where I remained until the talk was finished. Generals Surles and Handy were telling him that the situation was "dynamite" and he was to say nothing to anyone, nor was he to see anyone. That night at dinner in the small room of the club, we had General Stilwell's aides, Major Carl Arnold and Major Richard Young, with us. We were finishing dinner when a young man walked up and joined us without an invitation. He said at once to Joe:

"When are you leaving Washington, General?"

"What do you mean?" said Joe.

"Just that—when are you leaving?"

"That means I'm not wanted here—is that right?"

The young man, Colonel Frank McCarthy, acknowledged as much and Joe said: "Well, I'm not leaving Washington until I talk with General Marshall."

"I'm sorry," said Colonel McCarthy, "General Marshall is leaving Washington tonight and won't be back for several days."

"I know," said Joe, "but I shan't leave until I see him. And by the way," he added, "do you have a cell ready for me at Leavenworth?"

Colonel McCarthy reddened, got up, and excused himself.

We sat talking for a moment and Joe made a few remarks about fresh young men, which I won't repeat, and we went back to our apartment. Shortly, General Marshall, who lived around the corner, arrived at the apartment and again I took a walk—this time for over an hour. It was the same story: "Not a word—this is dynamite." Joe was already sick and tired of the entire proceedings and the atmosphere of crime. He was more than ready to start for Carmel.

We left by plane the following day, planning to break the trip at Dallas. Landing at Love Field, we were met by Colonel Higgins, who felt very troubled that there were no pleasant accommodations for us at the field. Since we had wired ahead for rooms in a Dallas hotel, we did not share his anxiety. However, we were shocked to learn that Colonel Higgins had received direct orders from Washington that no one from the plane was to leave Love Field. Exhausted, mentally and physically, we accepted the orders with as much grace as possible and I was given a room with the WASPS. The girls were very understanding and hospitable. General Stilwell and the crew of the plane were quartered in transient barracks, with an MP guard at the door, to make sure that no one interviewed him.

The next morning we had a very late start, due to bad weather, but eventually we neared Carmel. As we flew over the Salinas valley with its beautiful fields and air of peace, General Stilwell began to hum. He was nearing home. We circled Carmel so that he could look down on his home— the place he loved most in the world—and he leaned back and sighed. Could he rest, I wondered, with his mind and heart so full?

We landed at Del Monte Air Field on Monday, November sixth, at noon. It was a beautiful day for a homecoming. Our three daughters were there to meet us, and as their father stepped down from the plane I could see their expressions of shock and dismay at his gaunt, weary, and heartbroken appearance.

After days of seclusion and with the consent of the War Department, he received the press and photographers at our Carmel home. This was his first press interview since the recall. No word concerning China was spoken. This book is, in a sense, his first public report.

Winifred A. Stilwell

INDEX

Other DACAPO titles of interest

Available at your bookstore

OR ORDER DIRECTLY FROM

DA CAPO PRESS, INC.

233 Spring Street, New York, New York 10013